W9-DCM-495

elevate science

SAVVAS
LEARNING COMPANY

You are an author!

This is your book to keep. Write and draw in it!
Record your data and discoveries in it! You are
an author of this book!

Print your name, school, town, and state below.

My Photo

Name _Abbigaila Tran_

School _Winthrop Charter School_

Town, State _Brandon FL_

Autobiography _____

_____

_____

Copyright © 2019 by Savvas Learning Company LLC. All Rights Reserved. Printed in the United States of America.

This publication is protected by copyright, and permission should be obtained from the publisher prior to any prohibited reproduction, storage in a retrieval system, or transmission in any form or by any means, electronic, mechanical, photocopying, recording, or otherwise. For information regarding permissions, request forms, and the appropriate contacts within the Savvas Learning Company Rights Management group, please send your query to the address below.

Savvas Learning Company LLC, 15 East Midland Avenue, Paramus, NJ 07652

Cover: The cover photo shows a panther chameleon among leaves. FCVR: Klein & Hubert/Nature Picture Library; BCVR: Marinello/DigitalVision Vectors/Getty Images

Attributions of third party content appear on pages EM28–EM29, which constitute an extension of this copyright page.

Savvas® and **Savvas Learning Company®** are the exclusive trademarks of Savvas Learning Company LLC in the U.S. and other countries.

Savvas Learning Company publishes through its famous imprints **Prentice Hall®** and **Scott Foresman®** which are exclusive registered trademarks owned by Savvas Learning Company LLC in the U.S. and/or other countries.

Savvas Realize™ is the exclusive trademark of Savvas Learning Company LLC in the U.S. and/or other countries.

Unless otherwise indicated herein, any third party trademarks that may appear in this work are the property of their respective owners, and any references to third party trademarks, logos, or other trade dress are for demonstrative or descriptive purposes only. Such references are not intended to imply any sponsorship, endorsement, authorization, or promotion of Savvas Learning Company products by the owners of such marks, or any relationship between the owner and Savvas Learning Company LLC or its authors, licensees, or distributors.

SAVVAS
LEARNING COMPANY

ISBN-13: 978-0-328-94914-4
ISBN-10:   0-328-94914-0
11 23

Program Authors

ZIPPORAH MILLER, EdD

Coordinator for K-12 Science Programs, Anne Arundel County Public Schools
Zipporah Miller currently serves as the Senior Manager for Organizational Learning with the Anne Arundel County Public School System. Prior to that she served as the K-12 Coordinator for science in Anne Arundel County. She conducts national training to science stakeholders on the Next Generation Science Standards. Dr. Miller also served as the Associate Executive Director for Professional Development Programs and conferences at the National Science Teachers Association (NSTA) and served as a reviewer during the development of Next Generation Science Standards. Dr. Miller holds a doctoral degree from University of Maryland College Park, a master's degree in school administration and supervision from Bowie State University, and a bachelor's degree from Chadron State College.

MICHAEL J. PADILLA, PhD

Professor Emeritus, Eugene P. Moore School of Education, Clemson University, Clemson, South Carolina
Michael J. Padilla taught science in middle and secondary schools, has more than 30 years of experience educating middle grades science teachers, and served as one of the writers of the 1996 U.S. National Science Education Standards. In recent years Mike has focused on teaching science to English Language Learners. His extensive leadership experience, serving as Principal Investigator on numerous National Science Foundation and U.S. Department of Education grants, resulted in more than $35 million in funding to improve science education. He served as president of the National Science Teachers Association, the world's largest science teaching organization, in 2005–2006.

MICHAEL E. WYSESSION, PhD

Professor of Earth and Planetary Sciences, Washington University, St. Louis, Missouri
An author on more than 100 science and science education publications, Dr. Wysession was awarded the prestigious National Science Foundation Presidential Faculty Fellowship and Packard Foundation Fellowship for his research in geophysics, primarily focused on using seismic tomography to determine the forces driving plate tectonics. Dr. Wysession is also a leader in geoscience literacy and education, including being chair of the *Earth Science Literacy Principles*, author of several popular geology *Great Courses* video lecture series, and a lead writer of the *Next Generation Science Standards**.

---

*Next Generation Science Standards is a registered trademark of WestEd. Neither WestEd nor the lead states and partners that developed the Next Generation Science Standards were involved in the production of this product, and do not endorse it. NGSS Lead States. 2013. Next Generation Science Standards: For States, By States. Washington, DC: The National Academies Press.

Reviewers

Program Consultants

Carol Baker
Science Curriculum

Dr. Carol K. Baker is superintendent for Lyons Elementary K-8 School District in Lyons, Illinois. Prior to that, she was Director of Curriculum for Science and Music in Oak Lawn, Illinois. Before that she taught Physics and Earth Science for 18 years. In the recent past, Dr. Baker also wrote assessment questions for ACT (EXPLORE and PLAN), was elected president of the Illinois Science Teachers Association from 2011-2013 and served as a member of the Museum of Science and Industry advisory boards in Chicago. She is a writer of the Next Generation Science Standards. Dr. Baker received her BS in Physics and a science teaching certification. She completed her Master of Educational Administration (K-12) and earned her doctorate in Educational Leadership.

Jim Cummins
ELL

Dr. Cummins's research focuses on literacy development in multilingual schools and the role technology plays in learning across the curriculum. *Elevate Science* incorporates research-based principles for integrating language with the teaching of academic content based on Dr. Cummins's work.

Elfrieda Hiebert
Literacy

Dr. Hiebert is the President and CEO of TextProject, a nonprofit aimed at providing open-access resources for instruction of beginning and struggling readers, and a former primary school teacher. She is also a research associate at the University of California Santa Cruz. Her research addresses how fluency, vocabulary, and knowledge can be fostered through appropriate texts, and her contributions have been recognized through awards, such as the Oscar Causey Award for Outstanding Contributions to Reading Research (Literacy Research Association, 2015), Research to Practice Award (American Educational Research Association, 2013), William S. Gray Citation of Merit Award for Outstanding Contributions to Reading Research (International Reading Association, 2008).

Content Reviewers

Alex Blom, Ph.D.
Associate Professor
Department Of Physical Sciences
Alverno College
Milwaukee, Wisconsin

Joy Branlund, Ph.D.
Department of Physical Science
Southwestern Illinois College
Granite City, Illinois

Judy Calhoun
Associate Professor
Physical Sciences
Alverno College
Milwaukee, Wisconsin

Stefan Debbert
Associate Professor of Chemistry
Lawrence University
Appleton, Wisconsin

Diane Doser
Professor
Department of Geological Sciences
University of Texas at El Paso
El Paso, Texas

Rick Duhrkopf, Ph. D.
Department of Biology
Baylor University
Waco, Texas

Jennifer Liang
University Of Minnesota Duluth
Duluth, Minnesota

Heather Mernitz, Ph.D.
Associate Professor of Physical Sciences
Alverno College
Milwaukee, Wisconsin

Joseph McCullough, Ph.D.
Cabrillo College
Aptos, California

Katie M. Nemeth, Ph.D.
Assistant Professor
College of Science and Engineering
University of Minnesota Duluth
Duluth, Minnesota

Maik Pertermann
Department of Geology
Western Wyoming Community College
Rock Springs, Wyoming

Scott Rochette
Department of the Earth Sciences
The College at Brockport
State University of New York
Brockport, New York

David Schuster
Washington University in St Louis
St. Louis, Missouri

Shannon Stevenson
Department of Biology
University of Minnesota Duluth
Duluth, Minnesota

Paul Stoddard, Ph.D.
Department of Geology and Environmental Geosciences
Northern Illinois University
DeKalb, Illinois

Nancy Taylor
American Public University
Charles Town, West Virginia

Safety Reviewers

Douglas Mandt, M.S.
Science Education Consultant
Edgewood, Washington

Juliana Textley, Ph.D.
Author, NSTA books on school science safety
Adjunct Professor
Lesley University
Cambridge, Massachusetts

Teacher Reviewers

Jennifer Bennett, M.A.
Memorial Middle School
Tampa, Florida

Sonia Blackstone
Lake County Schools
Howey In the Hills, Florida

Teresa Bode
Roosevelt Elementary
Tampa, Florida

Tyler C. Britt, Ed.S.
Curriculum & Instructional
 Practice Coordinator
Raytown Quality Schools
Raytown, Missouri

A. Colleen Campos
Grandview High School
Aurora, Colorado

Ronald Davis
Riverview Elementary
Riverview, Florida

Coleen Doulk
Challenger School
Spring Hill, Florida

Mary D. Dube
Burnett Middle School
Seffner, Florida

Sandra Galpin
Adams Middle School
Tampa, Florida

Margaret Henry
Lebanon Junior High School
Lebanon, Ohio

Christina Hill
Beth Shields Middle School
Ruskin, Florida

Judy Johnis
Gorden Burnett Middle School
Seffner, Florida

Karen Y. Johnson
Beth Shields Middle School
Ruskin, Florida

Jane Kemp
Lockhart Elementary School
Tampa, Florida

Denise Kuhling
Adams Middle School
Tampa, Florida

Esther Leonard M.Ed. and L.M.T.
Gifted and Talented Implementation Specialist
San Antonio Independent School District
San Antonio, Texas

Kelly Maharaj
Science Department Chairperson
Challenger K-8 School of Science and
 Mathematics
Elgin, Florida

Kevin J. Maser, Ed.D.
H. Frank Carey Jr/Sr High School
Franklin Square, New York

Angie L. Matamoros, Ph.D.
ALM Science Consultant
Weston, Florida

Corey Mayle
Brogden Middle School
Durham, North Carolina

Keith McCarthy
George Washington Middle School
Wayne, New Jersey

Yolanda O. Peña
John F. Kennedy Junior High School
West Valley City, Utah

Kathleen M. Poe
Jacksonville Beach Elementary School
Jacksonville Beach, Florida

Wendy Rauld
Monroe Middle School
Tampa, Florida

Anne Rice
Woodland Middle School
Gurnee, Illinois

Pat (Patricia) Shane, Ph.D.
STEM & ELA Education Consultant
Chapel Hill, North Carolina

Diana Shelton
Burnett Middle School
Seffner, Florida

Nakia Sturrup
Jennings Middle School
Seffner, Florida

Melissa Triebwasser
Walden Lake Elementary
Plant City, Florida

Michele Bubley Wiehagen
Science Coach
Miles Elementary School
Tampa, Florida

Pauline Wilcox
Instructional Science Coach
Fox Chapel Middle School
Spring Hill, Florida

Topic 1

Earth's Patterns and Space

SC.4.E.5.1, SC.4.E.5.2, SC.4.E.5.3, SC.4.E.5.4, SC.4.E.5.5

 VIDEO

 eTEXT

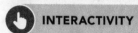 INTERACTIVITY

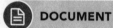 GAME

DOCUMENT

ASSESSMENT

Quest

In this Quest activity, you meet a planetarium curator who is putting together an exhibit about space. You will plan a trip around the world to observe patterns in the sky.

Like a planetarium curator, you complete activities and labs to observe a star, and research and describe moon phases. You use what you learn in the lessons to make a brochure for museum visitors that will explain patterns in the night sky.

Find your Quest activities on pages 2–3, 14, 22–23, 31, 34.

Career Connection Planetarium Curator page 35

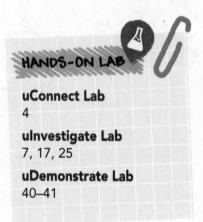

HANDS-ON LAB

Topic 2

Earth's Features

SC.4.E.6.1, SC.4.E.6.2, SC.4.E.6.3, SC.4.E.6.4, SC.4.E.6.5, SC.4.E.6.6

 VIDEO

 eTEXT

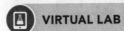 INTERACTIVITY

 VIRTUAL LAB

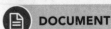 GAME

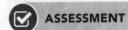 DOCUMENT

 ASSESSMENT

Quest

In this Quest activity, you meet a geologist who presents you with a challenge to find buried treasure. You will learn how to read maps and learn about the patterns of landforms and how they are made.

Like a geologist, you complete activities and labs to use what you learn about the effects of weathering and erosion on landforms. You use what you learn in the lessons to find the buried treasure.

Find your Quest activities on pages 44–45, 55, 65, 74–75, 85, 92, 94.

Career Connection Geologist page 95

The Essential Question

HANDS-ON LAB

Topic 3

Matter

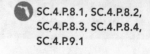

Quest

In this **STEM** Quest activity, you meet a metallurgist who wants you to identify an unknown metal. You need to apply what you know about the physical properties of matter to identify the metal.

Like a metallurgist, you complete activities and labs to explore the physical and chemical properties of matter. You use what you learn in the lessons to identify the unknown metal.

Find your Quest activities on pages 104–105, 115, 125, 134–135, 142, 144.

Career Connection Metallurgist page 145

SC.4.P.8.1, SC.4.P.8.2, SC.4.P.8.3, SC.4.P.8.4, SC.4.P.9.1

 VIDEO

 eTEXT

 INTERACTIVITY

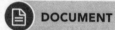 GAME

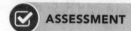 DOCUMENT

 ASSESSMENT

HANDS-ON LAB

Topic 4

Energy and Motion

Quest

In this **STEM** Quest activity, you meet a vehicle safety engineer who presents you with a design problem. You need to design a new safety feature for a car.

Like a vehicle safety engineer, you complete activities and labs to consider how speed and energy affect auto collisions and to learn about electric circuits. You use what you learn in the lessons to design a safety feature for a car.

Find your Quest activities on pages 154–155, 165, 174–175, 184, 192–193, 194.

Career Connection Vehicle Safety Engineer page 195

- ▶ **VIDEO**
- 📖 **eTEXT**
- 👆 **INTERACTIVITY**
- 🔬 **VIRTUAL LAB**
- 🎮 **GAME**
- 📄 **DOCUMENT**
- ☑ **ASSESSMENT**

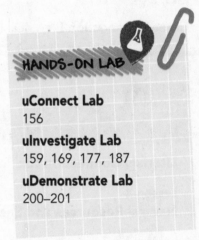

HANDS-ON LAB

Topic 5

Human Uses of Energy

SC.4.P.10.1, SC.4.P.10.2, SC.4.P.10.4

 VIDEO

 eTEXT

 INTERACTIVITY

 VIRTUAL LAB

 GAME

 DOCUMENT

ASSESSMENT

Quest

In this **STEM** Quest activity, you meet an electrical engineer who presents you with a design problem. You need to design an exercise bike that can power a cell phone.

Like an electrical engineer, you complete activities and labs to design and build your model. You use what you learn in the lessons to help with this design of an exercise device that charges a cell phone.

Find your Quest activities on pages 204–205, 215, 224–225, 232, 243, 244.

Career Connection Electrical Engineer page 245

The Essential Question

HANDS-ON LAB

uConnect Lab
206

uInvestigate Lab
209, 217, 227, 237

uDemonstrate Lab
250–251

Topic 6

Plants and Animals

VIDEO

eTEXT

INTERACTIVITY

VIRTUAL LAB

GAME

DOCUMENT

ASSESSMENT

Quest

In this **STEM** Quest activity, you meet a zoo engineer who presents you with a design problem. You will need to design a model wetland exhibit for zoo visitors.

Like a zoo engineer, you complete activities and labs to learn about different plant life cycles and the habitats of animals. You use what you learn in the lessons to help design a wetland habitat for zoo visitors.

Find your Quest activities on pages 254–255, 265, 275, 284–285, 292, 294.

Career Connection Zoo Engineer page 295

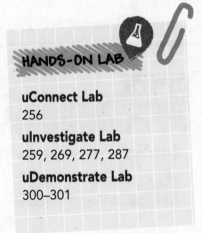

HANDS-ON LAB

Topic 7

Living Things and the Environment

SC.4.L.17.1, SC.4.L.17.2, SC.4.L.17.3, SC.4.L.17.4

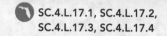

▶ VIDEO

📖 eTEXT

👆 INTERACTIVITY

🎮 GAME

📄 DOCUMENT

☑ ASSESSMENT

Quest

In this **STEM** Quest activity, you meet an ecologist who presents you with an important task. You need to evaluate whether or not animals should be kept in zoos.

Like an ecologist, you complete activities and labs to learn about the natural habitats of animals and where they belong in the food chain. You use what you learn in the lessons to decide whether or not animals should be kept in zoos.

Find your Quest activities on pages 304–305, 316–317, 325, 332, 341, 344.

Career Connection Ecologist page 345

The Essential Question

HANDS-ON LAB

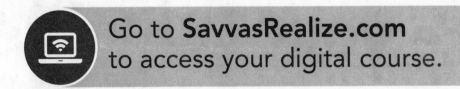

Go to **SavvasRealize.com** to access your digital course.

Elevate Science combines the best science writing with a robust online program. Throughout the lessons, look for digital support to increase your learning experience.

Online Resources

Savvas Realize™ is your online science class. It includes:

- Student eTEXT
- Teacher eTEXT
- Project-Based Learning
- Virtual Labs

- Interactivities
- Videos
- Assessments
- Study Tools
- and more!

Digital Features

 VIDEO

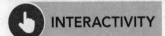 INTERACTIVITY

VIRTUAL LAB

ASSESSMENT

eTEXT

GAME

Look for these **symbols**. They tell you that there are more things to do and learn online.

 INTERACTIVITY

Complete an interactivity about chemical changes.

☺Elevate your thinking!

Elevate Science for Florida takes science to a whole new level and lets you take ownership of your learning. Explore science in the world around you. Investigate how things work. Think critically and solve problems! *Elevate Science* helps you think like a scientist, so you're ready for a world of discoveries.

Explore Your World

Explore real-life scenarios with engaging Quests that dig into science topics in Florida and around the world. You can:

- Solve real-world problems
- Apply skills and knowledge
- Communicate solutions

Make Connections

Elevate Science connects science to other subjects and shows you how to better understand the world through:

- Mathematics
- Reading and Writing
- Literacy

Quest Kickoff

STEM Find the Right Mix— and Step on It!

How can we mix ingredients to make a model stepping stone?

Hi, I'm Alicia Gomez, a materials scientist! Suppose a school is setting up a prairie habitat. In this problem-based learning activity, you will build a model stepping stone so that students can observe the habitat without damaging the plants.

Like a materials scientist, you will evaluate your design and learn how different combinations of materials can make your design solution more useful. And you can decorate your model stepping stones, too!

Follow the path to learn how you will complete the Quest. The Quest activities in the lessons will help you complete the Quest! Check off your progress on the path when you com...

Visual Literacy Connection

What is the matter?

All matter is made up of smaller particles. How can you observe the magnification of matter?

If you were to look at a solid object, such as cotton shirt closely, describe what you might observe with your unaided eye?

Sample answers: I might be able to see strands of threads.

Properties of Matter

Math ▸ Toolbox

Use Models Models can help you represent thoughts or ideas. How can you use the blocks in the image below to explain the idea that particles rearrange when they form new substances?

🌐 MAFS.K12.MP.4.1

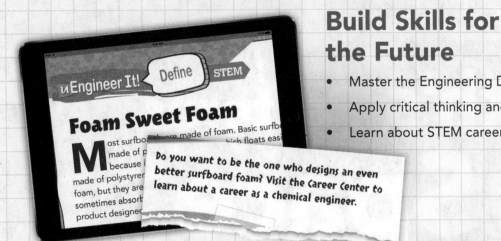

Build Skills for the Future

- Master the Engineering Design Process
- Apply critical thinking and analytical skills
- Learn about STEM careers

Do you want to be the one who designs an even better surfboard foam? Visit the Career Center to learn about a career as a chemical engineer.

Focus on Reading Skills

Elevate Science creates ongoing reading connections to help you develop the reading skills you need to succeed. Features include:

- Leveled Readers
- Literacy Connection Features
- Reading Checks

Literacy ▸ Toolbox 🔧

Use Evidence from Text
Water is formed by the combination of atoms of two different elements— hydrogen and ... smallest particl... atom or a mole... you think so?

LAFS.5.W.3...

☑ **READING CHECK** **Use Evidence from Text** Why do you think aerogels could be used to clean up oil spills in your community? Underline the important facts from th... text that support your claim with evidence.

Enter the Lab Zone

Hands-on experiments and virtual labs help you test ideas and show what you know in performance-based assessments. Scaffolded labs include:

- STEM Labs
- Design Your Own
- Open-ended Labs

Explore the Next Generation Sunshine State Science Standards for:

- Connecting Concepts to make connections
- Nature of Science standards to build inquiry
- Big Ideas, Benchmarks, and standards to master content

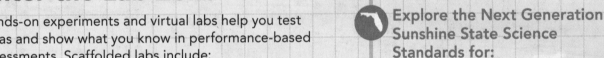

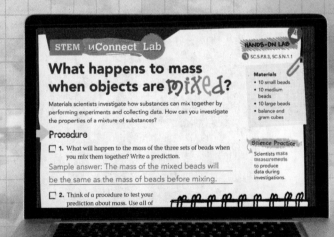

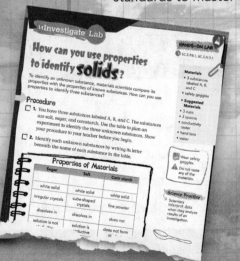

Earth's Patterns and Space

SC.4.E.5.1 Observe that the patterns of stars in the sky stay the same although they appear to shift across the sky nightly, and different stars can be seen in different seasons. **SC.4.E.5.2** Describe the changes in the observable shape of the moon over the course of about a month. **SC.4.E.5.3** Recognize that Earth revolves around the Sun in a year and rotates on its axis in a 24-hour day. **SC.4.E.5.4** Relate that the rotation of Earth (day and night) and apparent movements of the Sun, Moon, and stars are connected. **SC.4.E.5.5** Investigate and report the effects of space research and exploration on the economy and culture of Florida. (Also: **SC.4.N.1.1, SC.4.N.1.6, LAFS.4.RI.2.5, MAFS.4.MD.1.1, MAFS.4.NBT.2, SC.35.CS-CS.1.2**)

Go online to access
your digital course

▶ VIDEO

📖 eTEXT

👆 INTERACTIVITY

🎮 GAME

☑ ASSESSMENT

The Essential Question

How does what we see in the night sky change?

Show What You Know

Why does the moon not look like this every night?

_____

_____

_____

Quest Kickoff

Plan a Trip Around the World of Patterns

Where on Earth is it the middle of the night?

Hi, I'm Jackie Matters, a planetarium curator. I'm putting together an exhibit about patterns in space. In this problem-solving learning activity, you will go on a trip around the world to observe patterns in the sky.

At the end of your journey, you will make a brochure that identifies your destinations and explains the patterns you observed at each stop. We'll use your brochure at the museum to teach others about space patterns.

Follow the path to learn how you will complete the Quest. The Quest activities in the lessons will help you complete the Quest! Check off your progress on the path when you complete an activity with a QUEST CHECK ✓ OFF. Go online for more Quest activities.

Quest Check-In 1

Lesson 1

Learn about Earth's movement and use it to plan a trip around the world to see day and night.

SC.4.E.5.2 Describe the changes in the observable shape of the moon over the course of about a month. (Also **SC.4.E.5.1, SC.4.E.5.3, SC.4.E.5.4, SC.4.E.5.5**.)

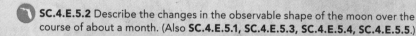

VIDEO

Watch a video about a planetarium curator.

Quest Check-In Lab 2

Lesson 2

Observe the same star as it sets each night over a period of time.

Quest Findings

Make a brochure to explain patterns in the sky. Include visuals in your brochure to illustrate the patterns.

Quest Check-In 3

Lesson 3

Research and describe moon phases at each of your destinations, including your last stop—home.

uConnect Lab

What causes seasons?

On December 21, it is winter in the United States and summer in South Africa. How can you make observations about seasons with a model to understand why?

Procedure

☐ **1.** On the globe, place a blue dot on the United States. Place a red dot on South Africa.

☐ **2.** Use the rest of the materials and the globe to model how sunlight strikes Earth. Make a plan so that you can model summer in the United States and then winter.

☐ **3.** Show your plan to your teacher. Observe how light strikes your locations. Record your observations.

Materials
- globe
- red dot
- blue dot
- light bulb and holder
- stack of books

⚠ Do not touch the light bulb; it will be hot.

Science Practice

Scientists gather data to find out more about the natural world.

Observations

Analyze and Conclude

4. Explain How did light strike different parts of Earth during different seasons?

_____

_____

_____

_____

_____

Sequence

GAME

Practice what you learn with the Mini Games.

When you read, you can identify events that take place. Sequence is the order in which the events take place. To help identify sequence, look for signal words such as *first, after, before, then, next, finally,* and *later.*

Read the text to find the sequence of events.

Seasons to Grow

Marco was planning to grow a garden. But it was winter where he lives. The ground was still frozen. Marco had to wait for the seasons to change before he could put plants in the ground. When springtime came, Marco was ready.

First, he dug some holes in the ground. Then, he put the seeds in the holes. After Marco covered the seeds with dirt, he poured water over them. During the summer, the days kept growing longer, and Marco's plants grew taller. The longer days of summer helped the plants grow faster. After a few weeks, flowers appeared on the plants. Then, the fruits started to grow. Finally, after the fruits turned red and plump, Marco harvested them. Marco really loved eating his tomatoes!

✓ **READING CHECK** **Sequence** How do signal words help you understand sequence? Underline any signal words in the paragraph.

_____

_____

_____

_____

_____

Earth's Movement

I can...

Show how Earth revolves around the sun and rotates on its axis. Explain how Earth's rotation is related to the apparent movement of the sun, moon, and stars.

Literacy Skill
Sequence

Vocabulary
axis
rotation
revolution
orbit
ellipse

Academic Vocabulary
impact

SC.4.E.5.3 Recognize that Earth revolves around the Sun in a year and rotates on its axis in a 24-hour day. **SC.4.E.5.4** Relate that the rotation of Earth (day and night) and apparent movements of the Sun, Moon, and stars are connected. **SC.4.E.5.5** Investigate and report the effects of space research and exploration on the economy and culture of Florida. (Also **SC.4.N.1.1., LAFS.4.RI.2.5, MAFS.4.MD.1.1**)

▶ **VIDEO**

Watch a video about Earth, the sun, and the moon.

STEM ▶ Connection

Suppose you want to watch the stars and see whether their position changes throughout the night. But you do not want to stay up all night. What could you do?

You could use time-lapse photography. Time-lapse photography is a way of showing change over time. The photo shows stars seeming to move in a swirl.

To take this photo, the camera was set to take one continuous photo for a longer time than with a regular photo. The photo shows any changes that happened during that time. The photo shows how stars seem to move in the night sky.

Time-lapse photography allows you to see at one glance the stars' apparent movement, which can take hours. A time-lapse photo can also show how the sun and moon seem to move across the sky.

📓 **Write About It** In your science notebook, tell how photography techniques can help show other patterns in the sky.

uInvestigate Lab

How are we spinning?

Scientists use models to study Earth's movements. How can you use a model to observe some effects of Earth's spinning motion?

Procedure

☐ 1. Make a plan to use the chair and the lamp to model Earth's spinning motion and some of its effects. Show your plan to your teacher before you begin.

☐ 2. Carry out your plan. Pause to record your observations. You can draw your observations on index cards or take photos.

☐ 3. Make your model creative. Combine your drawings or photos into a flipbook and "play" it from beginning to end.

Analyze and Interpret Data

4. **Explain** Which way did you spin? Which way did things appear to move as you were spinning?

_____

_____

5. **Infer** Based on your model, infer some effects of Earth's spinning motion. Explain your inference.

_____

_____

_____

_____

_____

_____

_____

_____

_____

Materials
- rotating chair
- lamp
- index cards
- yarn

Suggested Materials
- camera
- glue
- yellow crayon

 Be careful as you spin on the chair.

 Do not look directly at lamp.

Science Practice

Scientists investigate to find out more about the natural world.

Earth Moves

You cannot feel Earth's movement, but you can observe its effects. In the time-lapse photo, you can see that the sun seems to move across the sky. You can also observe the pattern of day and night. You know this is an effect of Earth's movement because the sun does not actually move across the sky.

Cause and Effect What causes the pattern of day and night that we observe on Earth?

_____

_____

_____

Earth's Rotation

Earth spins on its axis. An **axis** is an imaginary line that goes through the center of an object. Earth's axis passes through the North Pole, the center of Earth, and the South Pole. The spinning of a planet, moon, or star around its axis is called **rotation**. Each time Earth makes a full turn around its axis, it has made one rotation. Earth takes about 24 hours to make one rotation. So one rotation takes about one day. When Earth rotates, it turns from west to east.

Earth's rotation causes day to change into night and night into day. When a place on Earth is turned toward the sun, it has daytime. The opposite side of Earth has nighttime.

Because of Earth's rotation, objects such as the sun, other stars, and the moon appear to rise, move across the sky, and then set. Because Earth rotates from west to east, objects in the sky seem to move from east to west.

You cannot see the stars move across the sky in the daytime because the sun's light is too bright. If you watch for several clear nights, you can observe that the stars appear to change their positions in the sky. They will not change their positions relative to each other, though.

Cause and Effect How does Earth's rotation cause night and day?

_____

_____

_____

Shadows Change

Another result of Earth's rotation is that shadows change their positions and sizes during the day. When light shines on an object and does not pass through it, the object casts a shadow. As Earth rotates, sunlight shines on an object from different angles. The length and position of the object's shadow change. When the sun is low in the sky, shadows are long. When the sun is high in the sky, shadows are shorter.

uBe a Scientist

Changing Shadows
Measure the shadow of a tree at different times during the day. Rank the lengths of the shadows from shortest to longest. Explain your results.

Quest Connection

Is it night or day where you live? Are all places on Earth experiencing the same time of day? Why?

_____

_____

_____

How does Earth travel around the sun?

As Earth rotates, it travels around the sun. The movement of one object around another is a **revolution**. A complete trip around the sun by Earth is one revolution. The path an object follows as it revolves around another object is its **orbit**.

! Describe and contrast the characteristics of rotation and revolution.

GRAVITY

Gravity is a force that pulls two objects toward each other.

Earth's orbit is an ellipse. An **ellipse** is like a circle stretched out in opposite directions. As Earth moves in its orbit, its distance from the sun changes. Earth is farther from the sun in some parts of its orbit. It is closer to the sun in other parts.

Earth takes one year, or about 365 days, to complete a revolution.

The tilt of Earth's axis affects how directly the sun shines on Earth as it revolves.

INTERACTIVITY

Do an activity about Earth's motion.

The Space Program in Florida

You can look at the sky and observe patterns in space. You can also use data gathered by technology to study space. Much of what we know about space comes from data collected by spacecraft that were launched in Florida. How did Florida become a central part of our country's space program?

Before 1950, Brevard County, Florida, had many cattle ranches and citrus farms. In 1950, the U.S. Air Force began testing rockets at Cape Canaveral. The area's geography made it a good choice. As a result, between 1950 and 1970, many houses and hotels were built to serve the growing space industry. They replaced the ranches and farms.

In 1958, NASA began operations at Cape Canaveral. NASA stands for the National Aeronautics and Space Administration. This government agency runs the U.S. space program. In 1962, NASA opened what is now called the Kennedy Space Center on Merritt Island to launch larger rockets into space.

Infer Why do you think Cape Canaveral and Merritt Island are considered good locations to launch rockets?

_____

_____

_____

Kennedy Space Center

Space Research and Exploration

Over the years, the United States Air Force and NASA have launched many rockets from Cape Canaveral and Merritt Island. The U.S. government spends billions of dollars each year on space research and exploration. This money provides many jobs to Floridians and businesses involved in space research and exploration. Other area industries benefit as well, such as aviation, manufacturing, and construction.

Space research and exploration have had an **impact**, or effect, on the culture in Florida and around the world. For example, scientists must make equipment to keep astronauts safe in space. The research done by NASA is now used to make helmets for bike riding and playing sports stronger and safer. Another important effect has been in communication. Exploring space required improvements in reaching people over long distances. Today, satellites allow for very fast communication from most points on Earth. Satellites are used for TV, GPS technology, and some phones. These technologies have changed how Floridians and others interact with the rest of the world.

Literacy ▸ Toolbox

Sequence Identifying the order in which things happen can help you make connections between events. Make a time line on a separate sheet of paper. Show how the development of the space industry in Florida is connected to the growth of its towns and businesses.

LAFS.4.RI.2.5

✓ Lesson 1 Check

SC.4.E.5.4

1. **Explain Phenomena** The sun, moon, and stars appear to move across the sky. Design an experiment to prove that the Earth is rotating.

_____

_____

_____

_____

2. **Separate** Differentiate between the terms *revolution* and *orbit*.

_____

_____

_____

_____

Sun Up, Sun Down

What do you think the other side of Earth looks like outside right now? What might you see in the sky?

Look at the destinations shown in the table. These are the places you will visit on your trip around the world. You will fly to each of these cities and arrive on the day and time shown in the table. Your trip will begin in Seattle. For each city, describe what the sky is like when you arrive.

Quest Itinerary				
Location	Sunrise	Sunset	Time of arrival	Sky observations
Seattle	5:46 A.M	6:40 P.M	4:30 P.M. Monday	
Boston	5:38 A.M	6:22 P.M	8:00 P.M. Tuesday	
London	5:24 A.M	6:35 P.M	11:00 P.M. Wednesday	
New Delhi	7:08 A.M	6:49 P.M	6:45 P.M. Friday	
Tokyo	5:26 A.M	8:30 P.M	1:00 P.M. Saturday	

When you arrive in Tokyo, you will be on almost the opposite side of Earth from Boston. If it is the middle of the day in Tokyo, what will the sky look like in Boston?

_____

_____

_____

QUEST CHECK ✓ OFF

MAFS.4.MD.1.1

How long does it take to orbit?

You have learned that Earth orbits the sun. Other objects in the solar system orbit the sun too. Jupiter is a giant planet that moves around the sun. Halley's Comet, an object with a glowing tail, also blazes a path around the sun.

The table below shows the time it takes each space object to make one orbit around the sun. Study the table, and then rank the objects according to their orbit time. Start with the shortest orbit time and end with the longest.

Object in space	Orbit time	Rank (shortest to longest)
Earth	365.3 days	
Pluto	248 years	
Jupiter	11.9 years	
Halley's Comet	76.1 years	

Patterns of Stars in the Sky

I can...

See that star patterns in the sky stay the same but appear to change nightly and throughout the year. Explain how Earth's rotation is related to the apparent movement of the sun, moon, and stars.

Literacy Skill
Sequence

Vocabulary
constellation

Academic Vocabulary
appear

SC.4.E.5.1 Observe that the patterns of stars in the sky stay the same although they appear to shift across the sky nightly, and different stars can be seen in different seasons. SC.4.E.5.4 Relate that the rotation of Earth (day and night) and apparent movements of the Sun, Moon, and stars are connected. (Also SC.4.N.1.1, SC.4.N.1.6)

CURRICULUM Connection

Ancient people looked to the night sky and saw the same patterns of stars in different seasons. One star pattern would come into view in early spring each year. Another star pattern would appear in summer, and so forth. People used these patterns to help them figure out when to plant and harvest crops. Before there were calendars, people used star patterns to help them plan.

Ancient people also used star patterns to help them find their way from place to place. Stars seem to move across the sky at night. By tracking the apparent movements of stars, people could navigate on land and on sea.

Analyze Why do you think this ancient observatory was so important to scientists and others?

_____

_____

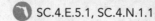
What star *patterns* can you **see**?

The time is 7 P.M. What star patterns can you see? Are these same stars still visible at 11 P.M.? Make a star finder to explore the night sky.

Materials
- Star Finder pattern
- folder
- scissors
- stapler
- glue

Procedure

☐ **1.** Use the Star Finder pattern to make a star finder.

☐ **2.** Choose a time and a date. Record the star groups you could see at that time.

_____

_____

☐ **3.** Describe how you can use the star finder to find out whether those same star groups are always in the same spot throughout the night.

_____

_____

_____

_____

_____

 Be careful using scissors.

Science Practice

Scientists **infer** when they explain their observations.

☐ **4.** Carry out your plan and record your observations.

_____

_____

Analyze and Interpret Data

5. Infer Use what you know about how Earth moves to explain your results.

_____

_____

_____

Lyra

Cygnus

Hercules

Stars

Scientists estimate that the universe may have more than 70 billion trillion stars! The sun is the star that is nearest to Earth and is most important to us. It provides energy to living things on Earth. Like all stars, the sun is a hot ball of gas. Although it seems to be the brightest star in the sky, many stars are much bigger, brighter, or hotter than the sun. Other stars are smaller, dimmer, and cooler.

For thousands of years, people have noticed that the stars **appear**, or can be seen, in shapes and patterns in the sky. You can see three star patterns in the picture. These star patterns are called **constellations**. Astronomers divide the sky into 88 constellations. People often identify the stars by the constellations they are part of. The constellations are so far away from Earth that they appear to be near each other. Actually, they may be very far apart in space.

As Earth rotates, stars appear to move across the sky. As Earth revolves, constellations appear to move as well. Some constellations, such as Draco, are visible during all the seasons. Some constellations are visible only during certain seasons. For example, Cygnus is visible in summer but not in winter. Orion can be seen in winter but not in summer. People in the Southern Hemisphere do not see the same constellations as people in the Northern Hemisphere.

📓 **Science Notebook** In your science notebook, write a story about one of the constellations in the picture.

Design It!

Why do patterns of stars stay the same but appear to shift across the sky each night? Why can different stars be seen in different seasons? Design a way to observe these star patterns. Describe each step you would take.

_____

_____

_____

_____

_____

Brightness of Stars

During the day, you cannot see stars because the sun is so bright. Even at night, if you are in a city that has many lights or if the sky is not clear, you may be able to see only a few of the brightest stars. The light from stars that are very far away appears faint when it reaches Earth. Many stars in the sky are so faint or far away that you cannot see them at all with only your eyes. But you can see some of them through a telescope.

Quest Connection

Would you see the same constellations at each of your destinations as you travel around the world? Explain.

_____

_____

_____

_____

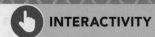
Science Practice
▸ Toolbox

Construct an Explanation
You can model parallax. Hold out your arm with your thumb sticking up. With both eyes open, center your view of your thumb so that it covers an object on the far side of the room. Wink one eye and then the other. How did your view of the object change? Write a summary of your results, explaining how they model parallax.

Distance from Earth

Stars are different distances from Earth. Some dim stars are closer to Earth, so they may appear brighter than bright stars that are farther away. Stars are too far away to directly measure their distance.

Explain How is it possible that a dim star can appear brighter than a bright star?

_____

_____

_____

_____

To measure the distance to stars, scientists use a process called parallax. Astronomers observe a star's position against a night sky of faraway stars. For example, in the picture, find the star where the blue arrows cross. If you observe that star from Earth in February, it will appear to be in a particular position in relation to certain distant stars. If you look at that star in August, it will appear to be in a different place in the sky in relation to those stars. Astronomers use this change in position to calculate the distance of the stars from Earth. The difference in where a star seems to be is because of Earth's movement around the sun.

Cause and Effect Would the star where the blue arrows cross seem to be in the same place in the sky in March and in September? Explain your answer.

_____

_____

_____

_____

_____

_____

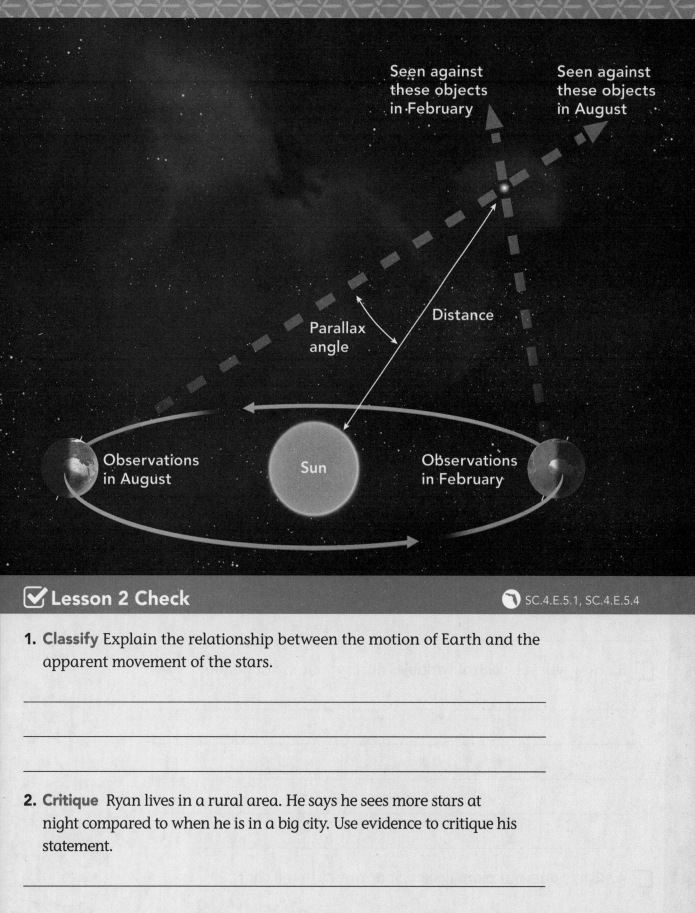

Seen against these objects in February

Seen against these objects in August

Distance

Parallax angle

Observations in August

Sun

Observations in February

✅ Lesson 2 Check

1. **Classify** Explain the relationship between the motion of Earth and the apparent movement of the stars.

_____

_____

_____

2. **Critique** Ryan lives in a rural area. He says he sees more stars at night compared to when he is in a big city. Use evidence to critique his statement.

_____

_____

_____

Quest Check-In Lab

How do stars make patterns?

Suggested Materials
Internet access

Now it's time to take a closer look at star patterns. What patterns can you observe about your star?

Science Practice

Scientists *organize data* to help them recognize patterns.

Procedure

☐ **1.** With the help of an adult, identify a bright star close to the western horizon. Observe the star from a window or online. Write the time it disappears from your view. Record your observations in the chart.

☐ **2.** How can you determine whether your star always disappears from view at the same time? Write your plan. Have your teacher approve the plan.

_____

_____

_____

☐ **3.** How will you control variables during your investigation?

_____

_____

_____

_____

_____

☐ **4.** Carry out your plan. Record your results in the chart.

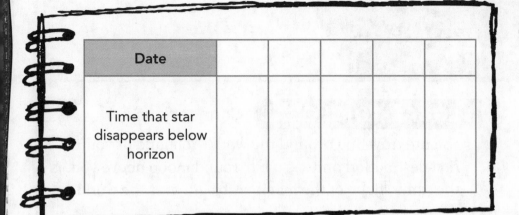

Date					
Time that star disappears below horizon					

Analyze and Interpret Data

5. Identify What pattern do you see in your results?

_____

_____

6. Cause and Effect What caused this pattern?

_____

_____

_____

_____

_____

7. Predict Look at the time and date of your first observation of the star. Predict when your star will disappear below the horizon at this time again.

_____

_____

_____

_____

_____

Moon Phases

I can...

Describe the phases of the moon.
Explain how Earth's rotation is related to the apparent movement of the sun, moon, and stars.

Literacy Skill
Sequence

Vocabulary
phase
eclipse

Academic Vocabulary
perspective

SC.4.E.5.2 Describe the changes in the observable shape of the moon over the course of about a month. (Also **SC.4.E.5.4, SC.4.N.1.1, MAFS.4.NBT.2, SC.35.CS–CS.1.2**)

LOCAL-TO-GLOBAL ⟩ Connection

You are traveling around the world. You land at your first destination and see a big, round moon above you. Is the same shape of the moon visible all over the world?

Everyone sees nearly the same shape of the moon during their night no matter their location on Earth. That is because the moon is in nearly the same place relative to Earth in the sky.

Draw What moon shapes have you seen? Draw them. After you read this lesson, label the moon shapes.

Moon's Movements

The gravity between the moon and Earth keeps the moon in its orbit. Because the moon stays in its orbit, it does not crash into Earth. In its orbit, the moon makes a complete trip around Earth in about one month. At the same time, the moon rotates around an axis. Each time the moon completes a rotation, it also travels once around Earth. As a result, the same side of the moon is always facing Earth. That is the only side you can see from Earth.

Why does the moon change shape?

Of all objects in the night sky, the moon is the easiest to spot. On most clear nights, it is shining above Earth, looking much larger than the stars. Why does the moon appear to change shape?

Materials
- 2 foam balls of different sizes
- light bulb with holder
- skewer

Suggested Materials
- camera

Procedure

☐ 1. How can you use the materials to model the sun, the moon, and Earth?

_____

_____

_____

☐ 2. Think about the moon shapes you have seen. Make a plan to use the model Earth, moon, and sun to show why the moon appears to have different shapes. Show your plan to your teacher before you begin. Record your observations.

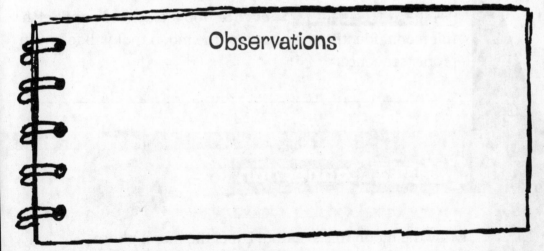

Observations

⚠ Do not touch the light bulb.

⚠ Be careful with sharp objects.

Science Practice

Scientists use models to observe very large objects.

Analyze and Interpret Data

3. Explain Why are only certain parts of the moon lit up at different times?

_____

_____

_____

Math ▸ Toolbox

Calculate About how many times does the moon go through its phases each year? Hint: 365 days/29.5 days.

🔧 MAFS.4.NBT.2

Moon Phases

Sometimes you can see a big, round moon at night. Sometimes you can even see it during the day. During both day and night, the moon looks as if it were shining with its own light. But the moon does not produce its own light. You can see the moon because sunlight reflects off the moon's surface.

If you look at the moon at different times of the month, its shape appears to change. Half of the moon faces the sun, and sunlight is reflected from the surface of that half. When the lighted half of the moon directly faces Earth, the moon appears as a full circle of light. It is called a full moon.

You see a full moon only briefly each time the moon revolves around Earth. The rest of the time, only part of the lighted half of the moon faces Earth. Then you can see only part of the full circle of light. For a short time, you cannot see any of the lighted part of the moon. So, from your **perspective**, or view, on Earth, the moon appears invisible. Between the time you see the full moon and the time you cannot see any moon at all, the moon appears to have different shapes. All the moon's shapes are called the **phases**, or stages, of the moon. The moon takes 29.5 days to complete one cycle of phases.

✅ **READING CHECK** **Sequence** You look outside and see a full moon. Identify the phases of the moon that will follow in proper sequence.

Quest Connection

▼▼▼▼ ▼ ▼▼▼ ▼ ▼ ▼ ▼▼ ▼▼▼ ▼▼▼▼ ▼ ▼ ▼ ▼▼ ▼ ▼ ▼ ▼ ▼ ▼

Draw the moon this evening. Label the moon phase.

Waxing gibbous

In the waxing gibbous phase, more and more of the moon's lighted half is visible.

First quarter

During a first-quarter moon, one half of the lighted half of the moon, or one quarter of the entire moon, is visible.

Waxing crescent

A waxing crescent moon follows a new moon. Waxing means the moon appears to be growing larger. You can see a sliver of the lighted moon.

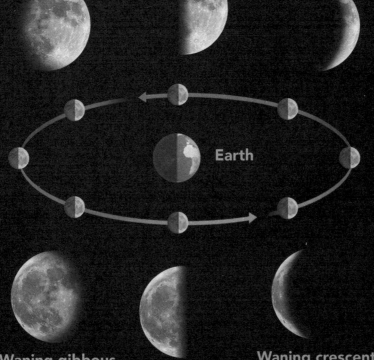

Earth

Sun

Full moon

During a full moon, the entire half of the moon that faces Earth is lighted. You see the moon as a full circle. A full moon appears about a week after the first-quarter moon.

Waning gibbous

Gradually, you see less and less of the moon. The moon is in the waning gibbous phase.

Last quarter

About a week after the full moon, the moon appears as half of a circle. This is the last-quarter phase.

Waning crescent

A waning crescent moon follows the last quarter. You can see a sliver of the lighted moon. Waning means the moon appears to be getting smaller.

New moon

During a new moon, the moon's dark, unlighted side faces Earth. You cannot see a new moon.

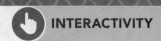

INTERACTIVITY

Do an activity about moon phases.

All About Eclipses

When one object in space gets between the sun and another object, it casts its shadow on the other object. This action is called an **eclipse**. Eclipses happen when the moon passes through Earth's shadow or when the moon's shadow falls on part of Earth. Eclipses are visible only in certain places. Where on Earth an eclipse can be viewed depends on the position of the sun, moon, and Earth.

Lunar Eclipse

Most of the time, reflected sunlight lights up the moon. However, during some full moons, the moon and sun are on exactly opposite sides of Earth. Often, the moon passes above or below Earth's shadow. A lunar eclipse occurs when the moon passes through Earth's shadow.

If only part of the moon is in Earth's shadow during the eclipse, the moon might look as if something took a bite out of it. This is a partial eclipse. If the whole moon is in Earth's shadow, the eclipse is a total lunar eclipse. Although the moon is in Earth's shadow during a total lunar eclipse, it stays visible. The photo shows the moon during a total lunar eclipse. A lunar eclipse can last for almost 4 hours, with the total eclipse lasting up to 100 minutes. One can occur several times in the same year. Each lunar eclipse is visible only from the half of Earth that is turned away from the sun.

moon during lunar eclipse

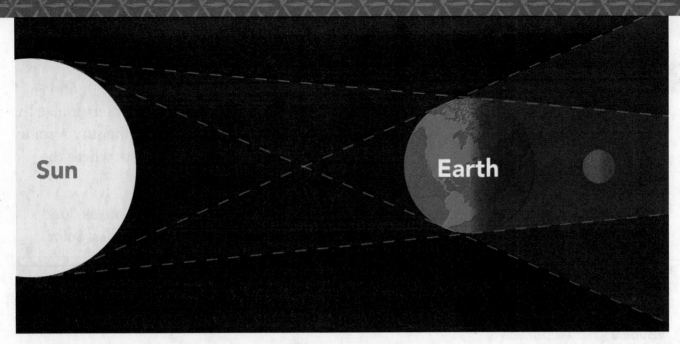

Sun

Earth

Classify Is the eclipse in the picture a total lunar eclipse or a partial lunar eclipse? How do you know?

_____

_____

_____

Model It! Use foam balls to model the positions of the sun, the moon, and Earth during a lunar eclipse. Draw your model below.

uBe a Scientist

Model Phases and Eclipses Revising is an important part of scientific investigations. Once scientists gain new knowledge, they may revise an investigation or model to incorporate new ideas. Now that you have learned about moon phases and eclipses, make a model to show all the phases of the moon. Include a lunar eclipse and a solar eclipse in your model.

Solar Eclipse

When the moon passes between the sun and Earth and casts its shadow on Earth, a solar eclipse occurs. From Earth, this looks like something slowly covering up the sun. A solar eclipse can be seen only at the places on Earth where the moon casts its shadow.

During a total solar eclipse, the day can become as dark as night. Total solar eclipses last up to 7.5 minutes. Solar eclipses occur 2 to 5 times each year.

Explain Why does the sky turn so dark during a total solar eclipse?

_____

_____

☑ Lesson 3 Check

 SC.4.E.5.4

1. **State** What happens during the waxing gibbous phase?

_____

_____

2. **Investigate** Sue reports that she saw a total eclipse. She does not remember if it was a solar or lunar eclipse. What question can you ask her to help you determine what type of eclipse this was?

_____

_____

Moon Sightings

On your trip, you will observe the moon phase at each of your destinations. Some of the phases are already identified for you in the table. Fill in the blank spaces to identify what the phase would be for each remaining city. Use what you observed in the Quest Check-In for Lesson 1 to help.

Quest Itinerary

Location	Day	Moon phase
Seattle	Monday	waxing crescent
Boston	Tuesday	
London	Wednesday	
New Delhi	Friday	first quarter
Tokyo	Sunday	

The moon orbits Earth about once a month. If you traveled around the world in a day or two, what would you notice about the moon phases?

_____

_____

_____

_____

Bonus question! Look at the moon phase for your first destination. Predict how many days until a full moon.

_____

_____

_____

Engineer It! Design STEM

INTERACTIVITY

Go online to learn about codes for computers.

Coding Moon Phases

A code is a way of using numbers, symbols, or words to represent things. Computer scientists use codes to instruct a computer to carry out tasks. People can also use codes to order a sequence of events, such as moon phases. How can you use a code to show the pattern of moon phases?

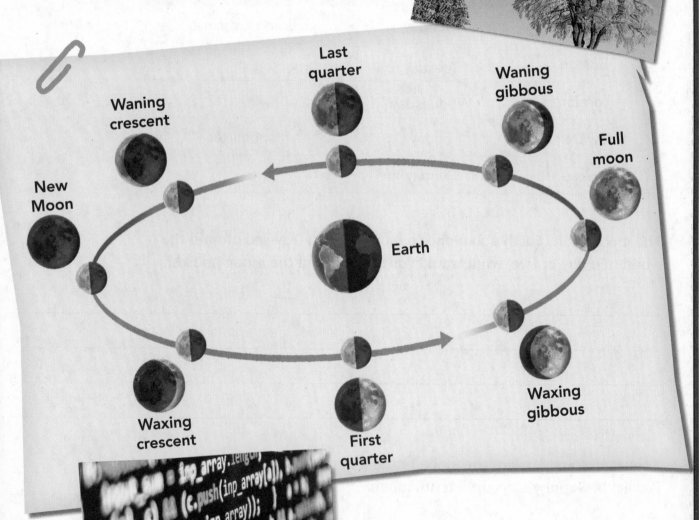

Last quarter

Waning gibbous

Waning crescent

Full moon

New Moon

Earth

Waxing crescent

First quarter

Waxing gibbous

Design It

- ☐ Look at the diagram of the eight moon phases. Calculate how many days the moon remains in each phase. Remember that a complete cycle of moon phases takes about 29.5 days.

- ☐ Choose a phase to start coding. Decide how many days this phase will be visible.

- ☐ Next, figure out how many days each of the remaining phases will be visible.

- ☐ Design a code that tells what moon phase it will be on different days.

Example starting code: If between Days 1 and 4, moon phase = Your Code

👆 **INTERACTIVITY**

Organize data to support your Quest Findings.

Plan a Trip Around the World of **Patterns**

Where on Earth is it the middle of the night?

Make a Space Patterns Brochure

In this Quest, you traveled around the world to observe patterns in space. Now use your observations to make a brochure that summarizes what you experienced on your trip. Remember that the purpose of the brochure is to help others learn about patterns in space. Consider the following questions as you make your brochure.

• Is it day or night?

• How long until sunrise or sunset?

• How will the moon look?

• How may the appearance of stars change over time?

Include drawings of Earth in space to illustrate Earth's patterns. Make pie charts that compare the length of day and the length of night at some locations.

Planetarium Curator

A curator is a person who is responsible for the items in a museum. A planetarium is a place where scientists study objects in the sky. The curator of a planetarium is in charge of the planetarium's collection. The collection includes space objects and historic items related to stars, the sun, the moon, and other objects in the universe. A planetarium curator gathers items for the planetarium's collection and makes sure the items are taken care of properly. He or she often decides how the items will be displayed for the public to see. The planetarium curator might also be involved with community activities for the museum.

Most planetarium curators must have at least four years of college education. Many planetariums look for curators with even more college training. Planetarium curators should have good critical thinking skills, be good at organizing things, and be able to talk with the public.

📕 **Reflect** In your science notebook, write why you think being able to think critically and organize things is important for a planetarium curator.

Read each question and choose or write the best answer.

1. **Vocabulary** The picture shows the movement of Earth. Which sentence best describes this diagram?

   A. Earth is rotating on its axis.

   B. Earth is revolving on its axis.

   C. Earth is orbiting around its axis.

   D. Earth is eclipsing.

2. **Explain** Describe the effects of space research and exploration on Florida's economy and culture.

   _____

   _____

   _____

   _____

   _____

   _____

   _____

   _____

3. **Develop a Logical Argument** Two friends live in different hemispheres. One friend lives in the Northern Hemisphere while the other lives in the Southern Hemisphere. When they describe the constellations in the night sky, what they see is different. Is it possible that they are seeing different constellations? Justify your response.

   _____

   _____

   _____

   _____

   _____

   _____

   _____

4. **Formulate** How can watching the sunrise or sunset help a person determine the direction they are facing?

   A. The sun appears to move across the sky, rising in the east and setting in the west, due to Earth's rotation.

   B. The sun appears to move across the sky, rising in the east and setting in the west, due to Earth's revolution.

   C. The sun appears to move across the sky, rising in the west and setting in the east, due to Earth's revolution.

   D. The sun appears to move across the sky, rising in the west and setting in the east, due to Earth's rotation.

5. Identify Which picture shows a crescent moon?

A.

B.

C.
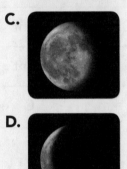

D.

6. Design Sophia has a large flashlight, a tennis ball, and a soccer ball. How can she use these materials to develop a model of a lunar eclipse?

_____

_____

_____

_____

_____

_____

_____

The Essential Question

How does what we see in the night sky change?

Show What You Learned

Describe how the moon appears to change shape over one month.

_____

_____

_____

_____

_____

_____

_____

_____

_____

_____

_____

_____

_____

_____

_____

_____

_____

Read the scenario and answer questions 1–3.

Elena lives in Jacksonville, Florida. Her father is on a business trip in Vietnam. When she gets home from school at 3:30 p.m., the time in Vietnam is 3:30 a.m. the next day.

1 Which information correctly completes boxes A and B?

Ⓐ 7:00 a.m.; day

Ⓑ 7:00 p.m.; day

Ⓒ 7:00 a.m.; night

Ⓓ 7:00 p.m.; night

Jacksonville		Vietnam	
Time	Day/Night	Time	Day/Night
7:00 a.m.	day	A	B
12:30 p.m.	day	12:30 a.m.	night
3:30 p.m.	day	3:30 a.m.	night
6:00 p.m.	night	6:00 a.m.	C

2 What time is it in Jacksonville when the sun is setting in Vietnam?

Ⓕ 7:00 p.m.

Ⓖ 12:30 a.m.

Ⓗ 3:30 a.m.

Ⓘ 6:00 a.m.

3 What is the best time for Elena to call her father when it is not too late or too early in either Jacksonville or Vietnam?

Ⓐ 7:00 a.m. in Jacksonville

Ⓑ 12:30 p.m. in Jacksonville

Ⓒ 1:00 a.m. in Vietnam

Ⓓ 10:00 a.m. in Vietnam

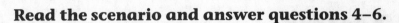
Read the scenario and answer questions 4–6.

Darius kept a moon journal for a month to record how the moon changes as it orbits the Earth. Each night he looked up at the sky and drew a picture to show the shape of the moon. He forgot to look at the moon a few nights.

NOVEMBER						
SUN	MON	TUE	WED	THU	FRI	SAT
			1	2	3	4
5	6	7	8	9	10	11
12	13	14	15	16	17	18
19	20	21	22	23	24	25
26	27	28	29	30		

4 Which statement supports Darius's moon journal observations?

Ⓕ The moon completes an orbit around Earth in about 7 days.

Ⓖ The moon completes an orbit around Earth in about 14 days.

Ⓗ The moon completes an orbit around Earth in about 21 days.

Ⓘ The moon completes an orbit around Earth in about 28 days.

5 Darius forgot to draw the moon on some nights, but one night, no moon appeared in the sky. This is called a new moon. Based on the pattern, which night was there a new moon?

Ⓐ November 7

Ⓑ November 13

Ⓒ November 19

Ⓓ November 21

6 Based on the calendar, which date is another full moon most likely?

Ⓕ December 3

Ⓖ December 8

Ⓗ December 17

Ⓘ December 25

How does a starry sky change?

Materials
• Star Chart sheet

Astronomers study the starry sky and watch how it changes. How can you model what happens to a constellation from season to season?

Science Practice

Scientists gather data to find out more about the natural world.

Procedure

☐ **1.** Use the Star Chart sheet to choose a constellation that is visible now in the night sky where you live.

☐ **2.** Draw the constellation in the correct box of the table.

Constellation Tracking Chart

Summer	Fall	Winter	Spring

☐ **3.** Make a plan to model the constellation and Earth during the remaining seasons. Students should represent each object in the model. One student should be the observer on Earth. Show your plan to your teacher before you begin. Record your observations. Test your model. Revise it if necessary. Sketch the constellation for the remaining seasons in the table.

Analyze and Interpret Data

4. Draw Conclusions Summarize the results in your chart. What happens to constellations from season to season?

_____

_____

_____

5. Cause and Effect What causes the pattern you observed?

_____

_____

_____

6. Explain How did you model your findings?

_____

_____

_____

_____

_____

_____

_____

Lyra

Earth's Features

SC.4.E.6.1 Identify the three categories of rocks: igneous, (formed from molten rock) sedimentary (pieces of other rocks and fossilized organisms) and metamorphic (formed from heat and pressure). **SC.4.E.6.2** Identify the physical properties of common earth-forming minerals, including hardness, color, luster, cleavage, and streak color, and recognize the role of minerals in the formation of rocks. **SC.4.E.6.3** Recognize that humans need resources found on Earth and that these are either renewable or nonrenewable. **SC.4.E.6.4** Describe the basic differences between physical weathering (breaking down of rock by wind, water, ice, temperature change, and plants) and erosion (movement of rock by gravity, wind, water, and ice). **SC.4.E.6.5** Investigate how technology and tools help to extend the ability of humans to observe very small things and very large things. **SC.4.E.6.6** Identify resources available in Florida (water, phosphate, oil, limestone, silicon, wind, and solar energy). (Also **SC.4.N.1.A, SC.4.N.1.1, SC.4.N.1.4, SC.4.N.1.5, SC.4.N.1.6, SC.4.N.1.7, SC.4.N.1.8, SC.4.N.3.1, LAFS.4.RI.1.1**)

Go online to access
your digital course.

▶ VIDEO

📖 eTEXT

👆 INTERACTIVITY

📱 VIRTUAL LAB

🎮 GAME

☑ ASSESSMENT

The Essential Question

How can you use maps to understand Earth's features?

Show What You Know

The movement of water shapes landforms over millions of years. If you were drawing a map of this area, how would you show the features seen here?

_____

_____

Does ✗ Mark the Spot? That's Up to You!

How can we use Earth processes to find buried treasure?

Hello! I am Salena Patrick, a geologist. I am an expert on landforms. I recently found a bottle with a map inside that shows there are hidden treasures buried deep within three land areas. There was also a clue that says the treasures are buried in locations that will one day be exposed through changes in Earth's surface.

In this problem-based learning activity, you will study maps, build landform models, test how those landforms may change over time, search for treasure, and present your findings.

Follow the path to discover what you need to do to complete the Quest. The Quest Check-In activities will help you complete the Quest. You can check off every step you complete with a **QUEST CHECK ✓ OFF**. Go online for more Quest activities.

Quest Check-In 1

Lesson 1
Learn how to read different types of maps. Find out how understanding parts of maps will help you locate the buried treasure.

Quest Check-In 2

Lesson 2
Learn about the patterns of some landforms, where they occur, and how they are made.

SC.4.E.6.4 Describe the basic differences between physical weathering (breaking down of rock by wind, water, ice, temperature change, and plants) and erosion (movement of rock by gravity, wind, water, and ice). (Also **SC.4.E.6.5, SC.4.E.6.6**)

VIDEO

Watch a video about a geologist.

Quest Check-In Lab 4

Lesson 4

See how the effects of weathering and erosion shape landforms. Learn how these processes can help you find the treasure.

Quest Check-In 5

Lesson 5

Florida has many resources. Find out how erosion can impact the availability of these resources.

Quest Check-In Lab 3

Lesson 3

Discover how rocks, minerals, and soil form and how they create Earth's landforms.

Quest Findings

Use what you have learned about maps, models, and Earth's features to describe changes your landform underwent and how you discovered the treasure.

uConnect Lab

How can rain affect land?

When geologists investigate landforms, they want to know how the feature formed. How can you model changes that rain causes in landforms?

Procedure

☐ 1. How will different amounts of rain affect differently sized soil mounds? Write your prediction.

_____

_____

☐ 2. Set up your "land" in the milk jug. Carefully, turn each cup upside down in the jug. Jiggle the cups to release the mounds of dirt.

☐ 3. Make a plan to test your prediction. Write your plan. Show it to your teacher before you begin. Record your observations.

Analyze and Interpret Data

4. **Use Evidence** How can rain affect land? Write your conclusions based on the evidence from your investigation.

_____

_____

_____

_____

_____

_____

_____

Materials

- bottom half of a gallon milk jug
- 3 plastic cups with different amounts of soil
- water

Suggested Materials

- watering can
- metric ruler
- graduated cylinder
- plastic spoon

Science Practice

Scientists plan and carry out investigations to answer questions.

Observations

	Water amount #1	Water amount #2
Small mound		
Medium mound		
Large mound		

Draw Conclusions

LAFS.4.RI.1.1

One important reading skill is drawing conclusions. It is like playing a mystery game. Here's how you do it.

- Collect clues when reading by finding important information.
- Underline the clues as you read them.
- Use the clues to understand what the text means.

Read the following passage to find out why engineers moved a whole lighthouse.

GAME

Practice what you learn with the Mini Games.

Lighthouse on the Move

Cape Hatteras sticks out into the Atlantic Ocean from the coast of North Carolina. In 1870, people put up a lighthouse at the tip of the cape to help ships avoid running into it. The lighthouse stood 1,000 meters from the shore. Over the years, powerful storms and constant waves wore away the coastline. By the 1990s, the lighthouse was almost surrounded by water. The lighthouse needed to be moved. The National Park Service built a base in a new spot and moved the lighthouse to it in one piece. Engineers raised the lighthouse onto a moving platform. Slowly, the lighthouse made the trip to its new, safe location. On November 13, 1999, the lighthouse lit up again. Today, its beacon continues to keep ships safe at sea.

☑ READING CHECK **Draw Conclusions** The lighthouse is currently 488 meters from the ocean. Draw a conclusion about how far the lighthouse may be from the ocean in 100 years.

_____

_____

_____

_____

Lesson 1

Maps and Data

I can...

Read maps to identify and compare Earth's surface features.

Literacy Skill
Draw Conclusions

Vocabulary
symbol
legend
compass rose

Academic Vocabulary
features

▶ **VIDEO**

Watch a video about maps and data.

🐾 **SC.4.E.6.5** Investigate how technology and tools help to extend the ability of humans to observe very small things and very large things. (Also **SC.4.N.3.1, SC.4.N.1.8, LAFS.4.RI.1.1**)

SPORTS ▸ Connection

If you run on a school track, getting lost is difficult. You just go around and around. On a cross-country race, getting lost can be a serious problem. Race organizers solve this problem by printing a map of the course. The map shows the path the race follows and the finish line. It also shows checkpoints and places to stop for water. Whether for a cross-country race or a cross-the-country vacation, maps are the tools that get you from here to there and back again!

Apply Look at the features on the map. How can this map help runners observe such a large park on a small sheet of paper?

_____

_____

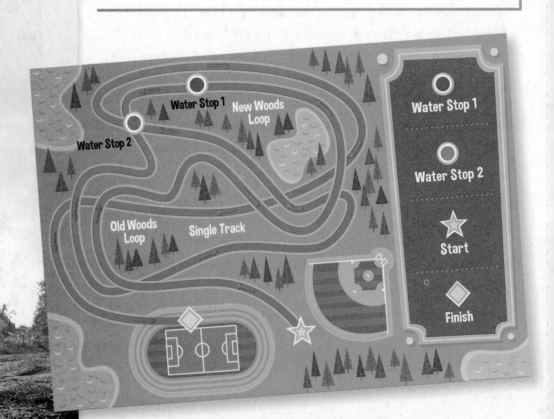

How do tools help us?

Geologists sometimes use tools to find their way in unfamiliar places. New students at a school also must find their way in an unfamiliar place. What are two different ways you could help new students at your school find their way around the school—to the gym, the playground, the cafeteria, the library, and even the principal's office?

Science Practice

Scientists **attempt reasonable answers** that are supported by evidence.

Procedure

☐ 1. Think of two different tools to help new students find their way around your school. Write your ideas.

_____

_____

☐ 2. How could you test your tools?

_____

_____

_____

_____

☐ 3. With your teacher's permission, test your tools. Record your data.

_____

_____

Analyze and Interpret Data

4. **Evaluate** Based on your data, which tool is most useful? How could you change it to make it more useful?

_____

_____

_____

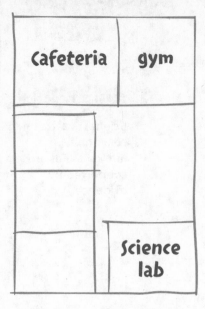

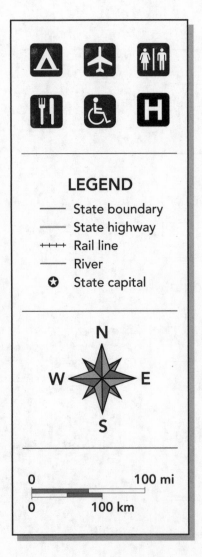

LEGEND

— State boundary
— State highway
++++ Rail line
— River
⊙ State capital

N
W — E
S

0   100 mi
0   100 km

Read a Map

The map shows the rooms in a school. For a map to be useful, it must have enough information. For example, a school map could include the location of the gym, cafeteria, and science lab.

Maps often have a legend, symbols, a compass rose, or a map scale.

- **Symbols** are small pictures, letters, lines, or colors that appear on a map. They should need little or no explanation. Draw a box around the symbols.
- A **legend**, or key, tells what map symbols stand for.
- A **compass rose** shows the directions north (N), east (E), south (S), and west (W). It is placed on the map with N pointing toward north.
- A map scale shows the distance a map covers. The scale on a map of a large area would be in miles or kilometers. A scale of a room would be in feet or meters. Circle the map scale.

☑ READING CHECK **Draw Conclusions** How would a map scale be useful?

_____

_____

Quest Connection

▼▼▼▼▼▼▼▼▼▼▼▼▼▼▼▼▼▼▼▼▼▼▼▼▼▼▼▼▼▼

Draw What might you include in a legend if you were making a map of an area that has both mountains and coastlines? Draw your map legend.

Types of Maps

A physical map shows an area's natural physical features, such as hills, valleys, rivers, lakes, waterfalls, and bays—usually by using different colors. A **feature** is a characteristic or part of something. In the map of the United States, several larger rivers are shown with blue lines. Water is usually shown as blue. The brown and darker green colors show areas where the land is higher, such as hills and mountains. The lighter green colors show areas that are flatter, such as plains.

Apply Circle part of the map where there are mountains. Put a box around where there are plains.

A political map shows countries, states, and cities. Capital cities on political maps are often marked with a star. Road maps show roads and highways in an area. Roads can be drawn using different colors or types of lines to show different kinds of roads. Road maps need to be changed when new roads are built or when old ones are closed.

Most of today's maps are drawn using information collected by space satellites. GPS, or the Global Positioning System, constantly sends out signals that a device uses to pinpoint almost exactly where it is.

Science Practice
▸Toolbox

Construct Explanations
Scientists use reliable sources of information to make an explanation. How does technology help you observe large and small areas to gather information?

How can you see the same place in different ways?

These maps are all maps of San Francisco. Each map shows different information. Look at each map and see what information it includes.

Street Map Use a marker to trace the most direct route to go from Daly City to the bridge that crosses the San Francisco Bay.

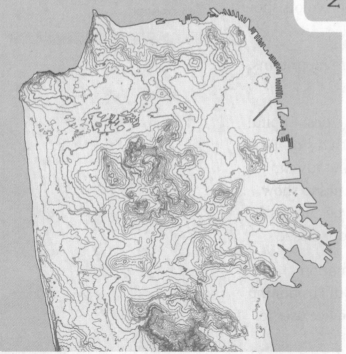

Topographic Map This map shows the land surface of San Francisco using contour lines. Contour lines that are closer together show steeper land. Contour lines farther apart show flatter land. Circle one of the highest points in San Francisco. Is San Francisco flat or hilly? How do you know?

_____

_____

_____

_____

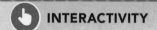
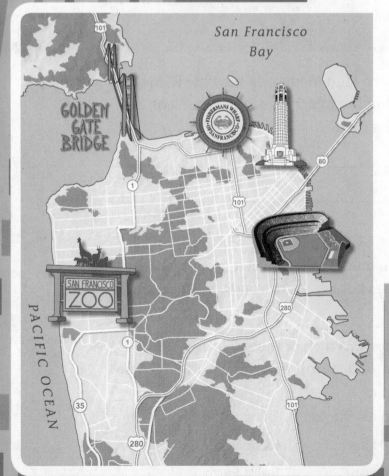

Local Attractions Map

What types of attractions are there to see in San Francisco?

_____

_____

_____

_____

_____

Literacy ▸ Toolbox 🔧

Draw Conclusions You draw a conclusion when you make a statement that summarizes what you think a specific collection of data or observations means. What conclusions can you draw about growing vegetables in Virginia?

 LAFS.4.RI.1.1

Resource Maps

Resource maps show what can be produced in or taken from an area. They may feature natural resources, such as forests, animals, plants, coal, silver, and gold. Resource maps could also show items made in the state or energy produced there. This map shows crops and livestock in Virginia.

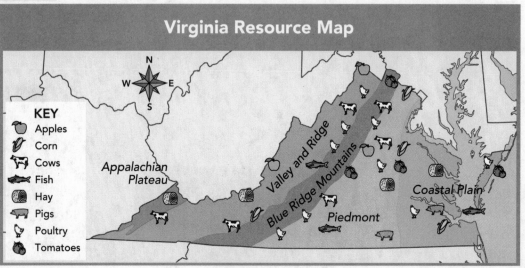

Virginia Resource Map

KEY
🍎 Apples
🌽 Corn
🐄 Cows
🐟 Fish
🧻 Hay
🐖 Pigs
🦃 Poultry
🍅 Tomatoes

☑️ Lesson 1 Check

 SC.4.E.6.5

1. **Analyze** Use the Virginia Resource Map to identify the Blue Ridge Mountain area. Using the key and the map, what conclusion can be drawn about the resources in this area?

_____

_____

_____

2. Jake finds a 100-year-old map in a book. He thinks it is a map of Elmdale, where he lives. Jake does not see many roads or other places he knows on the map.

   Jake gets a current map of his town. Which of these features normally marked on a map could Jake use to determine whether both maps are of Elmdale? Circle all that apply.

   Elm Lake   Elmdale Police Station   Duncan Creek

   Burdock Swamp   Hubbard's Hill   Hendricks Public Library

   Maple Lane Park   Rickard Canyon   Bell's Farm

The Making of a Legend

The Quest map in the bottle shows different areas of land. You will need to use symbols to represent land areas shown on the map. The drawing shows the area where the hidden treasures are buried.

1. Draw a physical map to show what this area would look like if you were looking at it from directly above. Include a legend with your map.

2. Place a star on the map next to the three areas where you think the treasures might be buried.

3. Suppose you gave your legend to some friends who did not have the map. How would the legend help them understand the kinds of features that are on the map?

_____

_____

_____

_____

_____

QUEST CHECK ✓ OFF   55

uEngineer It! Design STEM

INTERACTIVITY

Go online to identify rocks from around the world.

Take a Hike!

Desert terrain can be extremely difficult to cross. The desert is very dry and often very hot during the day. The temperature can become very cold at night or at certain times of the year. High winds can produce sandstorms.

Deserts are very sandy or rocky, so building on them is also difficult. Sandy soil tends to collapse over time. A road built on sand will crumble much faster than one built on more solid ground. Engineers must develop unique solutions to build any kind of structure in a desert.

A popular desert park wants to open a new hiking trail for visitors. The trail will bring visitors over difficult terrain to see some unique desert features. The engineers who will build the trail must come up with some unique solutions. The trail must be easy to walk on. It must also be built without disturbing the environment too much.

Design It

The design team at the park has asked for your help in designing the desert trail. They want the trail to be made of natural materials that can withstand both the extreme heat and cold. The materials should be relatively inexpensive. The trail should blend in with the surrounding environment so that it does not disturb the view of the desert.

☐ **1. Identify** What are the criteria for the trail?

_____

_____

_____

☐ **2. Identify** What are the constraints?

_____

_____

_____

☐ **3. Choose** What materials would you use to build the trail?

_____

_____

4. Design Draw a design for a sample section of your hiking trail. Be sure to include labels on features of your trail that will help it meet the criteria for success.

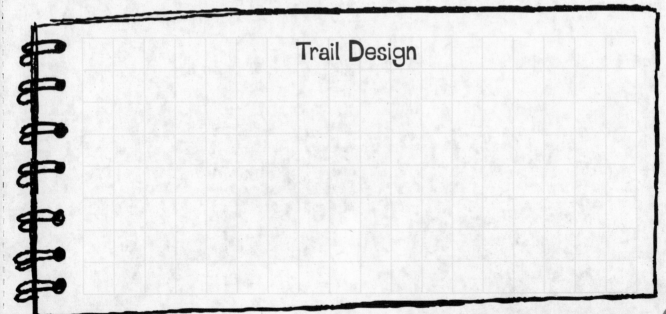

Trail Design

Patterns of Earth's Features

I can...

Identify patterns in Earth's surface features.

Literacy Skill
Draw Conclusions

Vocabulary
canyon
butte
fault
trench

Academic Vocabulary
patterns

VIDEO

Watch a video about patterns of Earth's features.

SC.4.N.1.A Scientific inquiry is a multifaceted activity. The processes of science include the formulation of scientifically investigable questions, construction of investigations into those questions, the collection of appropriate data, the evaluation of the meaning of those data, and the communication of this evaluation. (Also **SC.4.N.1.4, SC.4.N.3.1**)

ENGINEERING › Connection

Can you imagine how different your life would be if you only had limited electricity? Some places might face that situation if dams were not built. The water that moves through dams can be used to make electricity. In that way, a dam is good for most people. But dams can also change Earth's features. When water approaches a dam, it slows. As a result, the sediments—bits of rock and other materials—that the water carries settle here. The buildup of sediment before the dam can change the water's flow. In this way, the path of the river can change.

Write About It What effects do you think might occur if a river's path changes?

uInvestigate Lab

Where are major landforms?

Geologists study how huge pieces of Earth's surface, called plates, move. How can you model the movement of these plates?

Materials
• 2 rectangular sponges

Science Practice

Scientists base their explanations on *evidence.*

Procedure

☐ 1. Predict how Earth's plates and landforms are related.

_____

_____

☐ 2. Use the sponges to model how plates might interact. Draw three diagrams to show different ways you can make the sponges interact. Use arrows to show how the sponges moved.

Analyze and Interpret Data

3. **Draw Conclusions** What conclusions can you make about the movement of Earth's plates and how they shape landforms? Explain your ideas.

_____

_____

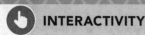

INTERACTIVITY

Complete an activity about landforms.

Science Practice
▶ Toolbox

Cite Evidence The movement of Earth's plates causes volcanoes to appear. What evidence suggests that it is the movement of Earth's plates that causes volcanoes to form?

 SC.4.N.1.4

Patterns of Mountains

Mountains are a type of landform found on Earth's surface. Mountain ranges are lines of mountains connected by high ground. **Canyons**, found in mountain ranges, are deep, narrow areas surrounded by a mountain's steep sides. Another landform, a **butte**, is a single hill that has steep sides and a flat top. A plateau is a large area of raised flat land that extends over a great distance. Cliffs are steep rock faces at the edge of a body of water.

Geologists study mountains because they are one kind of landform that occurs in pattterns across Earth's surface. A **pattern** is something that appears or occurs again and again in the same way. For example, mountains and volcanoes are common along the edges of Earth's plates. Earth's surface is divided into these plates, which are made up of rock. The plates move up and down and sideways. As the plates crash together, mountains and volcanoes form.

✓ **READING CHECK** **Draw Conclusions** Discuss with a partner how you think the Himalaya, a mountain range, formed.

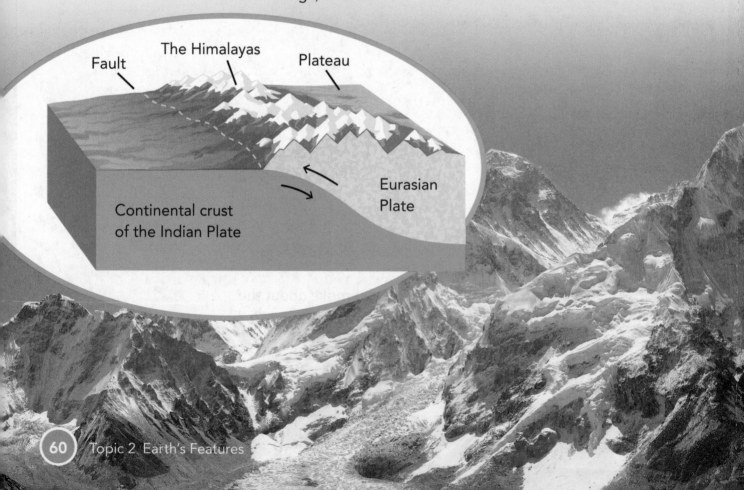

Fault

The Himalayas

Plateau

Continental crust of the Indian Plate

Eurasian Plate

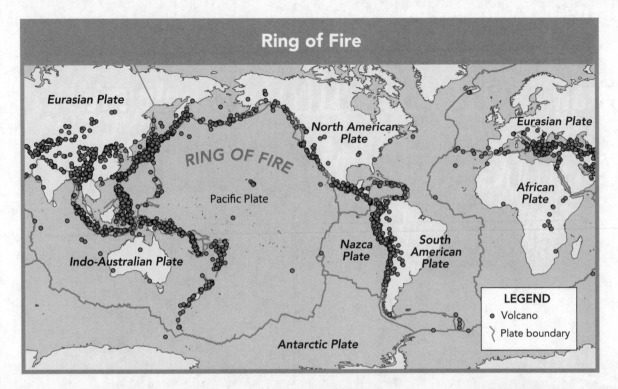
Ring of Fire

Patterns of Earthquakes and Volcanoes

Patterns of earthquake activity and volcanoes are closely related. Both occur along **faults**, or cracks in Earth's crust. Large faults often occur at plate boundaries. Smaller faults can occur in the middle of plates. Both earthquakes and volcanoes are the result of plates moving along these faults. Volcanoes form at places where magma, or molten rock, reaches Earth's surface. Volcanoes and earthquakes are common along a section of Earth called the Ring of Fire, which is the plate boundaries surrounding the Pacific Ocean.

Connecting Concepts ► Toolbox

Patterns Finding patterns helps scientists to organize and classify. Analyze the Ring of Fire map. Describe a pattern of Earth's features the map shows.

Quest Connection

How do the features of a mountain differ from the features of a plateau?

_____

_____

_____

Visual Literacy Connection

How can a physical map help me locate different landforms?

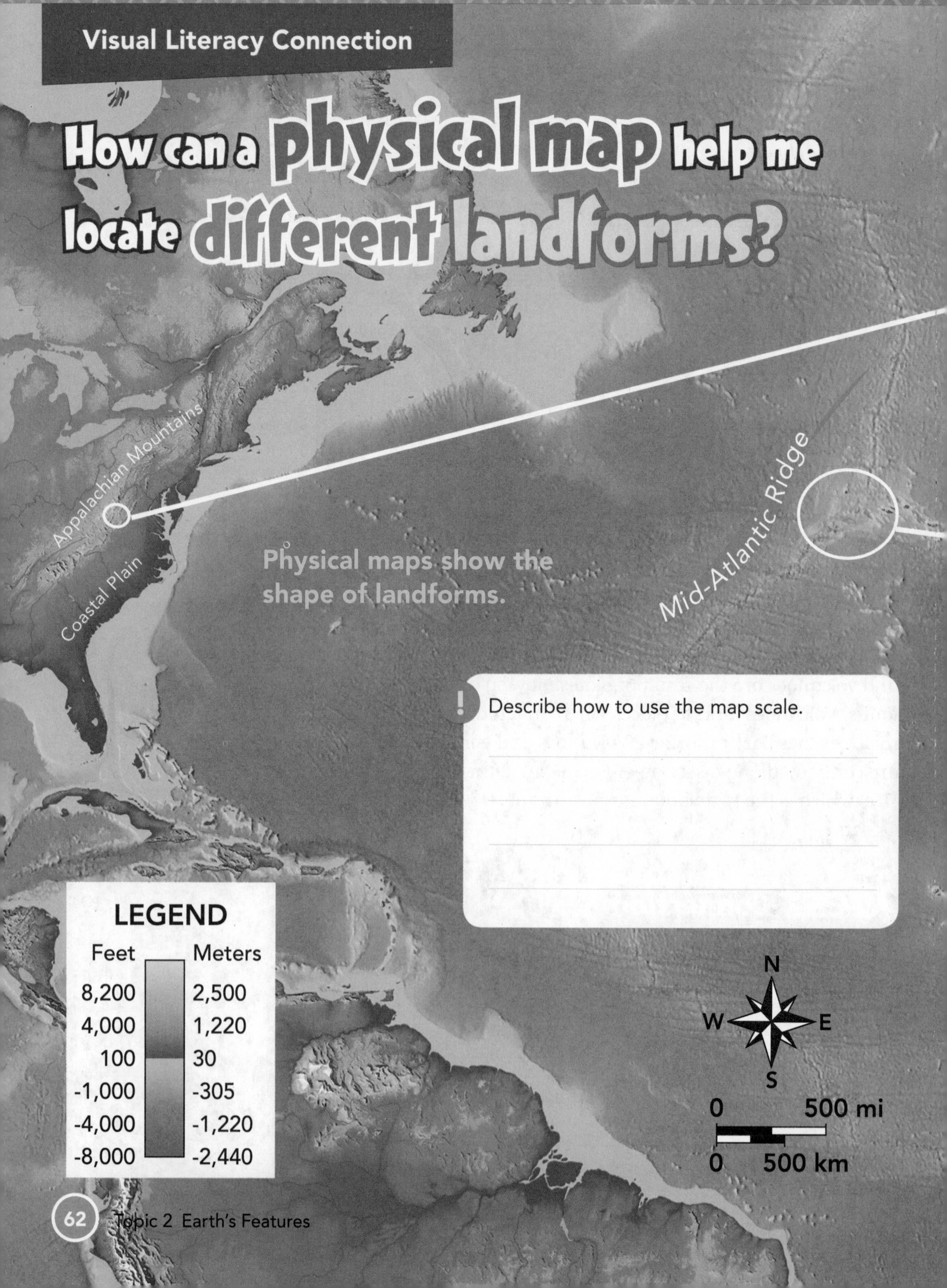

Appalachian Mountains
Coastal Plain
Mid-Atlantic Ridge
LEGEND
Feet
Meters
8,200
2,500
4,000
1,220
100
30
-1,000
-305
-4,000
-1,220
-8,000
-2,440
N
W
E
S
0
500 mi
0
500 km

Physical maps show the shape of landforms.

! Describe how to use the map scale.

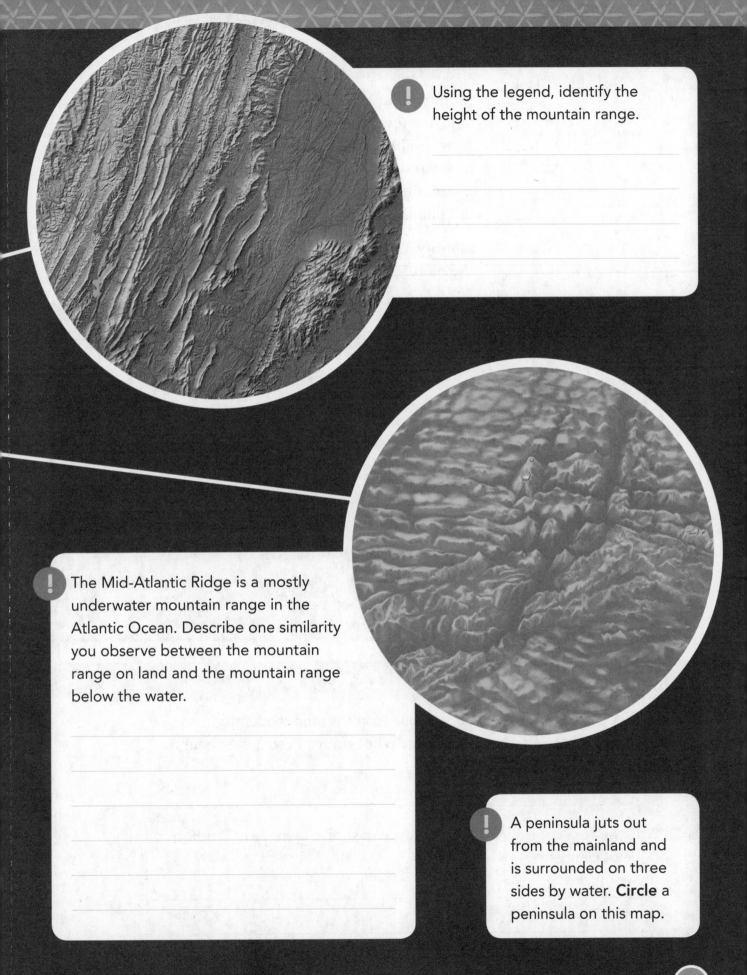

! Using the legend, identify the height of the mountain range.

_____

_____

_____

_____

! The Mid-Atlantic Ridge is a mostly underwater mountain range in the Atlantic Ocean. Describe one similarity you observe between the mountain range on land and the mountain range below the water.

_____

_____

_____

_____

_____

! A peninsula juts out from the mainland and is surrounded on three sides by water. **Circle** a peninsula on this map.

Patterns Under the Ocean

Many similar landforms lie under the oceans. **Trenches** are long, narrow, sunken areas in the ocean floor. Underwater canyons, like those above ground, are low areas surrounded by steep sides. Seafloors have ridges, which are like mountain ranges, and broad basins, which are like large, flat plains.

Identify Circle each kind of feature in a different color on the map.

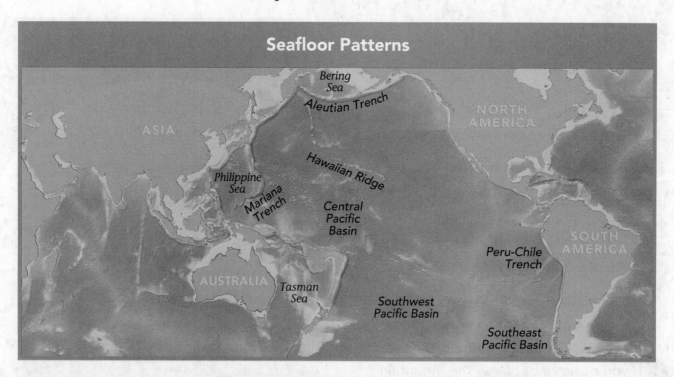

Seafloor Patterns

Bering Sea
Aleutian Trench
NORTH AMERICA
ASIA
Hawaiian Ridge
Philippine Sea
Mariana Trench
Central Pacific Basin
SOUTH AMERICA
Peru-Chile Trench
AUSTRALIA
Tasman Sea
Southwest Pacific Basin
Southeast Pacific Basin

☑ Lesson 2 Check

 SC.4.N.1.A

1. **Identify Patterns** Use the Seafloor Patterns map to identify the trenches beneath the ocean floor. What can you conclude about the location of the trenches?

_____

2. **Develop a Logical Argument** How can studying maps of landforms help scientists?

_____

_____

_____

A Changing Landscape

The Quest map in the bottle showed many landforms, including mountains, plateaus, and cliffs along the coast. Think about the features and patterns of these landforms.

1. Draw and label each landform in a space below.

2. **Compare and Contrast** How are these three landforms different?

_____

_____

_____

_____

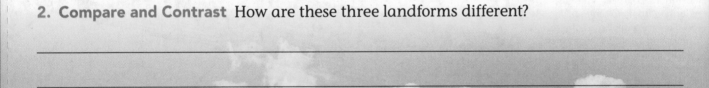

Rocks, Minerals, and Soil

I can...

Describe how rocks and soil form.
Identify the properties of minerals.

Literacy Skill
Draw Conclusions

Vocabulary
igneous
sedimentary
metamorphic

Academic Vocabulary
characteristic

▶ **VIDEO**

Watch a video about rocks, minerals, and soil.

🐢 **SC.4.E.6.1** Identify the three categories of rocks: igneous, (formed from molten rock) sedimentary (pieces of other rocks and fossilized organisms) and metamorphic (formed from heat and pressure). **SC.4.E.6.2** Identify the physical properties of common earth-forming minerals, including hardness, color, luster, cleavage, and streak color, and recognize the role of minerals in the formation of rocks. **SC.4.E.6.5** Investigate how technology and tools help to extend the ability of humans to observe very small things and very large things. (Also **SC.4.N.1.6, SC.4.N.3.1**)

ENGINEERING ▸ Connection

Can you see any rocks in the glass that makes up the windows of your home or school? Engineers often use rocks or minerals for developing products. You may be surprised to learn how many things that you use every day are made using these resources. Computers, cell phones, television sets, microwave ovens, and toasters contain materials made from rocks and minerals. The form of the rock may be different from a rock you find on the ground. For example, the glass of cell phones contains the element lead and quartz, a mineral found in rocks. Electrical circuits inside cell phones may have silicon, platinum, palladium, niobium, gold, arsenic, aluminum, zinc, and copper. All of these materials come from rocks!

📓 **Make Meaning** What other everyday items do you use that you think might contain rocks or the minerals in rocks?

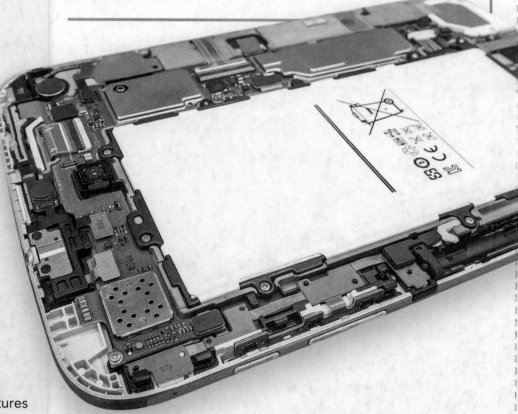

uInvestigate Lab

How can you classify minerals?

Materials
• mineral samples
• hand lens
• magnet
• nail

Geologists use properties of minerals to identify and classify them. How can you classify minerals according to properties?

Procedure

☐ 1. Choose three mineral samples. Write their names in the table.

☐ 2. Use the hand lens to make careful observations of each mineral. Choose three properties to test. Write them in the table. Then test the minerals. Record your observations.

Science Practice

Scientists *collect data* when they investigate a scientific question.

| Mineral | Properties | | |
	1	2	3
A			
B			
C			

Analyze and Interpret Data

3. **Explain** How did the hand lens help you observe and classify the minerals?

_____

_____

_____

igneous rock

Igneous Rocks

Rocks are sorted by certain **characteristics**, or features. Rocks are often sorted by their main characteristic, which is how they formed. Rocks form in three main ways. **Igneous** rocks form from molten rock, or magma. Magma heats up below or inside Earth's crust. Under heat and pressure, it can break through to Earth's surface as lava. When lava or magma cools, igneous rock forms.

☑ READING CHECK **Draw Conclusions** Igneous rock is found along plate boundaries. Why do you think that is?

_____

_____

_____

_____

sedimentary rock

Sedimentary Rocks

Sedimentary rock forms from particles in the environment that settle to form layers. The particles are called sediment. Sediment collects in layers in basins or flat surfaces. Over time, sediment becomes stuck together as if it were glued. Common sedimentary rocks include sandstone, limestone, and conglomerate. Sandstone forms from ribbons of different sand. Gray or white limestone is made from bones and shells of sea creatures. Conglomerate is made from chunks of rock glued together by other rock.

Recognize Label each type of sedimentary rock.

_____ _____ _____

Metamorphic Rocks

Rock can be changed by heat, pressure, or both. Rock that forms this way is called **metamorphic** rock. When either sedimentary, igneous, or other metamorphic rock is put under great pressure and very high temperature, the rock changes form. It usually develops new crystals. For example, marble is made when limestone or chalk is heated and squeezed. Metamorphic shale is slate, which breaks along neat, smooth lines. Igneous granite becomes the metamorphic rock gneiss (sounds like "nice").

Identify Draw an arrow in the white box to show the possible direction of the pressure that changed shale into this metamorphic slate.

Science Practice
▶Toolbox

Make Observations
What would you observe if you felt each of the rocks?

metamorphic rock

Quest Connection

In general, sedimentary rock wears away more quickly, and igneous and metamorphic rock wears away more slowly. Which type of rock might make up a coastal cliff? Explain your answer.

_____

_____

_____

_____

Visual Literacy Connection

How do rocks change?

Igneous, sedimentary, and metamorphic rock are formed in different ways. Over millions of years, these rocks continually change from one type to another type of rock. This process is called the rock cycle. The diagram shows one possible path rocks can take through the rock cycle. Follow the diagram and label each blank with the type of rock that is formed.

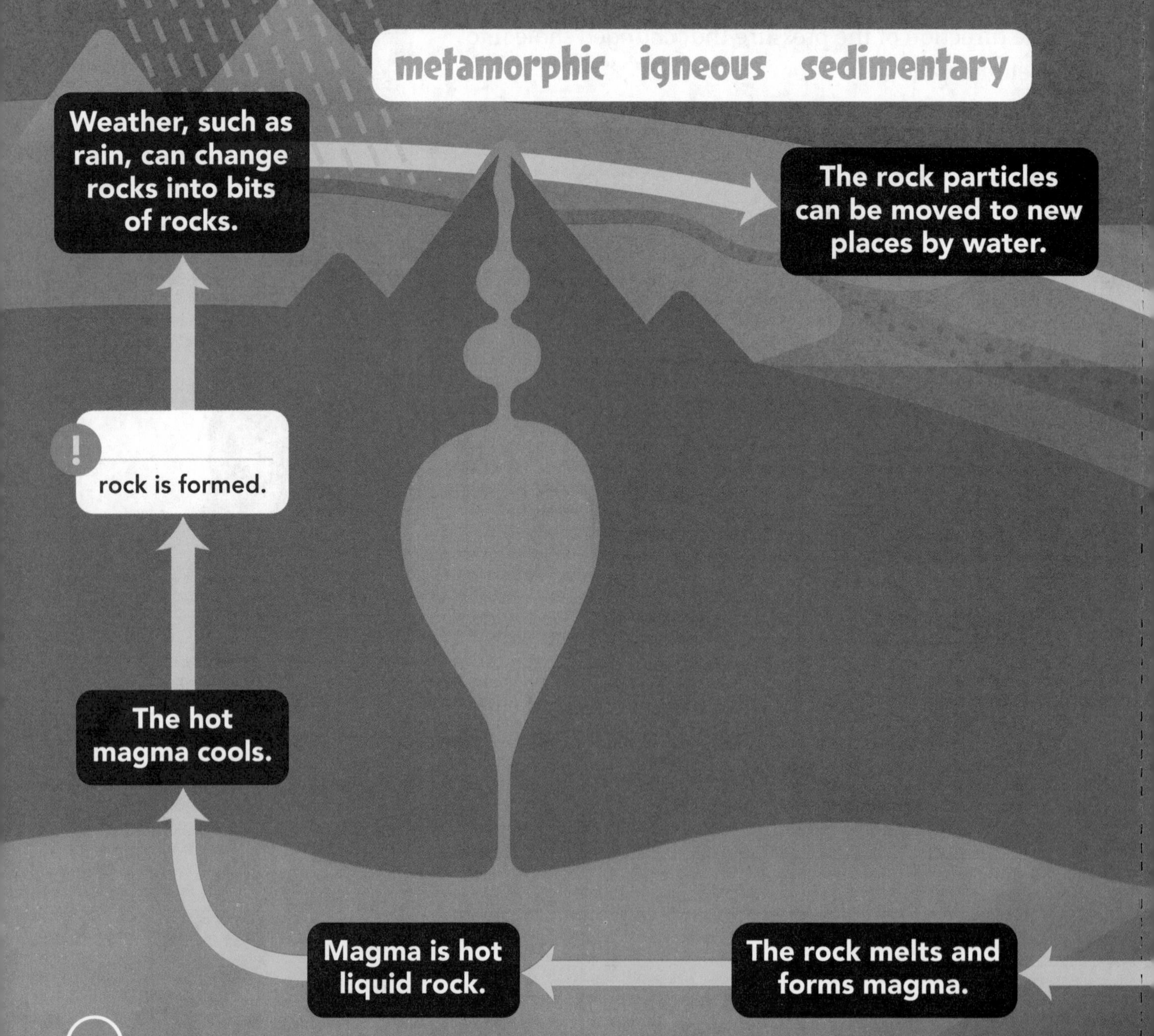

metamorphic igneous sedimentary
Weather, such as rain, can change rocks into bits of rocks.
The rock particles can be moved to new places by water.
!
rock is formed.
The hot magma cools.
Magma is hot liquid rock.
The rock melts and forms magma.

INTERACTIVITY

Complete an activity about the categories of rocks.

! **Connect** How does the rock cycle diagram help you identify types of rocks and the ways each type of rock is formed?

_____

_____

_____

The particles combine together.

! _____

rock is formed.

Heat and pressure change the rock.

! rock is formed.

Minerals

Rocks are made of one or more minerals. Minerals have properties, including color, texture, luster, streak, cleavage, and hardness. Some propeprties are easily observed. Luster is how a mineral's surface reflects light. A glassy luster is shiny, like glass. A metallic luster looks like polished metal. Luster can also be waxy, pearly, chalky, and other lusters.

A mineral's streak is its color in powdered form. This powder can be seen by rubbing a mineral across a streak plate. Minerals that break along smooth, flat surfaces have cleavage. Most minerals break in definite patterns. Some minerals with perfect cleavage break into flat, smooth layers. Other minerals do not have cleavage. They break into nonflat shapes or splinter. Hardness is how easily the surface of a mineral can be scratched. A mineral with greater hardness can scratch a mineral with lower hardness.

Minerals can be sorted into metals and gems. Gold and silver are metals. Diamonds are gems. Minerals can be soft or hard. Talc is the softest mineral. Diamond is the hardest mineral and may be used to make cutting tools. All minerals have a crystal, or organized, structure.

Compare and Contrast How are these minerals different?

_____

_____

uBe a Scientist

Identify Rocks How can you know what rocks are made of? Try the vinegar test. A drop of vinegar on marble or limestone will bubble. That's because they both contain a substance called calcium carbonate. Drop vinegar onto several different rocks. Record what you observe.

Soil

Soil is a mixture of rock particles, air, water, and decomposing matter. The main rock particles in soil are sand, silt, and clay. They come from parent material, which is broken down rock. The type of rock particles in the soil affects how the soil drains. Water pours quickly through sandy soil and less quickly through clay soil. Air enters soil as animals dig through it. As more organic matter, called humus, mixes in the soil, the soil becomes topsoil. Rich topsoil supports plant growth. If you dug down 15 meters or more into soil, you would most likely discover several layers of soil types. A cross section of soil, such as in the illustration, is called a soil profile.

Predict What might happen if you tried to grow crops in soil with little topsoil?

_____

_____

_____

_____

Topsoil —————

Subsoil —————

Parent material —————

 **Lesson 3 Check**   SC.4.E.6.2

1. Formulate When it rains, large puddles form in Braydon's backyard. Braydon says the puddles form because there is a lot of clay in his backyard. Evaluate and explain his statement.

_____

_____

_____

2. Classify Think about the properties of minerals. How might you sort those properties?

_____

_____

_____

How can you make a model of a landform?

Remember that the hidden treasures are buried deep within plateaus and coastal cliffs or near a mountain. In this lab, you will design and make a model of a rocky land form—a mountain, plateau, or cliff. You will use this model in the next Check-In to test how water affects your chosen landform.

Suggested Materials

- mineral samples
- cardboard
- paper plates
- craft sticks
- foam and plastic cups
- white glue
- bottom half of a gallon milk jug
- sand
- soil
- rock samples
- water

Design and Build

☐ **1.** Choose one of the rocky landforms to model—mountain, plateau, or coastal cliff. Discuss ways to use any of the materials to design and construct a model of your landform. Draw your ideas for the designs.

Engineering Practice

Engineers **design models** to explain natural phenomena.

2. Consider which materials will best show the characteristics of your landform. Make a list of those materials and tell why they best represent your landform.

_____

_____

_____

3. Build your model. Sketch or take a photo of your model. Save this for your Quest Findings.

Evaluate Your Design

4. Think about where your landform can be seen on the map from Lesson 1's Quest Check-In. What patterns of Earth's features might you expect to see around your landform?

_____

_____

5. **Compare and Contrast** How is your land model similar to and different from an actual landscape?

_____

_____

_____

6. **Infer** How might the rocks and your landform change over time?

_____

_____

_____

_____

Weathering and Erosion

I can...

Use evidence to show how weathering and erosion change Earth's surface.

Literacy Skill
Draw Conclusions

Vocabulary
weathering
erosion

Academic Vocabulary
evidence

▶ **VIDEO**

Watch a video about weathering and erosion.

🐢 **SC.4.E.6.4** Describe the basic differences between physical weathering (breaking down of rock by wind, water, ice, temperature change, and plants) and erosion (movement of rock by gravity, wind, water, and ice). **SC.4.E.6.5** Investigate how technology and tools help to extend the ability of humans to observe very small things and very large things. (Also **SC.4.N.1.1, SC.4.N.3.1**)

STEM ▷ Connection

Engineers design solutions to protect both land and people. One solution they have designed is a sea wall that can be built along a coastline. Most sea walls are built using concrete or large rocks. When rough seas threaten a town, a sea wall stops the water to prevent flooding. It also stops ocean waves from carrying away soil and sand. In these examples, a sea wall prevents problems. Other times, a sea wall can cause problems—especially with the environment. It can block the movement of sand along the coast, which is important in keeping the coast from washing away. It can also block animals, such as sea turtles, from coming onto a beach to lay their eggs.

📓 **Write About It** What do you think might be some factors that designers and engineers would have to consider when they plan a sea wall?

uInvestigate Lab

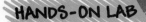
How can a rock wear away?

Geologists know that some rocks can break down because of water. What data can you gather about how water can break down rock?

Materials
- clear jar with lid
- hand lens
- water
- sandstone sample
- limestone sample
- chalk
- safety goggles

⚠ Wear safety goggles.

Procedure

☐ 1. Write a prediction about which rock sample will be affected more by water.

_____

_____

☐ 2. Write a procedure to test your hypothesis. Use all of the materials. Remember to include a control in your procedure. Show your procedure to your teacher before you begin.

☐ 3. Record your observations.

Science Practice

Scientists plan and carry out investigations.

Analyze and Interpret Data

4. Draw Conclusions What conclusions can you draw from your investigation?

_____

_____

_____

_____

_____

_____

_____

Observations

Chemical Weathering

Ocean waves, rushing rivers, pouring rain, and blustering winds can change rocks. **Weathering** is the process that wears away or breaks down rock. The two basic types of weathering are chemical and physical. Chemical weathering can happen when rain mixes with chemicals in the air and interacts with the rock. Chemical weathering can also happen when plants rot and produce chemicals. Those chemicals can interact with rock. In both examples, the surface of the rock can become rough or pitted. Deep pits, or holes, in rock are evidence that chemical weathering has taken place. **Evidence** is observable information that you can use to answer questions. Chemical weathering causes rock materials to turn into new kinds of materials.

✓ READING CHECK **Draw Conclusions** What do you think happened to the statue in the picture to make it change color?

_____

_____

_____

uBe a Scientist

Weathering Materials other than rocks can be weathered. Rub a piece of wood with coarse sandpaper. What do you see? Tap the wood dust onto a piece of paper. What conclusion can you draw from this investigation?

Physical Weathering

Physical weathering happens when wind, water, ice, or plants cause rock to flake or crack. The force of these materials causes rock to wear away or break into smaller pieces. As the wind blows, small particles of sand and other materials hit the rock, cutting and shaping it. Some plant roots can grow inside rock, forcing the rock to crack. Flowing water can cause rocks to hit one another and break apart. Water can also enter cracks in rock. If temperatures are cold enough, the water will freeze. The frozen water in the cracks expands and pushes against the rock, breaking it. Another way that ice weathers rock is in the form of glaciers. Glaciers are large sheets of slow-moving ice that cut and crack rock as they scrape over land.

Science Practice
► Toolbox

Ask Questions What questions would you ask if you were to design a way to prevent the physical weathering of an important stone monument?

Quest Connection

Describe how weathering affects mountains, plateaus, and cliffs by the coast.

_____

_____

_____

_____

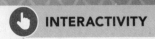
Erosion

Particles of weathered rock can be removed from the land by gravity, wind, water, and ice. **Erosion** is the process in which these weathered particles are removed from land. Rivers, streams, and water from rain and snow pick up broken particles and rock bits. Constant waves against the land can erode cliffs and shorelines. Erosion can cause slow changes over time.

Ice can also remove particles. Most often the ice that erodes land is in the form of glaciers. Gravity pulls those glaciers downward, causing particles to be picked up in the process.

Strong winds can remove rock and soil that have been loosened by physical and chemical weathering. Wind erosion can destroy landforms or make new ones.

Synthesize How are the processes of weathering and erosion related?

_____

_____

_____

_____

Movement of Particles

Wind, water, and ice carry particles from the places where they were weathered and eroded. Wind moves small particles over great distances, sometimes halfway across a continent. Waves can move sand on and off of beaches, carry sand along beaches, and carve structures along the shore. As glaciers move downward, particles get picked up and moved to new locations as well. Tiny rock particles in rivers are always moving along with the movement of the water.

Deposition

As particles are moved, they settle in new locations. Deposition is the settling of particles moved by wind, water, ice, or gravity. The weathered and eroded particles settle when wind or water slows down or when ice melts. The particles and other sediment build up in one location, often forming areas rich in nutrients. The area formed by the buildup of sediment is called a delta.

☑ **READING CHECK** **Draw Conclusions** Deltas and other areas that have large amounts of deposited sediment are often nutrient-rich. What are the benefits of a nutrient-rich area?

_____

_____

_____

HOW ARE weathering, erosion, AND deposition CONNECTED?

Weathering, erosion, and deposition are closely related. Weathering breaks off particles of rock. Erosion is the removal of those particles from larger rocks. The particles are carried away by wind and water and deposited in another place.

! Mark the diagram with W, E, and D in places that weathering, erosion, and deposition are shown.

2 Weathered and eroded particles are carried to new locations by wind and water.

Predict How might this structure have looked before wind changed the rock?

_____

_____

_____

3 Particles and sediment settle in one location when a river slows or changes direction. This causes a buildup of weathered and eroded material.

1 Wind can break off tiny pieces of rock.

Analyze How did water cause these cracks and ridges in the rock?

_____

_____

_____

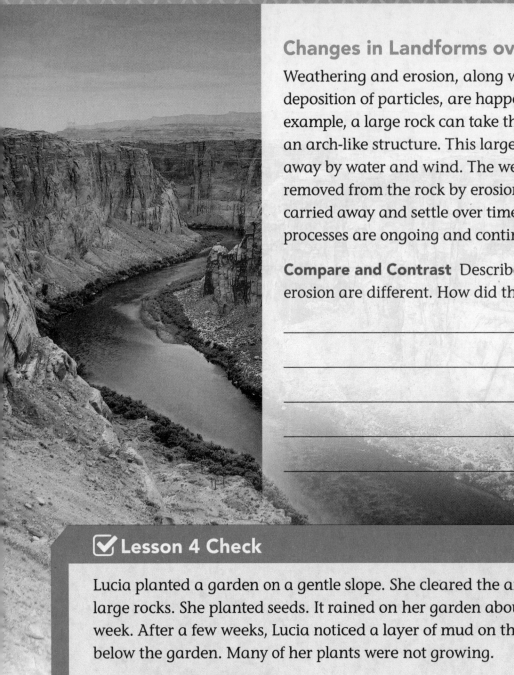

Changes in Landforms over Time

Weathering and erosion, along with the movement and deposition of particles, are happening all the time. For example, a large rock can take thousands of years to become an arch-like structure. This large rock can be weathered away by water and wind. The weathered rock particles are removed from the rock by erosion. Then the particles get carried away and settle over time in a new location. All these processes are ongoing and continue to shape landforms.

Compare and Contrast Describe how weathering and erosion are different. How did these processes form the river?

_____

_____

_____

_____

_____

☑ Lesson 4 Check

SC.4.E.6.4

Lucia planted a garden on a gentle slope. She cleared the area of five large rocks. She planted seeds. It rained on her garden about twice a week. After a few weeks, Lucia noticed a layer of mud on the concrete below the garden. Many of her plants were not growing.

1. **☑READING CHECK** **Draw Conclusions** What happened to Lucia's garden?

_____

_____

2. **Assess** What can Lucia do to prevent this situation from happening again?

_____

_____

_____

How does *water* affect landforms?

You know what causes weathering and erosion. Now you have the chance to demonstrate these processes as part of your Quest. Along the way, you may uncover the hidden treasure! You will use the model you made in the previous Check-In Lab. How will water affect your model?

Materials
- land model
- water
- plastic spray bottle
- cardboard cutouts

Suggested Materials
- paper towel

Test Your Design

☐ **1.** Predict what will happen to the landform model if it were ~~weathered and eroded.~~ exposed to heavy rain.

_____

_____

☐ **2.** Develop a procedure to model weathering and erosion of your landform. Have your teacher approve your plan. Then carry out your procedure. Sketch or take photos to show what happens along the way.

Engineering Practice

Engineers develop and test models to gather data.

Evaluate Your Design

3. **Compare and Contrast** Compare what happened to your landform with classmates who modeled a different landform.

_____

_____

_____

4. **Evaluate** Provide evidence of any effects of weathering or erosion you observed.

_____

_____

Natural Resources

I can...

Describe how renewable and nonrenewable resources are used.

Literacy Skill
Draw Conclusions

Vocabulary
renewable resource
nonrenewable resource

Academic Vocabulary
impact

SC.4.E.6.3 Recognize that humans need resources found on Earth and that these are either renewable or nonrenewable. **SC.4.E.6.6** Identify resources available in Florida (water, phosphate, oil, limestone, silicon, wind, and solar energy). (Also, **SC.4.N.1.5**)

STEM Connection

The eerie structures in the picture might look like something from a horror movie. But they are actually stalactites and stalagmites in a cave. Underground water dissolves limestone and then drips into a cave. The drips deposit tiny bits of limestone in the cave. These delicate shapes formed over thousands of years and billions of water drops. A stalactite might increase only 10 centimeters in 1,000 years, so imagine how old this cave is.

You may never visit a limestone cave, but you see limestone all the time. It is cut into building blocks and ground up to make concrete and brick mortar. It even helps make glass. Florida ranks second in the amount of limestone that is mined. Most of Florida's limestone is used for road construction.

Write About It Do you think people should be able to visit caves where they might break the limestone formations? Why?

uInvestigate Lab

How are resources used?

Scientists look at how people use resources. How do resources impact your life?

Procedure

☐ **1.** Choose a Florida natural resource from the Florida Resources sheet.

☐ **2.** Brainstorm ways you think people use the resource. Record your ideas.

☐ **3.** Show your list of uses to other students. See whether they can guess what your resource is.

Analyze and Interpret Data

4. Cause and Effect Revisit your list of uses. Determine whether another resource can be used in place of the resource you chose. What effect could using this alternative resource have on how you live?

_____

_____

_____

HANDS-ON LAB

SC.4.E.6.3, SC.4.E.6.6, SC.4.N.1.5

Materials
- Florida Resources sheet

Science Practice

Scientists compare methods and results.

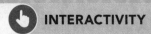

INTERACTIVITY

Complete an activity about how humans depend on the natural world

Renewable Resources

Earth has two types of natural resources: renewable and nonrenewable. **Renewable resources** can be replaced. Plants and animals are renewable resources. Sunlight and wind are two other types of renewable resources. Water is one of our most important renewable resources —if it is used wisely. Wasting or polluting water can affect the usable supply. The photos show how humans use sunlight, wind, and water to produce electrical energy. The air we breathe is another important renewable resource. Almost all living things need water and air to survive.

Identify Underline the resources available in Florida on these pages.

water

wind

sunlight

Nonrenewable Resources

All minerals are nonrenewable resources. **Nonrenewable resources** exist in limited amounts or are used up faster than they can be replaced in nature. People use nonrenewable resources to make products and to produce energy. Coal and oil are nonrenewable resources that we use as fuel. They are called fossil fuels because they were made from organisms that lived long ago.

As people use up more resources, fewer nonrenewable resources will be available for use by people in the future. It is important not to waste these valuable resources.

✓ READING CHECK **Draw Conclusions** In some areas, water has to be pumped up from underground. Groundwater levels have fallen because people are using water faster than it is replaced. Is this groundwater renewable or nonrenewable?

_____

_____

_____

.........**ⁿBe a Scientist**.........

Water Resources Fill a cup halfway with pebbles. Add water until just the tips of the pebbles are dry. Mark the water level on the cup. Remove 4 droppers of water (your water use). Add 1 dropper of new water (water replaced naturally). Repeat this process 10 more times. What happens to the water level? How does this show why everyone should conserve natural resources?

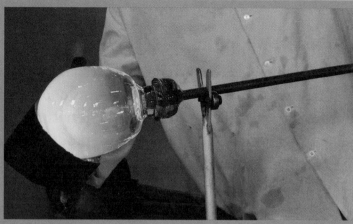

Raw sand, which is mostly quartz, must be processed to get pure silicon. Silicon is used in computer chips.

The quartz in sand is also used to make glass. The main ingredient in glass is silica.

Minerals in Florida

Florida has large deposits of several mineral resources. You may even use them every day without knowing it. Some of these minerals are shown in the pictures. Many people in Florida and elsewhere work to mine minerals. The minerals have a positive **impact**, or effect, on Florida's economy. Florida's minerals add $2 billion of value to the economy yearly.

Identify Underline the resources available in Florida on these pages. List the minerals that have had a positive impact on Florida's economy.

_____

_____

Quest Connection

▼▼▼▼▼▼▼▼▼▼▼▼▼▼▼▼▼▼▼▼▼▼▼▼▼▼▼▼▼▼

Many minerals can be obtained only by mining below Earth's surface. How do you think mining could affect the natural resources in a nearby cliff, mountain, or plateau?

_____

_____

People mine certain sedimentary rocks and process them to get phosphates. Phosphates are mainly used in plant fertilizer.

Limestone is a sedimentary rock often used in construction. It is also used in making concrete and brick mortar.

☑ Lesson 5 Check

 SC.4.E.6.3

1. **Recognize** Your classmate tells you that fossil fuels are renewable because they are formed from natural processes and more fuels are always being made. Critique their statement.

_____

_____

_____

_____

2. **Explain** What are the advantages of using renewable energy resources over fossil fuels?

_____

_____

_____

3. **Identify** Circle the resources below that are renewable Florida resources.

Oil	Limestone	Sunlight	Water
Cattle	Vegetables	Silicon	Phosphates

Washing Away Resources

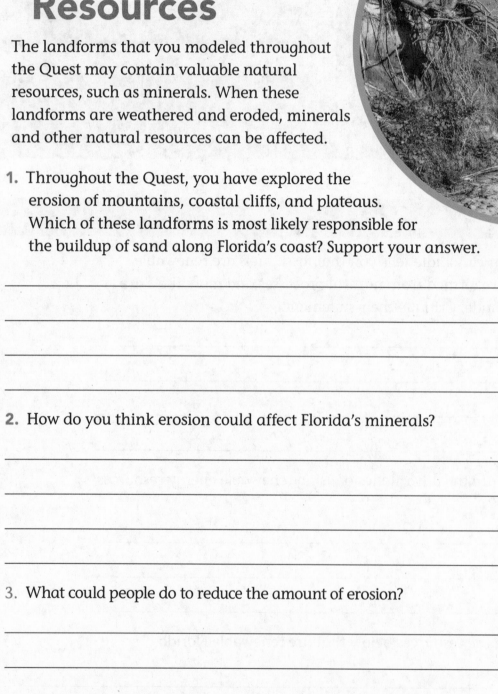

The landforms that you modeled throughout the Quest may contain valuable natural resources, such as minerals. When these landforms are weathered and eroded, minerals and other natural resources can be affected.

1. Throughout the Quest, you have explored the erosion of mountains, coastal cliffs, and plateaus. Which of these landforms is most likely responsible for the buildup of sand along Florida's coast? Support your answer.

_____

_____

_____

_____

2. How do you think erosion could affect Florida's minerals?

_____

_____

_____

_____

3. What could people do to reduce the amount of erosion?

_____

_____

_____

_____

QUEST CHECK ✓ OFF

Powerful Plants

Plants are more powerful than we think. Did you know that plants can cause damage to rocks? Rocks have little protection against the powerful roots of plants. Like wind and water, plants can weather rock!

Any time a plant seed falls into a crack in a rock, the seed may sprout. Roots of sprouting plants grow into cracks of rocks. The roots force bits of rock to crumble. The more the rock crumbles, the stronger the hold the plant has on the rock. This is an example of physical weathering.

Some plant roots produce strong chemicals that break apart the rock. The plants take minerals from the rocks, making the rocks weaker. This is an example of chemical weathering.

☑ READING CHECK Draw Conclusions

What might you expect to happen to a stone wall with many cracks over 200 years? Draw what you think the results would be.

Today	100 years in the future	200 years in the future

INTERACTIVITY

Organize your data to support your Quest Findings.

Does ✗ Mark the Spot? That's Up to You!

How can we use Earth processes to find buried treasure?

Plan and Prepare a Presentation

Produce a presentation that shows how a mountain, plateau, or coastal cliff is weathered and eroded. First, make notes to list what you will show. Then decide what visuals you will use as evidence for each stage of the process. Use the sketches you have drawn or the photos you have taken during Quest Check-Ins to provide evidence of your findings.

Provide a description of your evidence. Your audience should understand that what your presentation shows actually took place over millions of years.

Construct Explanations

What evidence did you use to explain that weathering and erosion can change a landform over time?

_____

_____

QUEST CHECK ✓ OFF

Geologist

Geologists study the Earth. They figure out how Earth's features form and change. They study mountain formations, volcanoes, and earthquakes. They learn about rocks, minerals, petroleum, coal, soil, and more. A geologist's job often involves collecting samples and analyzing data. Most geologists have a specialty, meaning they focus on a narrow topic. Some study volcanoes, wearing heat-protection gear as they sample bits of hot lava. Other geologists map ocean currents or test to see if land is stable enough to build on. Some collect and test rock samples.

Geologists may work in mining or engineering or may teach and carry out research at universities. At times, geologists use instruments, such as rock hammers or drills. They make charts, draw maps, and write reports. Geologists work in offices, labs, and often outdoors. So, if you love science AND enjoy the outdoors, you might make a great geologist!

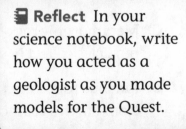

Reflect In your science notebook, write how you acted as a geologist as you made models for the Quest.

Read each question and choose or write the best answer.

1. **Classify** Which best explains how weathering and deposition are connected?

   A. Deposition breaks off rock particles, and weathering settles particles of rock in new locations.

   B. Weathering moves particles from larger rock by wind and water, and deposition settles particles of rock in new locations.

   C. Weathering breaks off rock particles, and deposition moves particles from larger rock by wind and water.

   D. Weathering breaks off rock particles, and deposition settles particles of rock in new location.

2. **Assess** Which statement about the rock cycle is the most accurate?

   A. Igneous rock is made of many small particles.

   B. Sedimentary rock forms from pressurized magma that cools above Earth's surface.

   C. Metamorphic rock forms when rock particles collect in shallow water.

   D. Igneous rock forms as liquid magma from Earth's crust cools.

3. **Use Diagrams** Identify and label the parts of the diagram.

   A. _____

   B. _____

   C. _____

   D. _____

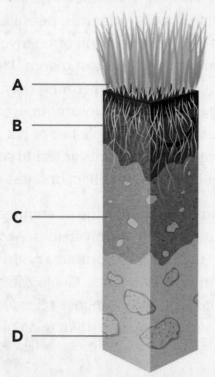

4. **Differentiate** Explain the differences between solar energy and coal energy. State a logical argument about which energy source your community should use.

   _____

   _____

   _____

   _____

   _____

SC.4.E.6.1, SC.4.E.6.3, SC.4.E.6.4, SC.4.E.6.5, SC.4.E.6.6

7. Explain Phenomena What evidence can you find to prove that the movement of Earth's plates causes Earth's surface features?

_____

_____

_____

_____

_____

_____

_____

_____

_____

5. Apply What processes produced this land feature?

_____

_____

_____

_____

_____

The Essential Question

How can you use maps to understand Earth's features?

Show What You Learned

Explain how you can use maps to locate specific landforms. Describe the tools that help you use the maps correctly.

_____

_____

_____

_____

_____

6. Compare Your family plans on taking a hike. What type of map(s) would you recommend your family brings along? Justify your answer.

_____

_____

_____

_____

_____

Read the scenario and answer questions 1–2.

Field geologists made a topographic map to help them study processes in a natural environment.

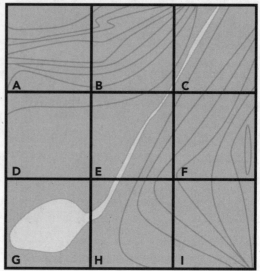

1 Which **best** describes the land that is featured in section I?

(A) steeper land than section B

(B) less hilly than section H

(C) flatter land than section A

(D) more mountainous than section B

2 The geologists study how the body of water in section G has impacted the land to the east of it. How does the topographic map help them understand why the land is shaped the way it is?

(F) The map shows that the water has eroded the land.

(G) The map shows that the water has shaped the land into steep cliffs.

(H) The map shows that the water has formed a deep crater.

(I) The map shows that the water has formed high mountains.

3 Which of the following describes the process of weathering by wind?

(A) Wind picks up small particles and forces them against solid rock.

(B) Wind carries away small particles broken off from solid rock.

(C) Wind weathers solid rock with the help of rain and ice.

(D) Wind deposits small rock particles into sand dunes.

SC.4.E.6.1, SC.4.E.6.2, SC.4.E.6.3,
SC.4.E.6.4, SC.4.E.6.5, SC.4.E.6.6

Read the scenario and answer questions 4–5.

Tara incorrectly recorded her observations about the three main ways rocks form.

Igneous	Sedimentary	Metamorphic
rocks that form from molten rock, or magma	rocks that change form by heat, pressure, or both	rocks that form from particles in the environment that settle to form layers

4 How should Tara revise her observations so that the information is correct?

F She should revise all three observations.

G She should switch the observations for sedimentary and metamorphic rocks.

H She should revise the observation for metamorphic rocks.

I She should switch the observations for igneous and sedimentary rocks.

5 Which is another way that Tara could use characteristics of the rocks she observed to help her identify how the rocks may have formed?

A She could compare the size, shape, and color of the rocks.

B She could compare how each rock sounds.

C She could compare how the rocks interact with water.

D She could compare the smell of each rock.

uDemonstrate Lab

How can you identify minerals?

When geologists need to identify unknown mineral samples, they compare the properties of the sample to the known properties of minerals. How can you identify mineral samples?

Materials
- 6 mineral samples
- hand lens
- streak plate
- nail
- penny

Procedure

☐ **1.** Study the table of known mineral properties.

Properties of Minerals

Mineral	Color	Luster	Streak	Hardness
Calcite	white/clear	glassy	white	3
Feldspar	varied	glassy	white	6
Hornblende	dark green to black	dull/glassy	pale gray	5.5
Mica (muscovite)	ruby, green, brown, black	pearly/glassy	white	2.5
Pyrite	gold	metallic	green to brown to black	6.5
Rose quartz	pink	glassy	white	7

Science Practice

Scientists plan and carry out investigations to answer questions.

☐ **2.** Make a plan to identify the six mineral samples. Use the tools to help you test for each property.

☐ **3.** Show your plan to your teacher before you start.

☐ **4.** Conduct your tests. Record your observations.

Observations of Mineral Samples

Sample	Color	Luster	Streak	Hardness	Identity of Mineral
Mineral **A**					
Mineral **B**					
Mineral **C**					
Mineral **D**					
Mineral **E**					
Mineral **F**					

Analyze and Interpret Data

5. Evaluate How does knowing the properties of minerals help you identify unknown samples?

_____

_____

_____

_____

6. Explain How could you test cleavage in minerals?

_____

_____

_____

Matter

SC.4.P.8.1 Measure and compare objects and materials based on their physical properties including: mass, shape, volume, color, hardness, texture, odor, taste, attraction to magnets. **SC.4.P.8.2** Identify properties and common uses of water in each of its states. **SC.4.P.8.3** Explore the Law of Conservation of Mass by demonstrating that the mass of a whole object is always the same as the sum of the masses of its parts. **SC.4.P.8.4** Investigate and describe that magnets can attract magnetic materials and attract and repel other magnets. **SC.4.P.9.1** Identify some familiar changes in materials that result in other materials with different characteristics, such as decaying animal or plant matter, burning, rusting, and cooking. (Also **SC.4.N.1.1, SC.4.N.1.2, SC.4.N.1.6, SC.4.N.1.7, LAFS.4.RI.2.6**)

Go online to access
your digital course.

▶ VIDEO

📖 eTEXT

👆 INTERACTIVITY

🎮 GAME

☑ ASSESSMENT

The Essential Question

How can matter be described and measured?

Show What You Know

This machinery in a junkyard is sorting some materials from the other materials. How do you think the machine is able to pick up the metals?

_____

_____

STEM The Mystery of the Unknown Object

How can I identify an unknown object?

Hi! My name is Gina Marcel, and I am a metallurgist. I see from the letter that you sent me that you were hiking in the mountains with a metal detector. While you were looking for buried treasure, your metal detector made a sound telling you that a metal was nearby. You dug a hole and found a small, flat, round object covered in mud. I would enjoy helping you find out what the metal is!

In this problem-based learning activity, you will learn about the properties of metals. You will be like a detective as you look for evidence to support your claims about the unknown metal object that you found.

Follow the path to learn how you will complete the Quest. Check off your progress on the path when you complete an activity with a QUEST CHECK ✓ OFF . Go online for more Quest activities.

Quest Check-In 1

Lesson 1
Learn about the physical properties of matter. Compare your unknown metal with known metals.

SC.4.P.8.1 Measure and compare objects and materials based on their physical properties including: mass, shape, volume, color, hardness, texture, odor, taste, attraction to magnets. (Also **SC.4.P.8.2**)

VIDEO

Watch a video about a metallurgist.

Quest Check-In Lab 3

Lesson 3

Apply what you know about classifying matter. Compare the mass of known coins with the mass of your coin.

Quest Check-In 4

Lesson 4

Narrow the list of possible metals in your coin. Write how you can use physical and chemical changes to identify your coin.

Quest Check-In 2

Lesson 2

Brainstorm and research ways you can use water to perform tests or procedures on your unknown metal.

Quest Findings

Report what you found out. Use the evidence you gathered in your Quest to tell what the object is made of.

How can objects be classified?

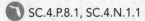
When metallurgists study objects, they put materials that have similar physical properties into groups. How can you group objects with similar properties?

Procedure

☐ 1. In the table, list three properties you want to observe.

☐ 2. Choose four objects. Write how you will test each property. Show your plan to your teacher before you begin.

☐ 3. Test each object and record your results.

☐ 4. Classify the objects into two groups—A and B. Circle the objects in Group A with one color. Circle the objects in Group B with a different color.

Suggested Materials

- button
- bead
- metal washer
- coin
- paper clip
- balance and gram cubes
- metric ruler
- 2 colored pencils
- magnet

Science Practice

Scientists carry out investigations to answer questions.

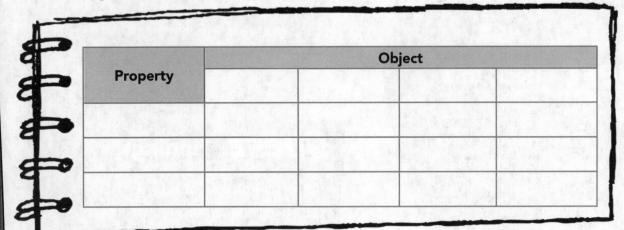

Property	Object			

Analyze and Interpret Data

5. Explain What properties do the objects in each group share?

_____

_____

_____

Compare and Contrast

An important skill in science is comparing and contrasting. When you compare things, you look for ways they are alike. When you contrast things, you identify how they are different.

🎮 **GAME**

Practice what you learn with the Mini Games.

- Key words and phrases that signal a comparison include *is like, as well as, same as,* and *both.*
- Key words and phrases for contrast include *but, is different from, although, except, unlike,* and *however.*

Read the text to find out how aluminum cans and plastic bottles compare and contrast.

Soft Drink Packaging

Soft drinks come in packages made of different materials. Aluminum metal cans and plastic bottles are commonly used. The packaging protects the soft drink. That way, it will reach your refrigerator in the same condition as it left the factory.

Aluminum metal is strong and lightweight. Plastic is also strong, but it can be heavier. Aluminum is easily recycled. The process for recycling plastic is more difficult. Can you think of other ways that aluminum cans and plastic bottles are the same or different?

Scientists choose the right material for packaging by analyzing and comparing the physical properties of different materials.

☑ **READING CHECK**
Compare and Contrast
Fill in the diagram to compare and contrast plastic bottles and aluminum cans.

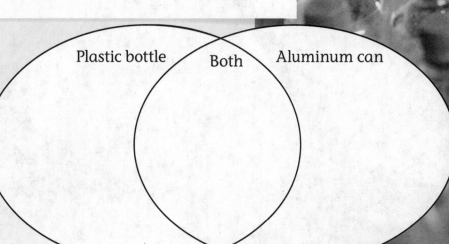

Plastic bottle   Both   Aluminum can

Properties of Matter

I can...

Measure and compare objects and materials based on their physical properties.
Demonstrate that magnets can attract magnetic materials and attract and repel other magnets.

Literacy Skill

Compare and Contrast

Vocabulary

property
texture
magnet
hardness

Academic Vocabulary

organize

SC.4.P.8.1 Measure and compare objects and materials based on their physical properties including: mass, shape, volume, color, hardness, texture, odor, taste, attraction to magnets. **SC.4.P.8.4** Investigate and describe that magnets can attract magnetic materials and attract and repel other magnets. (Also **SC.4.N.1.7, LAFS.4.RI.2.6**)

STEM ▶ Connection

The metal object in the photo gives few clues about what it is used for. It actually can alert a user when metal is near it. Metal detectors can sense metal without touching it. Some people use metal detectors to find coins for their collections, aluminum cans to recycle, or even a buried treasure.

You may think that all metals are shiny, hard, and gray. But metals can be very different. Lead is very heavy, but aluminum is very light. Gold is yellow, and copper is red. Iron is hard, but tin is soft. Silver turns dark, but platinum stays shiny.

📖 **Reflect** In your science notebook, list some metal objects you would like to find with a metal detector. Explain why you would like to find the objects.

uInvestigate Lab

What materials can a magnet **move?**

Materials
• magnet

Suggested Materials
• penny
• copper wire
• plastic paper clip
• bolt
• metal paper clip
• safety pin

Metallurgists know that they can use magnets to move objects. How can you find out whether a magnet can move a particular object?

Procedure

☐ **1.** Observe the objects. Predict which objects a magnet can move.

_____

_____

☐ **2.** Plan steps to test your prediction. Show your plan to your teacher before you begin. Record your observations.

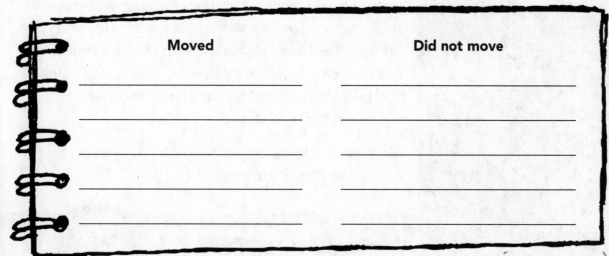

Moved	Did not move
_____	_____
_____	_____
_____	_____
_____	_____
_____	_____

Analyze and Interpret Data

3. Explain How are the objects that the magnet can move alike?

_____

_____

_____

_____

Properties of Matter

Matter is anything that has mass and takes up space. You, your desk, the air, and water are matter, but each kind of matter has its own set of properties. A **property** is a characteristic of an object. Scientists use properties to identify and organize matter. When you **organize** matter, you put matter with similar properties into groups.

Describe Choose two objects in the picture. Describe two properties of each.

_____

_____

_____

_____

Some properties of matter are easy to observe. For example, you can look at the color, size, and shape of some matter. You can touch some matter to observe its texture. **Texture** tells whether an object is rough or smooth. Properties such as mass, length, and height can be estimated, but we may want to accurately measure them with tools.

Identify Circle six properties in the paragraph that you can use to identify matter.

Quest Connection

Describe how you would classify an unknown object.

_____

_____

_____

_____

Magnetism

One property that you can easily test is whether an object is pulled toward a magnet. A **magnet** is a material that can pull some kinds of metal toward it. This pulling force is called attraction. Magnets come in different shapes. A bar, a stick, a U-shape, a doughnut, and a circle are just a few of the shapes a magnet can have.

Does the door of your refrigerator look like a scrapbook with papers, photos, notes, and reminders held in place by magnets? They can stick to the refrigerator because magnets attract magnetic materials, such as the steel found in many refrigerators. Steel is a mixture of iron and other materials. The iron in the steel is attracted to magnets.

Materials that are attracted to magnets have the property of magnetism. Iron and nickel have this property. Copper, another metal, is not attracted to magnets. So, it is not described as magnetic.

Identify Draw an arrow on the pictures where you see magnets sticking together.

...........uBe a Scientist...........

Magnet Hunt
Did you know that magnets are used all around your home? Have you ever noticed how your refrigerator door seems to pull shut as you close it? Find a metal paper clip and use it to look for a magnet inside your refrigerator door. Did you find a spot where the paper clip was attracted? Now take a refrigerator magnet and rub it over that same spot. What happens?

what do you sense?

You can use your senses to gather information about objects.

When you **look** at this dish, you use your **eyes** to gather information about its size, shape, and color. Use these properties to describe the dish.

_____

_____

_____

_____

By lifting an apple, you can observe whether it is heavy or light. **Circle** the apple you think would be heaviest.

If you **taste** an apple, your **tongue** will help you decide whether it is sweet, sour, salty, or bitter. What is something that has a sour taste?

_____

_____

_____

Your **nose** will quickly tell you what an object **smells** like. It might be a good odor or a bad odor. What is something that has a good odor?

_____

_____

_____

If you **touch** the lamp with your **fingers**, you can observe its texture. Describe how you think the lamp would feel if your rubbed your fingers over it.

_____

_____

_____

If you lightly tap the vase with a fork, your **ears** will **hear** the sound that is made. If you tapped the fork on the table, how might its sound be different?

_____

_____

_____

_____

Lesson 1 Properties of Matter 113

Hardness

Hardness is a physical property that describes how easily a material can be scratched. Some scientists use a scale to represent the hardness of different materials. The scale goes from 1 to 10. The hardest material would be rated as a 10. The softest material would be a 1. One of the hardest materials on Earth is diamond. It has a hardness of 10. Chalk is one of the softest materials. The hardness of chalk is 1. Metallurgists choose metals of the right hardness when they design objects. Very hard metals can be used as tools to cut through other materials. The sharp part of a drill is often made of steel. Softer metals, such as gold or silver, can be used to make jewelry.

Literacy ▸ Toolbox 🔧

Compare and Contrast
Scientists compare and contrast materials to see how they are alike and different. Underline two details that describe how scientists compare the hardness of materials. 🌊 LAFS.4.RI.2.6

☑ Lesson 1 Check

🌎 SC.4.P.8.1, SC.4.P.8.4

1. **☑ READING CHECK** **Compare and Contrast** Use physical properties to tell how a diamond and a piece of chalk are alike and different.

_____

_____

_____

_____

2. **Classify** Why is a paper clip attracted to a magnet, but chalk is not?

_____

_____

_____

Identify Properties

Research metals that your unknown object could be made of. Fill in the table below with your findings. Add any other information that might help you identify your unknown object in the notes column.

	Color	Magnetic?	Hardness	Notes
unknown	dark grey	yes	4	
copper				
nickel				
iron				

Summarize What do you know so far about the properties of your unknown object?

_____

_____

_____

_____

_____

_____

_____

_____

uEngineer It! Design STEM

Pancakes for Breakfast

▶ VIDEO

Go online to see how engineers program robots to do tasks.

A robot is a machine that can do some of the same tasks as humans. If you give a robot instructions, it will do the job on its own. Robots are found in more and more places these days, including in many homes. Someday, you may have a robot in your kitchen. The robot in the pictures is the world's first robotic chef! It can use different kitchen tools and ingredients to make meals. What kinds of food would you like to see a robot make?

Design It

Engineers choose materials to design systems that make our lives easier. The robot shown in the picture is making pancakes. Why might an engineer choose magnetic materials to design a robot like this one?

☐ Identify the parts of the robot that could be made of metals. Identify the parts that could be made of magnets.

_____

_____

_____

_____

☐ Define other tasks that a robot could perform when making your breakfast. Record your ideas.

_____

_____

☐ Design a robot to perform one of these tasks. Sketch your design here.

States of Matter

I can...

Identify uses and properties of water as a solid, liquid, or gas.

Literacy Skill
Compare and Contrast

Vocabulary
water vapor
solid
liquid
gas

Academic Vocabulary
differentiate

▶ **VIDEO**

Watch a video about states of water in the water cycle.

SC.4.P.8.2 Identify properties and common uses of water in each of its states. (Also **SC.4.N.1.1**)

CURRICULUM ⟩ Connection

Have you ever seen the lid on a pot of boiling water lift for no obvious reason? Energy from the steam is moving the lid. Steam energy can also be used to move heavier objects, such as the steam locomotive shown in the picture. The engine of a steam locomotive burns coal, wood, or oil. This process heats water to form steam. The steam moves parts of the locomotive that are connected to the wheels of the train.

During the 1700s, people learned to use steam to power machines. This new use improved people's lives by helping them move from place to place by train or boat. Steam energy also powered factories, mines, and mills. Steam energy had great advantages over human or animal energy. Advances in steam engine technology have made big changes in the world.

Explain What causes the train to move?

_____

_____

_____

How does freezing affect water?

Scientists use water in all three of its states. How can you find out how freezing affects the volume of water?

Materials
- graduated cylinder
- plastic bottle
- water

Procedure

☐ 1. What do you think will happen to the volume of water if you freeze the water? Write a prediction.

_____

_____

Science Practice

Scientists plan and carry out investigations to answer questions.

☐ 2. Make a plan and show it to your teacher before you begin. Record your observations.

Observations

Analyze and Interpret Data

3. Compare and Contrast How did freezing affect the volume of the water? What do you think will happen to the volume of the water if the water melts?

_____

_____

States of Matter

Scientists have learned that all matter is made up of tiny particles that are constantly moving. These particles are arranged in different ways. The arrangement and movement of the particles determine the matter's state. Three states of matter are solid, liquid, and gas. Substances on Earth usually exist naturally in only one state. Can you name the only substance that you can find naturally in all three states? If you said water, you are correct. Liquid water is the same substance as the solid ice in the photo and the gas form of water in the air, called **water vapor**. Read on to see how you can **differentiate**, or recognize differences, between the states of matter.

Describe In which two states does water fall to Earth as precipitation?

_____

_____

Solids

At a temperature of 0°C (32°F) or colder, the shape of an ice cube is the same whether it is on a plate or in a container. A **solid** is matter that has a definite shape and takes up a definite amount of space. The particles of a solid are closely packed together, and they have some energy. They move back and forth, but they do not change places with each other. Solid water has a hard surface and can support weight. It is also soft enough to carve into different shapes, such as the carved ice in the photo. People use solid water for cooling drinks and making ice-skating surfaces.

Identify What properties make ice a good material for a sculpture?

_____

_____

_____

_____

Liquids

Water takes the shape of the container it is in. If you pour all of the water in a pitcher into a glass, the shape of the water changes. The volume of water stays the same. Matter that does not have a definite shape but takes up a definite amount of space is a **liquid**. In a liquid, the particles are not held together as tightly as in a solid. The particles are able to slide past one another. This allows a liquid to be poured into different containers. Liquid water can be used for drinking, cleaning, or putting out fires.

✅ READING CHECK **Compare and Contrast** Why does liquid water pour but solid water does not?

_____

_____

Science Practice
▸ **Toolbox**

Construct an Explanation
Explain how heating affects the particles of water.

Gases

Like a liquid, a **gas** takes the shape of its container. Unlike a liquid, a gas spreads out to fill whatever space is available. A gas always fills the container it is in. The particles in a gas are very far apart from one another, and they move in all directions. They move around more easily and more quickly than the particles in a liquid. You can see evidence of water vapor, the gas form of water, as it cools and condenses in the atmosphere. The tiny droplets form into fog and clouds. Water vapor and several other gases make up the air that is all around us. Water vapor can be used for heating, cleaning, or moving machines.

Quest Connection

By now you know that your unknown object is made from metal. Did you know that when metals are heated to very high temperatures, they soften and can be shaped and formed? Why do you think that coins are made of metal?

_____

_____

What are physical changes of water?

The arrangement of the particles that make up matter changes when its state changes. For most matter, the particles get farther apart when going from a solid to a liquid to a gas. What makes water unique?

1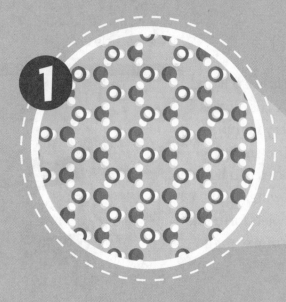

The particles of ice are like those of all solids—they move back and forth in place. Ice is different from other solids because the ice particles are farther apart than the particles of liquid water.

0°C

INTERACTIVITY

Do an activity about using water.

Describe why an **ice cube** would float if placed in water.

_____

_____

_____

25°C   energy added

3

Why do gas **molecules** leave the beaker?

_____

_____

_____

_____

_____

_____

energy added

100°C

Lesson 2 States of Matter 123

Liquid, Solid, Gas

With an adult, measure how long liquid water takes to go from liquid to solid and from liquid to gas. Determine your own procedure and materials.

Unique Properties of Water

Water has different properties as a solid, liquid, and gas. Solid water is a poor heat conductor and can be used to cool hot objects. Some people use ice to keep food fresh. Ice is also easy to carve, making it good for sculptures.

Liquid water is useful for turning wheels that generate electricity. It can be used to wash things. It can be sprayed with so much force that it can remove paint! Of course, liquid water is also needed to keep organisms alive.

Water vapor, or steam, is used to cook food and to clean things, such as carpets. Most homes get their electricity from machines that are powered by steam.

Reflect The picture shows a hotel that is made from ice. In your science notebook, tell whether you would like to stay in an ice hotel. How would it be different from staying in a typical hotel?

✓ Lesson 2 Check

SC.4.P.8.2

1. **Explain Phenomena** When boiling water in a tea kettle, the top may move around slightly if it is not on tight. What evidence explains why this happens?

_____

2. **Categorize** Describe one common use for each state of water.

_____

_____

Ways of Water

How can you use water to perform tests and procedures on your unknown object? Brainstorm ways to use water other than simply washing to help you identify your unknown object. Record your ideas in the table.

What I will do	Why I will do it

Measure Matter

I can...

Measure matter.
Demonstrate the Law of
Conservation of Mass.

Literacy Skill
Compare and Contrast

Vocabulary
mass
physical change
volume

Academic Vocabulary
compute

SC.4.P.8.1 Measure and compare
objects and materials based on their
physical properties including: mass,
shape, volume, color, hardness,
texture, odor, taste, attraction to
magnets. **SC.4.P.8.3** Explore the
Law of Conservation of Mass by
demonstrating that the mass of a
whole object is always the same as
the sum of the masses of its parts.
(Also **SC.4.N.1.2, SC.4.N.1.6**)

LOCAL-TO-GLOBAL Connection

When you follow a recipe, you measure matter. When
making cookies, you will want to measure the amount
of each ingredient correctly. This way, the cookies will
look and taste the same each time that you make them.

In the United States, we often measure both solid and
liquid ingredients by their volume. The measuring tool
might be a teaspoon or a cup. In other countries, solid
ingredients are often measured by their mass in grams.
Liquids are measured by volume in liters or in milliliters.

Describe Would measuring solid ingredients by mass
instead of volume be an advantage, a disadvantage, or
both? Why?

_____

_____

_____

How does mass compare?

Scientists may investigate a whole object or its pieces. Does the mass of an object change if it is broken into pieces?

Materials
- ball of clay
- balance and gram cubes

Procedure

☐ **1.** Examine the ball of clay. Do you think its mass will change if you reshape it? If you break the clay into smaller pieces, will the mass change? Write a prediction.

_____

_____

_____

Science Practice

Scientists keep records to analyze data.

☐ **2.** Write a plan to test your prediction. Show it to your teacher before you begin. Record your data.

Mass before change	Mass after change	How it changed

Analyze and Interpret Data

3. Infer What can you infer from the data you collected?

_____

_____

_____

_____

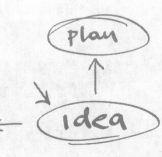

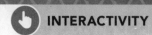

INTERACTIVITY

Complete an activity about the conservation of mass.

Mass

Anything that is made of matter and takes up space has mass. **Mass** is a measure of how much matter something has. Solid objects have mass. So do water and other liquids. Even the air we breathe has mass. The metric unit for mass is the gram. One gram is about the same as the mass of a paper clip. Smaller amounts of mass might be measured in milligrams. One milligram is equal to 0.001 gram. Larger masses are often measured in kilograms. A kilogram is equal to 1000 grams.

You can use a pan balance to compare a mass that you know with one that you do not know. When the pans are level, the two masses are equal.

The total mass of an object will not change when a physical change occurs. In a **physical change**, the size, shape, or state of matter changes, but the type of matter stays the same. An empty plastic bottle has a certain mass. If you crush the bottle, it will still have the same mass. If you cut it into two pieces, the mass of the combined two pieces will be the same as the mass of the whole bottle.

Compare and Contrast Each block on the balance has a mass of 1 g. What is the mass of the toy car? How does that mass compare with the mass of the eraser?

_____

_____

_____

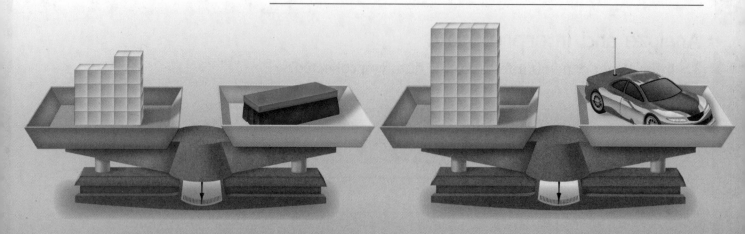

Question It!

You have entered a robot-building competition. One of the requirements is that the finished robot has a mass of 250 g or less. When you finish your robot, you find that it has a mass of 208 g. You realize that the robot needs four batteries.

What questions will you ask to find out whether your robot's mass will be within the 250 g or less requirement?

_____

_____

Law of Conservation of Mass

The Law of Conservation of Mass states that the parts of an object will have the same total mass as the mass of the whole object. For example, suppose you measure the mass of the toy in the picture and find that it is 23 g. You take the toy apart and measure the mass of each part separately. If you added the masses of the parts, the total would be 23 g, or the same as the mass of the assembled toy.

☑ READING CHECK **Compare and Contrast** Suppose you measure the mass of a wet sponge. Then you squeeze out the water in the sponge. You measure the sponge again. How will the mass of the wet sponge compare with the mass of the sponge in which you squeezed out the water? Why?

_____

_____

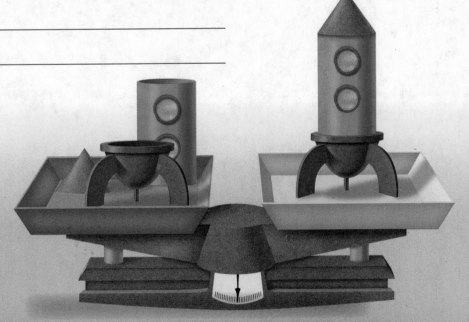

what is the mass?

Each pizza is on a scale. How can you use the scale and the Law of Conservation of Mass to compute the mass of the missing pieces of pizza?

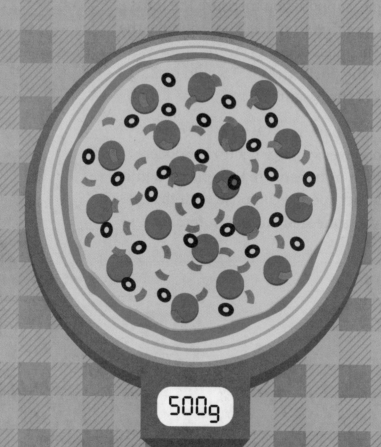

500g

! **What is the mass of the whole pizza?**

_____

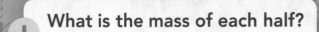

! **What is the mass of each half?**

_____

! **What is the mass of the piece of pizza that is missing?**

_____

How do you know?

_____

_____

_____

_____

Volume

All matter takes up space. The amount of space that matter takes up is called **volume**. Like mass, volume is a property of matter that can be measured.

✓ READING CHECK **Compare and Contrast** As you blow up a balloon, what happens to its volume? Why?

_____

_____

Volume of Liquids

To measure a liquid, use a measuring container, such as a graduated cylinder or a graduated beaker. A measuring container is marked with metric units. Some metric units used to measure volume are milliliter (mL) and liter (L). One liter is equal to 1000 milliliters. The units marked on the beaker are milliliters (mL).

Volume of Solids

If a solid is a cube, you can measure its length, width, and height. You can then **compute**, or determine, its volume by multiplying the measurements.

Explain Circle the cube that will have a greater volume. Tell why you think so.

_____

_____

_____

_____

A measuring container can be used to find the volume of solids that sink in water. To measure the volume of a solid, first put some water into a measuring container. Record its volume. Then place the solid into the container and record the volume of the water again. The object takes up space and pushes the water away. The water level rises by the same number of milliliters as the volume of the solid.

Compute Use the diagrams of the beakers to complete the sentences.

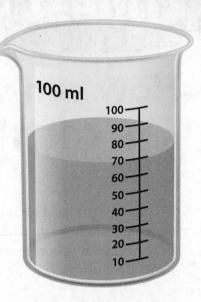

The volume of water is_____mL.

The volume of water and the cube is_____mL.

What is the volume of the metal cube? _____mL.

What might happen if the cube is made of a different material?

_____

Quest Connection

Describe how you would measure the volume of your unknown coin.

_____

_____

_____

_____

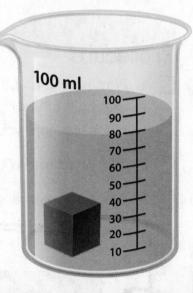

☑ **Lesson 3 Check**   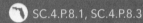 SC.4.P.8.1, SC.4.P.8.3

1. ☑ **READING CHECK** **Compare and Contrast** If you can cut a wooden cube in half, how would the mass of the two halves compare with the mass of the cube before it was cut?

_____

_____

2. **Explain** Why would it be difficult to find the volume of a rock using a ruler?

_____

_____

How can we measure and compare objects?

Scientists compare unknown objects to known objects using measurements. How can you compare masses to help identify an unknown object?

Materials
- balance and 30 gram cubes
- 10 U.S. pennies
- 10 nickels
- 10 dimes
- 2 quarters

Science Practice

Scientists **measure** properties to produce data during an investigation.

Procedure

☐ **1.** Plan how you will compare the masses of known coins to the mass of your unknown coin. Share your plan with your teacher before you begin.

☐ **2.** Construct and complete a data table.

☐ **3.** Compare your data with that of your classmates.

Data Table

Object	Mass
Unknown	4.8 g

Analyze and Interpret Data

4 How might your results be different from the results of another group? Why?

_____

_____

_____

_____

5. **Evaluate** Why is one measurement not enough evidence to determine the identity of an unknown object? What additional data could you consider?

_____

_____

_____

_____

_____

_____

_____

_____

Changes in Matter

I can...

Explain how some materials change and become materials with different characteristics.

Literacy Skill
Compare and Contrast

Vocabulary
chemical change
decay
rust

▶ **VIDEO**

Watch a video about changes in matter.

SC.4.P.9.1 Identify some familiar changes in materials that result in other materials with different characteristics, such as decaying animal or plant matter, burning, rusting, and cooking. (Also **SC.N.4.1.6**)

SPORTS ▸ Connection

Spelunking is the sport of exploring caves. While climbing around and squeezing through small passageways, a spelunker can observe some interesting-looking matter. As liquid water seeps through Earth's surface, it dissolves materials. As the water slowly drips into a cave from the ceiling, it leaves behind materials that continue to build up and make strange formations that hang from the cave ceiling. As water drips from these formations onto the cave floor, solid structures begin to build upward from the floor.

The natural formations found in caves can be destroyed by human activity. When a cave is visited often for recreation, people may want to make changes to the cave, such as widening passageways or adding stairways to hard-to-reach places.

Explain Should people be allowed to make changes to caves in order to make it easier for visitors? Why or why not?

_____

_____

uInvestigate Lab

How can you tell whether *matter changed*?

Scientists record their observations about matter and its changes. How can you show that matter changes when substances are mixed?

Procedure

☐ 1. Choose two materials that you think will change when they are mixed. Write a plan to test the materials to see whether they change.

☐ 2. Show your plan to your teacher before you begin. Record your observations.

Materials

- safety goggles
- beaker
- aluminum foil
- thermometer

Suggested Materials

- water
- vinegar
- baking soda
- steel wool

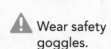
⚠ Wear safety goggles.

Observations

> **Science Practice**
>
> Scientists **record observations** during investigations.

Analyze and Interpret Data

3. **Use Evidence** Did the materials you mixed change? How do you know?

_____

_____

Plan It! Both baking powder and salt appear as white powders. What properties could you observe or test to help you tell the difference between them without tasting them? Write a plan.

_____

_____

_____

_____

Matter Changes

Sometimes matter changes, and new substances form. For example, burning wood will change the wood into ashes and gases. The new substances formed have very different properties than the original wood. Burning wood is an example of a chemical change. In a **chemical change**, new kinds of matter are produced. During a chemical change, the particles that make up the original substances rearrange to make new substances.

☑ **READING CHECK** **Compare and Contrast** Tell how the properties of ashes are different from the properties of the wood.

_____

_____

_____

_____

Common Chemical Changes

You may be familiar with the way fresh fruit changes over time. When fruit and other foods spoil, they go through a chemical change called **decay**. As matter decays, it can change color, produce an odor, or become very soft. These new properties are a sign that a chemical change has happened.

Some chemical changes happen quickly, such as when wood burns. When a firework explodes, the chemical change happens very quickly. Other chemical changes happen slowly. **Rust** is the substance that forms when oxygen and iron chemically change. As the hinge rusts, more and more of the iron in the hinge chemically changes. Over time, the amount of rust on the hinge will increase.

Apply Give one example of a chemical change that occurs slowly and one that occurs quickly.

_____

_____

_____

_____

Quest Connection

▼▼▼▼▼▼▼▼▼▼▼▼▼▼▼▼▼▼▼▼▼▼▼▼

Why might metals be good materials for coins?

_____

_____

_____

_____

u Be a Scientist

Chemical Change
Wear safety goggles. Measure 100 mL of vinegar and 25 mL of water. Pour them into a bowl. Add a pinch of salt. Stir. Find a penny. Describe it. Drop it into the solution. Wait a few minutes. Observe any changes. Describe what happened to the penny. Why does an older penny look different from a new penny?

What is an example of a chemical change?

Decay is an everyday chemical change. Describe how the apple appears as it moves through the process of decay.

Describe the apple in this picture.

_____

_____

_____

_____

_____

_____

Describe how the apple has changed in this picture.

_____
_____
_____
_____
_____
_____

How do you know that the fruit in the picture is undergoing chemical change?

_____
_____
_____
_____
_____
_____

☑ Lesson 4 Check

SC.4.P.9.1

1. **Critique** Several small red, yellow, and green paper squares are mixed together. Explain why this is not an example of a chemical change. Use evidence to justify your response.

_____
_____
_____

2. **Explain** Why is a burning match an example of a chemical change?

_____
_____

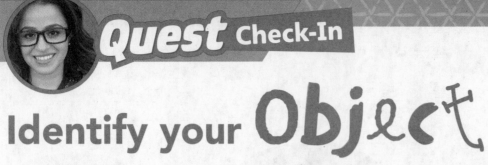
Identify your Object

Based on the evidence from previous Check-Ins and the information that you learned so far, narrow your choices for the possible metals that your unknown coin might be made of. List your choices and reasons for your choice.

Possible metal	Reasons for my choice

How could you narrow your choices? Write how you could do an investigation to use a physical or chemical change to help identify the metal your coin is made of.

_____

_____

_____

_____

_____

_____

_____

The Extreme Power of Water

How might you cut through thick pieces of metal without a sharp blade? Would you believe that you could use water? Water-jet cutters are tools that use a stream of water under extremely high pressure. Ordinarily, liquid water is soft and flowing. But when pressure is applied, look out! Water can be very hard. You may have noticed this when you did that last belly flop into a swimming pool!

Water-Jet cutters are extreme tools that are able to quickly perform very fine cuts in many different materials by making the stream of water smaller and smaller.

How could this tool be useful in the design of new products?

_____

_____

_____

_____

_____

STEM

The mystery of the unknown Object

How can I identify an unknown object?

INTERACTIVITY

Complete an activity to help you identify your coin.

It is time to let the metallurgist know what you think the metal in your coin is. Tell her what tests you have performed and their results. Explain why you identified your choice as you did.

_____

_____

_____

_____

_____

_____

_____

_____

_____

_____

_____

QUEST CHECK ✓ OFF

Metallurgist

If you want to know how to find, investigate, and design products with metals, talk to a metallurgist. A metallurgist is a materials scientist who studies the physical and chemical properties of metals. Metallurgists know how to extract and use metals for specific purposes.

Not all metallurgists perform the same jobs. For example, one metallurgist might test metal safety and quality. Another metallurgist might design processes to shape metals. Still others investigate accidents where the cause might be the failure of a metal part. Wherever you find a product made of metal, a metallurgist was probably involved in its development.

A metallurgist needs a college degree in areas such as metallurgy, materials science, physics, or chemical engineering. Knowledge of the physical and chemical properties of metals is not all that a metallurgist needs. Metallurgists also must be able to make observations and predictions, run investigations, design solutions to problems, prepare detailed drawings, and communicate their findings in a variety of ways.

▤ Write About It
What are some things you would make as a metallurgist?

Read each question and choose the best answer.

1. **Assess** Neil was given three substances to identify. He recorded his observations of the substances in the table.

Property	Substance A	Substance B	Substance C
color	green	green	green
particle appearance	powder	crystals	crystals
makes bubbles in vinegar	yes	no	yes

Is color a useful property to identify substances in Neil's investigation? Explain.

_____

_____

_____

2. **Analyze** How could Neil identify whether the substances are made of metal?

_____

_____

_____

_____

3. **Classify** If Neil used a balance to measure the substances, which physical property did he observe?

   A. color

   B. odor

   C. mass

   D. texture

4. **Differentiate** Which pair of changes are both physical changes?

   A. baking bread and melting crayons

   B. cutting paper and rolling modeling clay

   C. tarnishing silver and burning logs

   D. freezing water and rusting nails

5. Compare Look at the picture of the two objects.

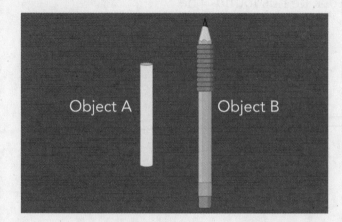

Object A   Object B

Compare the two objects by using their physical properties.

_____

_____

_____

_____

_____

6. Formulate Would the mass of Object A change if it were broken into three pieces? Explain.

_____

_____

_____

_____

7. Predict What will happen to an iron nail in the presence of air and moisture?

A. It will harden.

B. It will melt.

C. It will evaporate.

D. It will rust.

The Essential Question

How can matter be described and measured?

Show What You Learned

You described and measured the properties of metals. What properties do some metals have that made it possible for junkyard machinery to pick up the metals?

_____

_____

_____

_____

_____

_____

_____

_____

_____

_____

Read the scenario and answer questions 1–2.

Phillipe uses a bar magnet to test an unknown rock he has found. The results of his investigation are shown below.

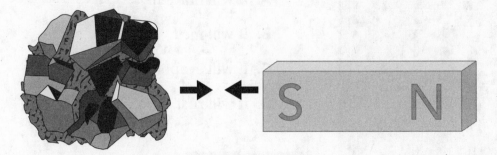

1 What can Phillipe conclude about the rock?

Ⓐ The rock contains a magnetic material.

Ⓑ The rock contains non-magnetic metal.

Ⓒ The rock is made of metal and is a magnet.

Ⓓ The rock is made of multiple types of minerals.

2 How could Phillipe test the hardness of the unknown rock?

Ⓕ He could feel the rock with his hand.

Ⓖ He could scratch the rock with a known rock.

Ⓗ He could weigh the rock on a scale.

Ⓘ He could measure the rock with a meter stick.

3 Which would be a function of a design solution that uses magnets?

Ⓐ sorting plastic recycling from garbage

Ⓑ separating particles of sand from water

Ⓒ finding nails buried under the dirt

Ⓓ holding a piece of paper onto a wooden door

Read the scenario and answer questions 4–5.

Layla placed two solid cubes into a graduated cylinder with 25 mL of water. She drew a diagram to show the results of her investigation.

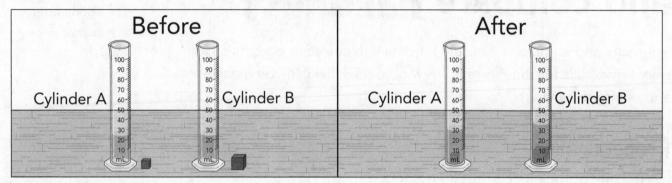

4 Which statement supports Layla's observations from her investigation?

F Cube A has more mass than cube B.

G Cube B has more mass than cube A.

H Cube A has more volume than cube B.

I Cube B has more volume than cube A.

5 How could Layla demonstrate a chemical change in the cubes?

A She could allow the cubes to rust.

B She could melt the cubes.

C She could cut the cubes in half.

D She could remove mass from the cubes.

6 Nadia claims that water vapor is a gas. Which statement **best** supports her claim?

F A gas spreads out to fill whatever space is available.

G A gas has a definite shape and takes up a definite amount of space.

H A gas does not have definite shape but takes up a definite amount of space.

I A gas does not take the shape of its container.

How can **you** measure and compare **hardness**?

Materials
- safety goggles
- chalk
- wooden stirrer
- quarter

Scientists and engineers measure hardness to compare objects or to select materials for the design of new objects. How can you measure and compare hardness?

 Wear safety goggles.

Procedure

☐ **1.** Look at the objects, but do not touch them. How does the hardness of the materials compare? Write a prediction about the order of the materials from hardest to softest.

_____

_____

_____

Science Practice

Scientists carry out investigations to answer questions.

☐ **2.** Write a plan to test how the hardness of the materials compares. Show your plan to your teacher before you begin.

☐ **3.** Record your observations.

Observations

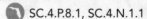

Analyze and Interpret Data

4. Analyze Do your results support your prediction? What is the order of hardness of the materials from hardest to softest?

_____

_____

_____

5. Compare and Contrast Do your results match those of other students? If not, why do you think this is so?

_____

_____

_____

_____

6. Evaluate How could you test the same materials for a different property of matter?

_____

_____

_____

_____

_____

Energy and Motion

SC.4.P.10.1 Observe and describe some basic forms of energy, including light, heat, sound, electrical, and the energy of motion. **SC.4.P.10.2** Investigate and describe that energy has the ability to cause motion or create change. **SC.4.P.10.3** Investigate and explain that sound is produced by vibrating objects and that pitch depends on how fast or slow the object vibrates. **SC.4.P.11.1** Recognize that heat flows from a hot object to a cold object and that heat flow may cause materials to change temperature. **SC.4.P.11.2** Identify common materials that conduct heat well or poorly. **SC.4.P.12.2** Investigate and describe that the speed of an object is determined by the distance it travels in a unit of time and that objects can move at different speeds. (Also **SC.4.N.1.1, SC.4.N.1.7, SC.4.N.3.1, LAFS.4.RI.2.5, MAFS.4.MD.1.2**)

Go online to access
your digital course.

▶ VIDEO

📖 eTEXT

👆 INTERACTIVITY

📱 VIRTUAL LAB

🎮 GAME

☑ ASSESSMENT

The Essential Question

What is energy, and how is it related to motion?

Show What You Know

The race cars are moving around the track. In what ways do you think energy is important for car racing?

_____

_____

_____

Energy Changes in Collisions

How can you design a safe car?

Hi, my name is Anna Alomar, and I am a vehicle safety engineer. I study what happens to cars and trucks involved in accidents. In this problem-based learning activity, you will design a new safety feature for a car. The most important criterion for your design is the safety of your passengers. You will consider how speed and energy affect auto collisions. Then you will find out how energy changes and transfers during a collision. You will use what you learn about energy to design a new safety feature.

Follow the path to learn how you will complete your Quest. The Quest activities in the lessons will help you complete the Quest. Check off your progress every time you complete an activity with a QUEST CHECK ✓ OFF . Go online for more Quest activities.

GAS

Quest Check-In 1

Lesson 1
Learn how energy affects the speed and direction of moving vehicles.

SC.4.P.10.2 Investigate and describe that energy has the ability to cause motion or create change. (Also **SC.4.P.10.1**)

VIDEO

Watch a video about a vehicle safety engineer

Quest Check-In 3

Lesson 3

Look at evidence from crash tests to find out how energy was transformed during a collision.

Quest Check-In Lab 4

Lesson 4

Learn about electric circuits, and design an alert system to prevent car crashes.

Quest Check-In Lab 2

Lesson 2

Review some data from crash tests, and use a model to study the motion of cars before, during, and after a collision.

Quest Findings

Use everything you have learned to design a safe vehicle.

How can you compare the energy of objects?

Scientists measure the amount of energy that is transferred during events. How can you compare the amount of energy of two objects with different sizes?

Materials
- golf balls
- large marbles
- ruler
- balance and gram cubes
- pan
- fine sand
- safety goggles

Procedure

☐ 1. Predict which object will have more energy: a larger or smaller object.

_____

_____

☐ 2. Use all the materials to plan an investigation that tests your prediction.

☐ 3. Show your plan to your teacher before you begin. Record your observations.

⚠ Wear safety goggles.

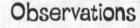 Science Practice

Scientists *collect data* to use as evidence.

Analyze and Interpret Data

4. **Interpret** Did your results support your prediction? Explain.

_____

_____

_____

5. **Explain** What evidence did you use to compare the amount of energy of each object?

_____

_____

_____

_____

Observations

Cause and Effect

LAFS.4.RI.2.5

GAME

Practice what you learn with the Mini Games.

Cause-and-effect relationships can explain how two events are related. A cause is the reason something happens. An effect is what happens. Use these strategies to help you identify causes and effects when reading informational texts.

- Ask yourself questions such as *What happens?* or *How did it change?* to identify an effect.

- Ask yourself *why* to identify the cause.

- Look for clue words such as *because* and *so.* They can signal cause and effect.

Just One Tiny Push

Have you ever seen a long line of falling dominoes? Dominoes have to be carefully set up to ensure that energy can move from domino to domino. With a tiny push, the dominoes fall because energy is transferred from one to the next. If enough energy moves from domino to domino, they will keep falling. Sometimes, all the dominoes fall. Other times, the dominoes stop falling, and some dominoes are left standing.

✓ **READING CHECK** **Cause and Effect** Circle words that identify a cause. Underline words that identify an effect.

Energy, Speed, and Moving Objects

I can...

Explain what energy is and describe some forms of energy. Explain how a moving object's speed and energy are related.

Literacy Skill
Cause and Effect

Vocabulary
energy
potential energy
kinetic energy
speed

Academic Vocabulary
transfer
transform

▶ **VIDEO**

Watch a video about moving objects.

SC.4.P.10.1 Observe and describe some basic forms of energy, including light, heat, sound, electrical, and the energy of motion. **SC.4.P.10.2** Investigate and describe that energy has the ability to cause motion or create change. **SC.4.P.10.3** Investigate and explain that sound is produced by vibrating objects and that pitch depends on how fast or slow the object vibrates. **SC.4.P.12.2** Investigate and describe that the speed of an object is determined by the distance it travels in a unit of time and that objects can move at different speeds. (Also **SC.4.N.1.7, LAFS.4.RI.2.5**)

ENGINEERING ❯ Connection

Have you ever noticed how many cars have a similar shape? Most cars are curved in the front. They have a gentle slope over the hood, windshield, and roof. The side mirrors are curved as well. The gentle curves and slopes of the car's design allow air to pass easily over the car.

Air is matter, so energy is needed to move it. Cars that come in contact with less air lose less energy, which means the cars can go faster and use less fuel. Engineers study how air can affect objects so that they can design cars that are faster and more fuel efficient.

📓 **Write About It** How would you design a new car? List criteria you may consider when developing your design.

How does starting height affect an object's energy?

When doing work involving vehicle safety, engineers consider factors that affect the speed and direction of a vehicle. How can you study the energy of a moving object?

Materials
- toy ball
- meterstick
- stopwatch
- masking tape
- several books
- smooth, flat board

Procedure

☐ **1.** Predict how the height of a ramp will affect how fast an object travels down it.

_____

_____

_____

Science Practice

Scientists construct explanations based on evidence.

☐ **2.** Use the materials to make a plan to test your prediction. Show your procedure to your teacher before you begin.

☐ **3.** Conduct your test. Record your observations.

Observations

Analyze and Interpret Data

4. Explain How does the starting height of an object traveling downward affect how fast it moves? Support your answer with evidence from this lab.

_____

_____

_____

_____

_____

Literacy ▸ Toolbox

Cause and Effect A cause can result in more than one effect. Find a cause in the photo that has two effects.

LAFS.4.RI.2.5

Energy

Energy is the ability to do work or to cause change. Energy is involved when anything moves or changes. Energy cannot be made nor destroyed, but it can change form and be transferred. When energy is **transferred**, it moves from one object to another.

Infer Some forms of energy are more easily observed than others. Suppose you were riding this roller coaster. What forms of energy do you think you would observe?

_____

_____

_____

Quest Connection

▼▼▼▼▼▼▼▼▼▼▼▼▼▼▼▼▼▼▼▼▼▼▼▼▼▼▼▼▼

How can energy be transferred in a car?

_____

_____

Energy at Rest

When these dominoes are first set up, they have stored energy. Stored energy in an object at rest is called **potential energy**. The potential energy of the dominoes comes from how they are positioned. As soon as each domino starts to fall, its potential energy changes into energy of motion. The amount of potential energy an object has depends on its shape or position.

Energy in Motion

The energy of a moving object is called **kinetic energy**. The kinetic energy of an object depends on its mass and how fast it is moving. We see the effects of kinetic energy when something moves from place to place. Falling dominoes have kinetic energy. Some kinetic energy is transferred from one domino to the next when they collide. When energy is **transformed**, it is changed from one kind of energy to another kind. When the dominoes fall, some energy is transformed into sound energy. That is why you hear the dominoes click. Heat, light, and electricity are some other forms of kinetic energy.

☑️ **READING CHECK** **Cause and Effect** How would kinetic energy of the dominoes be affected if the first domino did not hit the second one?

_____

_____

_____

_____

_____

INTERACTIVITY

Complete an activity on kinetic and potential energy.

How does energy affect particles of matter?

Just like larger objects, the smallest particles of matter have energy, too.

Potential Energy

Potential energy is involved when objects are bent, stretched, or compressed.

normal pillow

compressed pillow

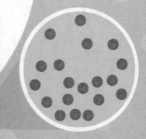

cold water

Thermal Energy

Thermal energy is energy that an object has because of the movement of its particles.

hot water

Electrical Energy

Electrical energy is energy caused by charged particles that flow through a path.

electrical particles

Chemical Energy

When you fill your car with gas, you are filling up on potential energy. When gasoline burns in the engine of a car, its chemical energy becomes kinetic energy and heat.

gasoline molecule

Draw and label another example of an object that uses energy.

Force and Speed

Find a ball that you can easily roll. With an adult, measure how far the ball travels if you give it a small push. Then measure how far it goes with a big push. How are the force and distance traveled related?

Motion and Energy

Motion is a characteristic of all matter, including the particles that make up matter. Motion can be observed, described, and measured. Two characteristics that are often used to describe motion are direction and speed. **Speed** is the distance an object travels in a particular amount of time, such as a minute or an hour. Speed is often described as *fast* or *slow*. Direction is which way an object is moving, such as north or south.

The speed or direction of an object is affected by forces. For example, a large force is needed to launch a rocket because the rocket's weight pulls downward on it. An upward force is applied to the rocket. If the upward force on the rocket is greater than the downward force, the rocket will launch upward. The greater the force pushing upward, the faster the rocket will move. That is because the faster an object moves, the more energy it has.

Apply A ball slowly starts to roll downhill, but its speed increases as it rolls. How are the ball's speed and energy related?

_____

_____

☑ Lesson 1 Check

 SC.4.P.10.2

1. **Differentiate** A ball is released from the top of a 3-foot ramp. The distance the ball travels is measured. The same ball is released from the top of a 6-foot ramp. How would the distance the ball travels differ the second time? Explain your reasoning.

_____

_____

2. **Explain** How do you know that a falling domino that causes another domino to move has energy?

_____

_____

Energy, Speed, and Motion

How are energy, speed, and motion related? Vehicle safety engineers use test crashes to investigate how energy, speed, and motion interact. The results from the investigations can help design safer cars.

1. Draw an arrow that shows the direction you think the cars were moving in each crash.

2. Why do you think vehicle safety engineers test vehicles at different speeds and directions in the test crash investigations?

_____

_____

_____

_____

_____

_____

_____

_____

INTERACTIVITY

Go online for interactivities related to this feature.

Toys on the Move

Almost anywhere you look, you are likely to see a machine that can move. Each kind of machine is designed to do a certain job. For example, a car is designed to move forward. A helicopter is designed to move both forward and straight upward. Some machines are toys. Guiding a remote-controlled toy car around a sidewalk can be a lot of fun. People love to watch toy helicopters do aerial stunts. In order for people to enjoy playing with a toy that moves, an engineer first had to build it. Engineers consider what the toy needs to do. Then they use their science knowledge and problem-solving skills to get the job done. If you could build any kind of moving toy, what would you build?

Design It

You have been asked by a toy company to build a moving toy that will race against other moving toys. Your toy must travel a distance of at least 1 meter in 10 seconds or less. There is no one way to build your machine. Figuring out how to do it will be up to you!

☐ Identify what form your toy will take.

☐ Describe how the parts of your toy will have to work together.

☐ Decide on which materials you will use to build your machine.

☐ Draw the design for your toy. Label each part. Include a sentence or two that tells how the parts work together.

Collisions

I can...

Predict changes in energy that occur when objects collide.

Literacy Skill
Cause and Effect

Vocabulary
collision

Academic Vocabulary
simulate

SC.4.P.10.2 Investigate and describe that energy has the ability to cause motion or create change. **SC.4.P.12.2** Investigate and describe that the speed of an object is determined by the distance it travels in a unit of time and that objects can move at different speeds. (Also **SC.4.N.1.1, SC.4.N.3.1**)

▶ **VIDEO**

Watch a video about sound energy.

SPORTS ⟩ Connection

SLAM! A stick hits a hockey puck. The motion requires an energy transfer from the hockey stick to the hockey puck. Hockey players use the force from their bodies to hit the puck. The harder the puck is hit, the farther the puck will travel. Hockey players are not the only athletes to use energy transfer to their advantage. Tennis, baseball, and cricket are sports where players also use transfer of energy to their advantage.

Identify What are two other sports that involve energy transfers between objects? Where do the transfers happen?

_____

_____

_____

_____

uInvestigate Lab

How does energy *transfer* between objects?

Vehicle safety engineers investigate the factors affecting collisions. What happens to the energy of objects when they bump into each other?

Materials
- marbles of different sizes and masses
- small ramp or chute

Procedure

☐ **1.** Choose a variable that you want to investigate about two objects that bump into each other. Choose between different masses, different speeds, moving or not moving, or starting from different heights. Make a prediction about what will happen to the objects when they collide.

_____

_____

_____

_____

Science Practice

Scientists design investigations to answer a scientific question.

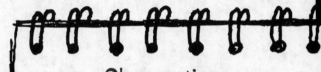

Observations

☐ **2.** Use the materials to make a plan to test your prediction. Show your plan to your teacher before you begin.

☐ **3.** Conduct your investigation and record the data.

Analyze and Interpret Data

4. Explain What energy transfer occurred in your investigation? How do you know?

_____

_____

_____

_____

_____

Energy Changes IN A COLLISION

When one object bumps into another object, the action is called a **collision**. During a collision, energy is transferred. Observe what happens when a basketball strikes the floor of the basketball court.

Energy is transformed as the ball moves downward.

Objects slightly compress when they collide. The ball becomes compressed as if it were made of springs.

The ball stretches back out after it bounces off the floor.

! **What changes in energy occur when the bowling ball strikes the pins?**

_____

_____

_____

_____

_____

_____

_____

Other Energy Changes

When a bowling ball strikes the pins, a loud sound is heard. The sound is evidence of an energy change. Some of the bowling ball's kinetic energy is changed into sound energy. Collisions can also result in a change of kinetic energy to light energy, thermal energy, or other types of energy.

Model It!

Draw a picture of two objects that are colliding and transferring kinetic energy into another type of energy. Label the energy changes that are happening.

Engineering Practice ▸ Toolbox

Design a Solution A company wants to improve its bowling ball so that it rolls in a straighter line. Define one problem that engineers would have to solve when improving the design of the ball.

Quest Connection

Why would the collision between two cars both traveling at a fast speed most likely cause more damage than a collision between two slow-moving cars?

_____

_____

_____

_____

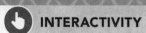
INTERACTIVITY

Complete an activity on kinetic energy.

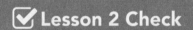 **Be a Scientist**

Construct a Cradle
With an adult, find some objects around your home that you can use to make your own version of a Newton's cradle. How do the energy transfers of different objects compare? What properties do you think make objects better for this purpose?

The device in the picture is a Newton's cradle. It shows how energy can move between objects in a collision. It can **simulate**, or model, larger collisions. When you lift one of the spheres and drop it, the first sphere's energy is transferred to the other spheres. This causes the sphere on the opposite side to fly upward. Then the second sphere comes down, and the first sphere you dropped pops back up. The spheres in the middle barely move. Much of the kinetic energy is transferred through them.

☑ Lesson 2 Check

 SC.4.P.12.2

1. **☑ READING CHECK** **Cause and Effect** In Newton's cradle, why do the spheres in the center barely move?

_____

_____

2. **Hypothesize** Suppose you are bowling. You want to see how the number of pins knocked down changes when a ball is rolled slowly down the lane with little force compared to when a ball is rolled quickly with a great deal of force. What do you predict the difference would be?

_____

_____

How does modeling help you understand a collision?

Materials
- toy cars
- colored pencils or markers
- paper

Vehicle safety engineers use models to understand what happens in a collision. By studying the effects of the collision, engineers can use the data to develop designs that improve the safety of the car. How can a model help you understand what happened in the collision shown in the picture?

Engineering Practice

Scientists use models to help identify cause and effect relationships.

Procedure

☐ **1.** Identify any evidence that helps explain the causes and effects of the car crash. What chain of events do you think led to the collision? Write the information on the Accident Report.

☐ **2.** Use the toy cars and other materials to model the collision. Re-create the crash. Draw pictures on the Accident Report to show the scene before, during, and after the collision.

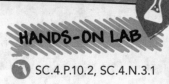

Accident Report

_____
_____
_____
_____
_____
_____
_____

Evaluate Your Model

3. Evaluate Does your model provide enough information to determine what caused the crash? How could you improve the model to make it more useful?

_____
_____
_____

4. Draw Conclusions Based on your data, what do you think caused the crash?

_____
_____
_____

5. Infer What can you infer from your model about the energy changes that occurred in the crash?

_____
_____
_____

Energy Transfer

I can...

Give examples of energy being transferred from place to place.
Explain that heat flows from hot objects to cold ones.
Demonstrate that some materials are good conductors of heat and others are not.

Literacy Skill
Cause and Effect

Vocabulary
heat
radiation
light
sound
wave

Academic Vocabulary
generate

SC.4.P.10.1 Observe and describe some basic forms of energy, including light, heat, sound, electrical, and the energy of motion. **SC.4.P.10.3** Investigate and explain that sound is produced by vibrating objects and that pitch depends on how fast or slow the object vibrates. **SC.4.P.11.1** Recognize that heat flows from a hot object to a cold object and that heat flow may cause materials to change temperature. **SC.4.P.11.2** Identify common materials that conduct heat well or poorly. (Also **SC.4.N.1.1, MAFS.4.MD.1.2**)

STEM Connection

Many animals, such as bats and owls, are active only at night. Scientists want to know how animals behave in their natural habitat. However, a normal camera needs visible light to make an image, so it would not work well at night. How can we see animals at night?

To help capture images in the dark, scientists use thermal cameras, or cameras that sense the warmth of an animal's body rather than the visible light that common cameras use. The images that thermal cameras produce do not show the same images you see with your eyes. Instead, the images look like those shown here, which show differences in temperature. In a thermal photo of an animal in its habitat, the red areas show the warmest parts of an animal and its surroundings, and the blue areas show the coolest parts. Plants are also detected by using thermal imaging.

Write About It In your science notebook, tell how you would use thermal imaging to analyze an animal in its habitat.

uInvestigate Lab

How does heat move?

Scientists study how easily heat can move through different materials. How can you identify materials that allow heat to move easily?

Procedure

☐ **1.** Look at the suggested materials. Make a hypothesis about which materials will allow heat to move easily through them and which ones will not.

_____

_____

☐ **2.** Make a plan to test your hypothesis. Show your plan to your teacher before you begin. Record your observations.

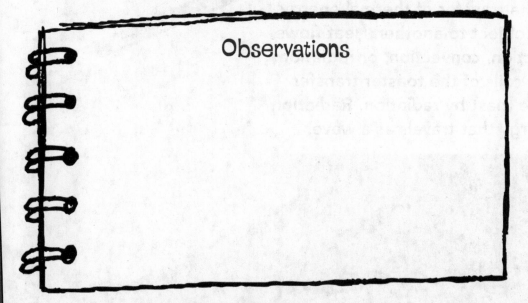

Observations

Materials
- ice bath
- hot water
- thermometer
- graduated cylinder

Suggested Materials
- plastic cups
- foam cups
- paper cups
- metal cups
- glass cups
- ceramic cups

⚠ Be careful handling hot water.

⚠ Be careful using glassware.

Science Practice

Scientists collect evidence by performing experiments.

Analyze and Interpret Data

3. Summarize What did the results of your experiment show? Did they support your hypothesis?

_____

_____

_____

How is ENERGY transferred?

Energy can be transferred through heat, sound, light, and electricity.

Heat is the transfer of thermal energy from one object to another. Heat flows by conduction, convection, or radiation. The hot coils of the toaster transfer heat to the toast by radiation. **Radiation** is energy that travels as a wave.

Infer Circle examples of where you think energy is being transferred.

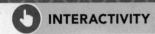
Energy and Particle Motion

All matter, including your body, is made of moving particles. These moving particles have kinetic energy. When you use a thermometer to find the temperature of a substance, you are finding the average kinetic energy of its particles. The energy is carried away from the matter by radiation.

Compare Look at the particles in the two diagrams. What difference do you see?

_____

_____

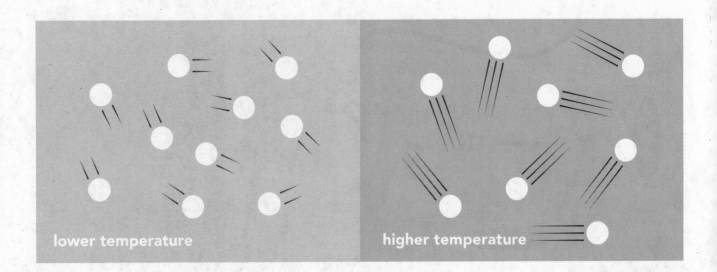

lower temperature   higher temperature

When heat is transferred to an object, the object's particles move faster. That is why the temperature of the object increases. When radiation carries energy from the sun to your skin, you feel hotter. The sun's radiation is making the particles of your skin move faster.

✓ READING CHECK **Cause and Effect** What do you think happens to the particles of matter of the object that is transferring the heat to another object? How will this affect its temperature?

_____

_____

Light Energy

Any object that is a source of light has light energy. **Light** is a form of energy that we can see. Some of the energy that is radiated to Earth from the sun can be seen as light. The same kind of radiation is given off by other stars, which is why we can see them in a dark sky. You can also see light produced when lightning streaks across the sky. Some animals, such as these jellyfish, **generate**, or produce, their own light. Many of these animals live deep in the ocean where the sun's energy does not reach. The light these animals produce are examples of natural sources of light energy. Scientists have also developed ways to generate other forms of light energy, such as light bulbs, flashlights, and lasers.

Question It!

What are some other forms of light energy that you can identify? How do you use different forms of light energy every day?

_____
_____
_____
_____
_____
_____
_____
_____

Sound Energy

When you strike a bell, you hear a sound—the bell's ring. To ring the bell, the kinetic energy of your hand is transferred to the bell, causing it to vibrate. **Sound** is energy in the particles that vibrate as they pass through matter. As the vibrating particles bump into each other, they form a pattern similar to the one in the picture. Sound can travel through solids, liquids, or gases. Sound is often described in terms of pitch, or how fast or slow the particles vibrate as they pass through matter. A sound with a high pitch has particles that vibrate faster than a sound with a low pitch.

✓ **READING CHECK** **Compare and Contrast**
Which sound has more energy—the croak of a frog or the squeal of a pig? _____

Quest Connection

Each time an air particle interacts with another air particle, some, but not all, kinetic energy is transferred. What do you think ultimately happens to the energy of the sound as it moves through the air?

_____

_____

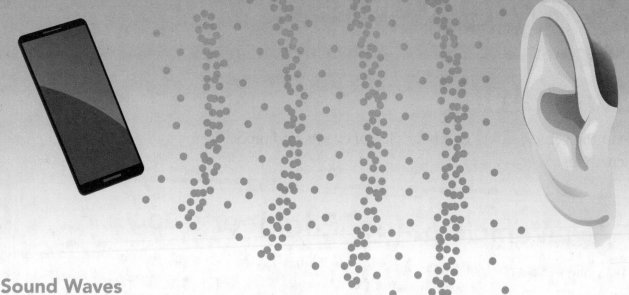

Sound Waves

Sound energy travels outward as a wave from the source of the sound, such as a cell phone. A **wave** is a form of the transfer of energy. When a wave moves through matter, the matter does not move with the wave. A sound wave moves in all directions from the source of the sound.

Think again about the ringing bell. You may not be able to see it vibrate, but you can feel it. The metal of the bell moves back and forth as it vibrates. Each time it moves forward in a vibration, it pushes against air particles, and the air particles move outward and closer together. When the metal moves backward in a vibration, the air particles spread out again. That is what causes the pattern.

☑ Lesson 3 Check

🕐 SC.4.P.10.3, SC.4.P.11.1

1. **Cite Evidence** What evidence can you use to prove that sounds can be different pitches?

   _____

   _____

   _____

2. **Draw Conclusions** A hot pot is placed on a cool table. Which way will heat flow between the pot and the table? Why?

   _____

   _____

Crash It!

Read the vehicle safety engineer's log of events and report from a crash test.

 Vehicle Safety Engineer's Log

The following vehicle crash test was conducted on January 20, 2017. The vehicle was a passenger vehicle. It was tested for safety during a front-end collision at 35 miles per hour (mph), or about 56 kilometers per hour (kph).

1:00 P.M. – Vehicle placed on test track with crash-test dummies inside. Electric tow cable attached.

1:10 P.M. – Pretest safety check conducted. All safety engineers in position to safely monitor the test.

1:12 P.M. – Crash sequence started. Electric tow cable began pulling the vehicle.

1:13 P.M. – Vehicle impacted concrete barrier at 35 mph.

1:15 P.M. – Final safety check completed. Vehicle crash test completed.

Crash Test Results

A loud boom sounded at the time of impact. The front end of the vehicle was compressed by 30%. The frame of the car was also bent. The vehicle's windshield was cracked over 90% of its surface. All other windows were completely shattered. The vehicle's restraints (seat belts) and airbags worked correctly. Crash-test dummies showed only minor signs of damage.

1. What are three pieces of evidence from this investigation that show energy was transferred?

_____

_____

2. What are two ways that energy was transformed in the test?

_____

_____

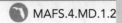
Relative Distance

The pitcher stands on the mound 60 feet away from home plate. She looks over her shoulder to see the runner on first base. She winds up and throws the ball to the catcher. The ball takes exactly 1 second to get to the catcher's glove. How fast was the ball going?

As you have learned, speed is how fast an object goes. The pitcher threw the ball 60 feet in 1 second. Usually, the speed of a pitch is measured in miles per hour (mph). But a baseball never actually goes a mile. The distance from the pitcher to home plate is about 60 feet. One mile is the same as 5,280 feet! How many pitches fit inside a mile? Complete this equation to find out.

[feet in a mile] / [feet between pitcher and catcher] = _____

If the ball went 60 feet per second, what was the ball's speed in mph? To answer this question, first find out how long it would take the ball to travel 1 mile. How many seconds would it take the ball to travel 1 mile?

_____

There are 3,600 seconds in an hour. How many miles could the baseball go in 1 hour if its speed did not change? Round your answer to the nearest whole number.

3,600 / _____ = ~ _____

Convert your answer to kilometers. _____

1 mile = 1.6 kilometers

Electric Circuits

I can...

Use models to describe how electric currents flow in circuits.

Literacy Skill
Cause and Effect

Vocabulary
electric charge
electric current
conductor
insulator
resistor

Academic Vocabulary
source

▶ **VIDEO**

Watch a video about electric currents.

SC.4.P.10.1 Observe and describe some basic forms of energy, including light, heat, sound, electrical, and the energy of motion. SC.4.P.10.2 Investigate and describe that energy has the ability to cause motion or create change. (Also SC.4.N.1.1, SC.4.N.3.1)

CURRICULUM ⟩ Connection

The tubes of neon signs are filled with certain gases that produce light when they absorb energy. Each kind of gas produces a particular color of light. For example, neon produces red light, and argon gas produces blue light. The gases can be mixed to make many different colors of light. If you mix argon gas with a gas that gives off yellow light, the light that fills the tube will be green. The source of energy to make these different colors of light is electricity.

📓 **Describe** What kind of energy change does electricity cause in the sign's tube?

_____

_____

How does *electric energy* flow in circuits?

Engineers use models to design products that use electrical energy in newer and safer ways. How can you use a model to describe how electrical energy flows?

Materials
• 2 pieces of wire
• bulb and holder
• battery and holder

Science Practice

Scientists make observations to gather evidence.

Procedure

☐ **1.** Look at the materials. How can you connect them to make the bulb light? Draw a picture.

☐ **2.** Show your plan to your teacher before you begin. Test your idea. If the bulb does not light, revise your plan. Keep testing until you have put the materials together in a way that makes the bulb light.

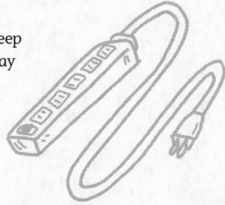

Analyze and Interpret Data

3. Assess How does energy move in this system? Draw arrows on your drawing to show the path.

Connecting Concepts ▸ Tool box

Systems A system is a group of different parts that work together. When you turn on a light bulb, you are using an electrical system. How many parts of the system can you identify?

Electric Charge

When you turn on a light, electrical energy moves. The flow of electrical energy happens because the particles that make up matter move. These particles have an **electric charge**. The electric charge is a property that causes matter to have a force, called electric force, when it is placed near other charged matter. Electric charges can be positive (+) or negative (–). Two particles that have the same charge will repel, or push away, each other. If their charges are opposite, they will attract, or pull toward, each other.

Infer Do you think the balloon and the towel have opposite charges? Explain your answer.

_____

_____

Model It! The circles in the diagram represent particles with electric charges. Draw arrows to show whether each pair of particles will attract or repel each other.

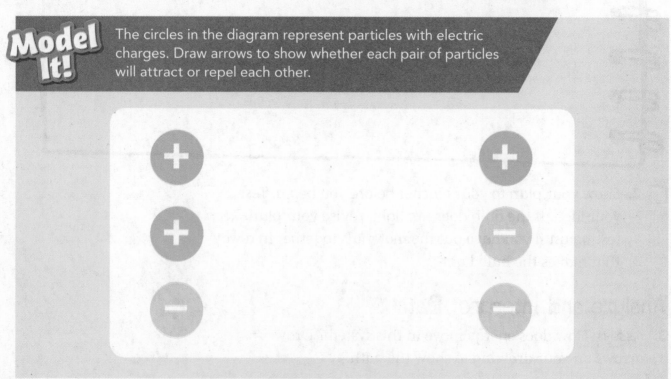

Moving Electric Charges

Particles with electric charge can move from place to place. The flow of charged particles in the same direction is called **electric current**.

Some materials allow electric current to easily flow through them. A material that allows electric current to flow through it is called a **conductor**. Metal is a good conductor of electricity. For that reason, copper is a metal that is used to make electrical wires.

Other materials do not allow current to flow. A material that does not allow electrical current to flow through it is called an **insulator**. Plastic is an insulating material.

Infer Why do you think that the inside and the outside of electrical wires are made from different materials?

_____

_____

_____

_____

Quest Connection

▼▼▼ ▼▼▼ ▼ ▼ ▼▼ ▼ ▼▼ ▼ ▼ ▼▼▼ ▼ ▼▼▼ ▼ ▼ ▼▼ ▼ ▼

How can you use what you know about conductors and insulators to improve the safety design of your vehicle?

_____

_____

_____

_____

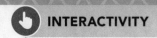

INTERACTIVITY

Complete an activity on how electricity is transferred.

Electric Circuits

In a conducting material, such as a wire, the electric current needs a **source**, or starting point, of energy to keep it moving. The electric current must flow in a complete path. This path is called an electric circuit. The photo shows the path of an electric circuit.

✅ **READING CHECK** **Cause and Effect** How do you think the switch can stop the electric current from flowing in this electric circuit?

_____

_____

_____

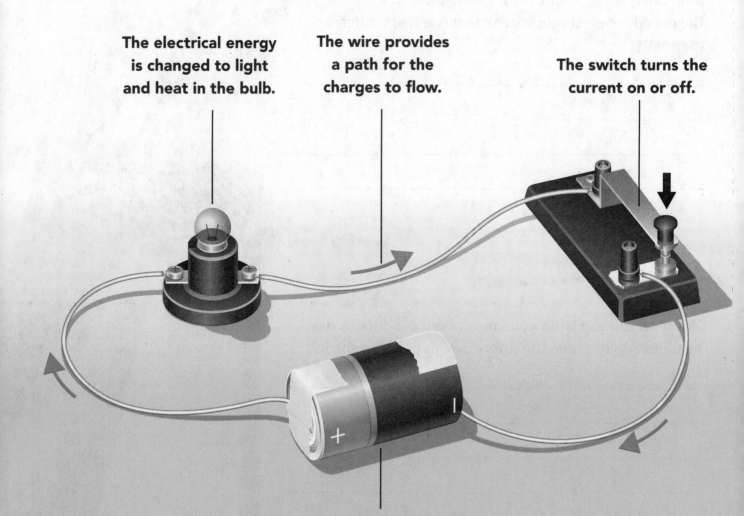

The electrical energy is changed to light and heat in the bulb.

The wire provides a path for the charges to flow.

The switch turns the current on or off.

The battery is the power source.

Resistance

In the circuit, current flows through both the wire and the bulb. The bulb glows, but the wire does not. The difference is that the light bulb has a wire made of a material that does not allow electric current to flow easily. The wire is a **resistor**, which is a device to control the flow of electricity. When current is pushed through a resistor, often the electrical energy is changed into another form of energy, such as light or heat. The wire that carries the current to and from the light bulb is made of a conductor.

Make Meaning Do a survey of your home to see how many objects make heat or light. Which of these do you think result from electric current flowing through a resistor?

resistor

✓ Lesson 4 Check

1. **Explain Phenomena** Several small squares of tissue paper are on a table. A negatively charged balloon is brought near the squares and they stick to the balloon. What charge do the papers have? Justify your response with evidence.

_____

_____

_____

_____

2. **Recognize** What is a source in a circuit? Why is a source necessary in an electric current?

_____

_____

How can an electric circuit help prevent collisions?

The red-signal traffic lights that are common almost everywhere in the United States were designed by engineers to control traffic and prevent accidents. But they cannot control all accidents, such as the collision you learned about in the earlier Quest Check-Ins. How can you use an electric circuit to design an alert system to prevent rear-end collisions?

Materials
- electric buzzer
- battery with holder
- insulated wire
- scissors

Suggested Materials
- light with holder
- cardboard
- aluminum foil

Plan and Build

☐ 1. List two ideas for using an electric circuit to develop an alert system.

_____

_____

_____

_____

☐ 2. Choose one idea and write or draw a plan to make a model of it. Include the materials you will use and how you will test your model. Use all the materials and any of the suggested materials.

  ⚠ Be careful using scissors.

Engineering Practice

Engineers use models to design and test devices.

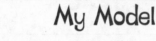
My Model

☐ **3.** Share your plan with another classmate. What suggestions does the classmate have for a design improvement?

_____

_____

_____

☐ **4.** Incorporate any useful suggestions into your plan. Show your final plan to your teacher before you begin.

☐ **5.** Build your model, and test it. Record your observations.

Observations

Evaluate Your Design

6. Did your model work the way you thought it would? Based on your observations, do you think your new safety feature would help prevent collisions?

_____

_____

_____

_____

INTERACTIVITY

Get support to design your safe car.

STEM Energy Changes in Collisions

How can you design a safe car?

Design a Solution

Throughout the Quest, you learned about energy and how forms of energy change. You designed a safety device for a car. Now you will make a model drawing of a car that shows where the device will be located. You will also show how energy will turn on the device.

My Model

Communicate Your Solution

Present the design of your vehicle to your classmates. Explain how your design will keep passengers safe.

QUEST CHECK ✓ OFF

Vehicle Safety Engineer

Do you like cars or trucks? Do you want to make the world a safer place? Vehicle safety engineers use their knowledge of energy, forces, and materials to design safer vehicles. They use data from the real world, computer simulations, and crash-test experiments to develop their designs.

Vehicle safety engineers can work in government labs or for private companies. They are an essential part of the teams that design new cars and trucks. If you want to be a vehicle safety engineer, you will need a degree in engineering. Vehicle safety engineers can help make the world a safer place!

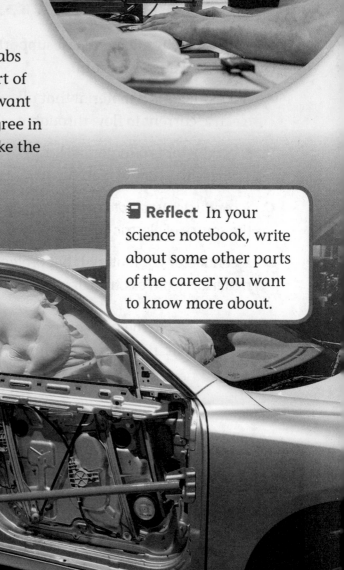

Reflect In your science notebook, write about some other parts of the career you want to know more about.

**Read each question and choose or
write the best answer.**

Peter drew a diagram of an electric circuit.

conductor

1. Identify Which statement best supports
the label on Peter's diagram?

  A. A conductor is a material that allows
electric current to flow through it.

  B. A conductor is a material that
controls the flow of electric currents.

  C. A conductor is a material that provides
the source of electric currents.

  D. A conductor is a material that protects
materials from electric currents.

2. Explain Describe the path of the
electric current in Peter's diagram.

_____

_____

_____

_____

_____

_____

_____

3. Summarize Which statement describes
heat?

  A. Heat moves from hot objects to cold
ones.

  B. Heat only moves by conduction.

  C. Heat increases as objects become
colder.

  D. Heat is the temperature of an object.

4. Assess Which of the following
variables could affect how fast a
baseball travels after being hit?
Select all that apply.

  ☐ height of the player

  ☐ weight of the ball

  ☐ amount of light energy

  ☐ speed of the pitch

5. Formulate Bernard rolled four different-colored bowling balls with the same mass down a bowling lane. He recorded each ball's average speed in the table.

Ball color	Average speed (m/sec)
	7.15
	6.26
	8.94
	6.71

Which ball has the most kinetic energy? Use data from the table to support your claim.

_____

_____

_____

6. Draw Conclusions Which vehicle is moving at the fastest speed?

A. a car that travels 96 kilometers in 2 hours

B. a bus that travels 160 kilometers in 5 hours

C. a bike that travels 64 kilometers in 4 hours

D. a truck that travels 320 kilometers in 5 hours

The Essential Question *What is energy, and how is it related to motion?*

Show What You Learned

What energy transformations take place in a race car during a race?

_____

_____

_____

_____

_____

_____

_____

_____

_____

_____

_____

_____

Read the scenario and answer questions 1–3.

A scientist was watching a baseball game. He became curious about what happens when a player swings the bat to hit the ball. He collected data about the bat's speed as it hits the ball and the ball's speed just after it is hit by the bat. He recorded the data in a table.

Swing	Bat Speed	Ball Speed
1	9 m/s	24 m/s
2	12 m/s	30 m/s
3	15 m/s	34 m/s
4	18 m/s	37 m/s
5	21 m/s	40 m/s
6	24 m/s	20 m/s

1 Which question could be answered using the data in the table?

Ⓐ How would the ball speed change if a bigger ball were used?

Ⓑ Which direction is the ball moving in and where will it likely land?

Ⓒ Does the speed of a ball change when the weight of the bat changes?

Ⓓ How is the speed of the bat related to how fast a ball travels when hit?

2 During swing 6, the player's bat broke. Which of these conclusions does this observation support?

Ⓕ Energy from the player was lost to inertia.

Ⓖ Energy from the ball was absorbed by the bat.

Ⓗ Energy from the player was transformed to heat.

Ⓘ Energy from the bat was transferred to the player.

3 Given the same bat speeds, what would likely happen if the bat used were heavier?

Ⓐ The baseball would travel more slowly.

Ⓑ More kinetic energy would be transferred.

Ⓒ Less kinetic energy would change to sound energy.

Ⓓ More energy would be changed to potential energy.

Read the scenario and answer questions 4–6.

Ms. Alba makes her afternoon tea each day by filling a kettle with cold water. She puts the kettle on a hot stove and heats it until the water boils. She pours the hot water into her cup that has a tea bag.

4 When do the particles in the water in the kettle begin to move faster?

Ⓕ when the kettle is being filled

Ⓖ when the kettle is being heated

Ⓗ when the kettle is taken off the stove

Ⓘ when the water is poured from the kettle to the cup

5 Which description related to the scenario does NOT describe a transfer of thermal energy from one object to the next?

Ⓐ The burner plates on the stove heat the kettle.

Ⓑ The metal from the kettle heats the water.

Ⓒ The water from the kettle heats the cup.

Ⓓ The steam from the kettle heats the water.

6 Which **best** describes how heat flows through the scenario above?

Ⓕ kettle > stove > cup > spoon

Ⓖ stove > kettle > cup > spoon

Ⓗ kettle > cup > spoon > stove

Ⓘ stove > cup > spoon > kettle

What affects energy transfer?

Materials
- rubber ball, 1-inch
- meterstick
- safety goggles
- paper bowl
- sand

Vehicle safety engineers use what they know about different materials to make new and safer vehicles. How does speed affect how much energy is transferred during a collision?

 Wear safety goggles.

Procedure

☐ **1.** Predict how the height from which an object is dropped affects the amount of energy it transfers.

_____

_____

_____

_____

Science Practice

Scientists **collect data** to use as evidence.

☐ **2.** Use all the materials. Make a plan to test your prediction. Show your plan to your teacher before you begin.

_____

_____

_____

_____

_____

_____

_____

☐ **3.** Record your data.

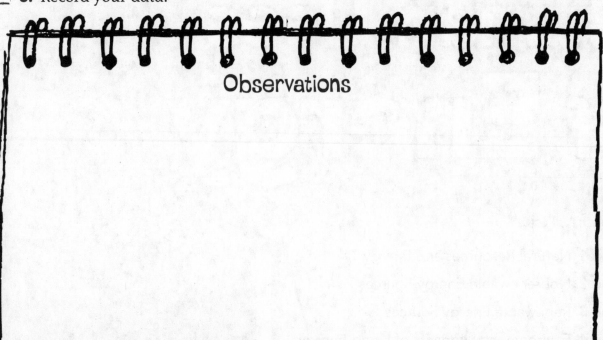

Observations

Analyze and Interpret Data

4. Use Evidence Do the data you collected support your prediction? Use evidence to support your answer.

_____

_____

_____

_____

_____

_____

5. Explain How does the speed of an object relate to its energy?

_____

_____

Topic 5

Human Uses of Energy

SC.4.P.10.1 Observe and describe some basic forms of energy, including light, heat, sound, electrical, and the energy of motion. **SC.4.P.10.2** Investigate and describe that energy has the ability to cause motion or create change. **SC.4.P.10.4** Describe how moving water and air are sources of energy and can be used to move things. (Also **SC.4.N.1.1, SC.4.N.1.5, SC.4.N.1.7, SC.4.N.1.8, SC.4.N.2.1, SC.4.N.3.1, LAFS.4.RI.3.7**)

Go online to access
your digital course.

▶ VIDEO

📖 eTEXT

👆 INTERACTIVITY

🧪 VIRTUAL LAB

🎮 GAME

☑ ASSESSMENT

The Essential Question

How do we convert energy to meet our needs?

Show What You Know

People use a lot of electrical energy in homes, schools, and businesses. What are some ways to produce electrical energy from other kinds of energy?

_____

_____

_____

Power from the People

How can a device convert energy from one form to another?

Hi, I'm Barry Arnold, an electrical engineer. I work for a company that designs exercise equipment. That might sound like an unusual job for an electrical engineer, but it isn't. Right now, my big project is designing an exercise bike that provides power to your home as you work out. A one-hour ride on your bike can provide enough power to keep your laptop computer working for ten hours.

I need your help to design a mechanical device that provides electric power. Maybe it could charge your cell phone. To test the device, you will use it to run a small electric motor. Then you will demonstrate how your device works and think about ways to improve it.

Follow the path to learn how you will complete the Quest. The Quest activities in the lessons will help you complete the Quest! Check off your progress on the path when you complete an activity with a

QUEST CHECK ✓ **OFF** . Go online for more Quest activities.

Quest Check-In 1

Lesson 1
Identify some criteria and constraints of your energy device.

SC.4.P.10.1 Investigate and describe some basic forms of energy, including light, heat, sound, electrical, chemical, and mechanical. **SC.4.P.10.2** Investigate and describe that energy has the ability to cause motion or create change.

VIDEO

Watch a video about an electrical engineer.

Quest Check-In Lab 3

Lesson 3

Convert your charging device from a battery-operated device to a solar-powered one.

Quest Check-In 4

Lesson 4

Evaluate the environmental impact of your device.

Quest Check-In Lab 2

Lesson 2

Build a device that uses a battery to create motion.

Quest Findings

Build your final exercise device that charges the cell phone.

How are energy resources used?

Electrical engineers consider the availability of an energy source. How can you show the effect of use on renewable and nonrenewable energy sources?

Materials
- 160 tokens
- number cubes

Procedure

☐ **1.** Decide who will be the 2 energy suppliers and the 2 energy users in this lab. Energy supplier A and energy supplier B each have 45 units (tokens) of energy to start. Each supplier has one user.

☐ **2.** Users take turns rolling a number cube. At each turn, the user gets the number of tokens that shows on the number cube. On each turn, supplier B gets 10 additional tokens. Supplier A gets 0 additional tokens. Write the amounts in the table.

☐ **3.** Repeat rolling the cubes until each user has had 5 turns.

Science Practice

Scientists **construct explanations** for observations and results of investigations.

	Supplier A			Supplier B		
Turn	Added	Used	Total	Added	Used	Total
0	45	0	45	45	0	45
1	0			10		
2	0			10		
3	0			10		
4	0			10		
5	0			10		

Analyze and Interpret Data

4. Predict Which supplier will be able to provide units longer? Construct an explanation.

_____

_____

Use Text Features

LAFS.4.RI.3.7

Text features help organize the information given to you in the text. They help you better understand the text's overall meaning. Some common types of text features are images, captions, headings, and highlighted words.

Read the following text about energy alternatives. Pay special attention to text features.

GAME

Practice what you learn with the Mini Games.

Energy of the Future

Finding and using energy sources other than fossil fuels is an important goal of scientists and people around the world. Here are two newer alternatives.

Wave Energy

The energy of moving water can be used to turn the blades of a turbine. The turbines change this moving energy into electricity. Wave energy can be captured on or below the ocean surface, near or far from the shore. Like wind energy, it is a safe and clean source.

Solar Energy

Many homes now use solar panels to collect solar energy that can be changed to electricity for their homes. Scientists are currently developing window glass that acts as a solar collector. The glass will capture the energy in sunlight that we cannot see while letting regular visible light pass through.

☑ READING CHECK **Use Text Features** Circle the text features that helped you understand what you read.

Natural Resources and Energy

I can...
Describe how natural resources are converted to energy and fuel.

Literacy Skill
Use Text Features

Vocabulary
fuel
combustion
turbine
generator
battery

Academic Vocabulary
device
primary

▶ **VIDEO**

Watch a video about chemical and electrical energy.

🔹 **SC.4.P.10.1** Observe and describe some basic forms of energy, including light, heat, sound, electrical, and the energy of motion.
SC.4.P.10.2 Investigate and describe that energy has the ability to cause motion or create change. (Also **SC.4.N.1.8, LAFS.4.RI.3.7**)

STEM ▶ Connection

The world has more than a billion cars! Almost all of them use a gasoline engine for power. Some new kinds of cars are very different, though. Many people now drive hybrid cars. These cars use both gasoline and electricity to run. Other cars use only electricity. These cars have electric motors connected to large batteries and use only electricity. They get their batteries recharged instead of gas tanks filled. Electric cars are much more efficient than cars that use gas—they use less total energy.

What if the batteries did not need to be recharged? Some research engineers have built solar cars. Solar panels charge the batteries whenever enough light is available, so you do not have to plug the car into an electric station. These new cars are experiments, so you cannot buy one yet. Someday, though, you might travel in a car that needs no fuel other than sunlight.

📑 **Make Meaning** In your science notebook, explain why a solar car might have trouble traveling at night. Write a plan to solve this problem.

How can a potato provide energy to a light bulb?

Engineers design devices that use natural resources as an energy source. How can a potato provide the energy to light a bulb?

Materials
- copper strips
- zinc strips
- LED light bulb
- fresh potatoes
- safety goggles
- alligator clips

Suggested Materials
- lemons

Build and Improve

☐ 1. Insert a piece of copper into the potato. Then insert a piece of zinc into the potato. Connect one end of an alligator clip to the copper. Connect the other end of the alligator clip to the zinc. Connect the LED wires to the two metal strips, and observe what happens. Record your observations.

☐ 2. Improve your circuit by designing one that produces more electrical energy. Show your design to your teacher before you begin. Record your observations.

⚠ Wear safety goggles!

⚠ Do not taste lab items.

Observations

Engineering Practice

Engineers use creativity when they design solutions.

Evaluate Your Design

3. **Use Evidence** How do you know whether a change in energy occurred in the electric circuit?

_____

_____

Use Text Features Text features include ways that text is marked so that the reader knows that the marked text is especially important. In the text on this page, four words are highlighted in yellow. What does the highlighting tell you about those words?

 LAFS.4.RI.3.7

Using Energy

People use a lot of energy to heat and light buildings and to power tools, cars, and other electric devices. A **device** is something made for a particular purpose. All devices that plug into wall outlets need electrical energy. The electrical energy is produced by changing some other form of energy.

Some of this energy comes from burning fuel. A **fuel** is a material that releases energy as heat when it burns. Common fuels include coal, natural gas, petroleum, and wood. The process of burning a fuel to produce heat and light is called **combustion**. During combustion, the fuel combines with oxygen. A chemical change occurs that releases energy stored in the fuel.

✓ READING CHECK **Use Text Features** How does the photo on this page help you understand the text?

_____

_____

Fuels

The **primary**, or original, source of energy of almost all fuels is the sun. Plants change the energy of sunlight into plant materials that store energy, such as wood. Other fuels, such as coal, oil, and natural gas, formed when living things died and went through changes underground over a very long time. These living things were plants or animals. Their stored energy originally came from sunlight.

Chemical Energy

Fuels burn and produce energy as heat and light. This energy comes from a chemical change. The energy is stored in the fuel as chemical energy. During combustion, substances in the fuel combine with oxygen to form new substances. These new substances do not have as much chemical energy as the original fuel.

Transportation is an important use of fuel. In a car engine, gasoline and air mix. Combustion of the mixture changes the chemical energy stored in the mixture into heat. Hot gases in the engine expand and push against engine parts. The motion of the engine parts moves the car. You can tell that combustion of gasoline releases heat by touching the hood of a car after it has been running a long time.

Plan It!

You are a city official who must make sure your city has enough electricity. You know you will need to use some kind of chemical energy. List the steps that must take place to get electricity to your people.

How is **electrical power** generated from **chemical energy?**

Label In the space below each part of the power plant, write what energy change occurs in the part.

steam

Boiler

In a coal power plant, the primary source of energy is the coal. When coal is burned in the plant, chemical energy changes to heat that turns water into steam. Because the water vapor is so hot, it has a lot of energy.

_____

_____

Turbine

The hot steam flows through a turbine. The **turbine** is a device that spins as the gas flows and changes the heat energy of the steam into energy of motion.

_____

_____

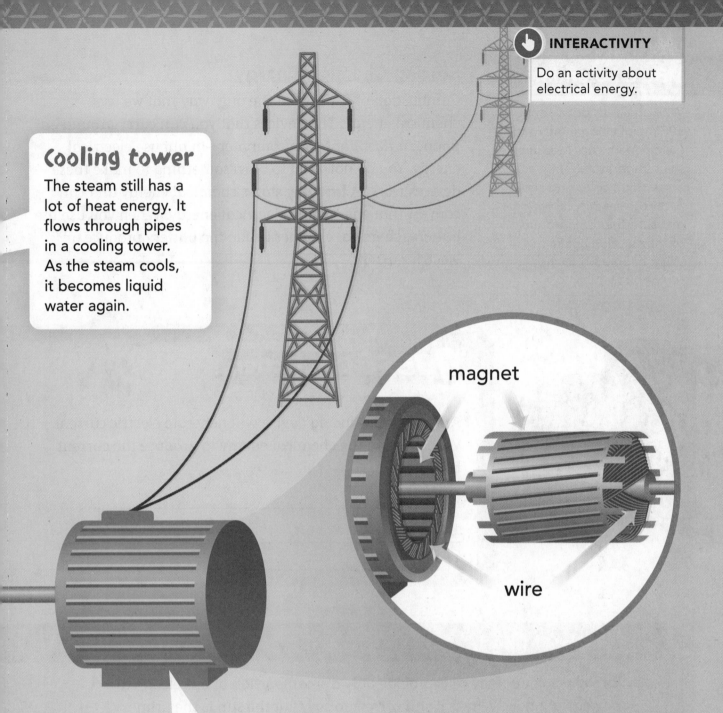

Cooling tower

The steam still has a lot of heat energy. It flows through pipes in a cooling tower. As the steam cools, it becomes liquid water again.

magnet

wire

Generator

As the turbine spins, it turns a shaft that causes motion in the generator. A **generator** is a device that changes energy of motion into electrical energy. Inside the generator, a magnet is surrounded by a coil of copper wire. As the magnet turns, an electric current is generated in the wire coil.

uBe a Scientist

With an adult, pour about 100 mL of vinegar into a tall plastic foam cup. Measure the temperature. Then add a teaspoon of baking soda. After the reaction slows, measure the temperature of the solution again. What happened to the temperature?

Storing Chemical Energy

Combustion of fuels is not the only way that we use chemical energy. The devices that you can carry around—a phone, a flashlight, or a computer—might use electrical energy. You do not want to burn something to make these devices work. A **battery** stores chemical energy and can convert that energy into electrical energy. When you use the battery, chemical changes inside the battery produce an electric current.

Quest Connection

An energy-producing device will generate electric current. Where might the chemical energy to produce the current be stored?

_____

_____

✓ Lesson 1 Check

SC.4.P.10.1, SC.4.P.10.2

1. **Explain** Solar energy cells provide only a small portion of our electrical power right now. Why is it still correct to say that the sun is the primary source of most of the electricity that we use?

_____

_____

2. **Evaluate** In a car engine, what happens during combustion of gasoline and air? What type of change is this?

_____

_____

_____

Human Power

In this Quest, you will design a device that changes the mechanical energy of a moving person into electrical energy that can power a motor. Your teacher will identify the materials you can use. You must build your device by the end of this topic. Your device will help me design an exercise bike that will power a laptop computer.

1. Define the problem you must solve.

_____

_____

_____

2. What are the criteria for success? What are the constraints? Write your answers in the table.

Criteria	Constraints

3. Use the criteria and constraints to write a plan.

_____

_____

_____

_____

Nonrenewable Energy Sources

I can...

Investigate how people extract and use natural resources.
Give examples of nonrenewable energy sources.

Literacy Skill
Use Text Features

Vocabulary
fossil fuel
coal
petroleum
natural gas
nuclear fuel
uranium

Academic Vocabulary
outcome

▶ **VIDEO**

Watch a video about energy resources.

SC.4.P.10.1 Observe and describe some basic forms of energy, including light, heat, sound, electrical, and the energy of motion. **SC.4.P.10.2** Investigate and describe that energy has the ability to cause motion or create change. (Also **SC.4.N.1.5, SC.4.N.1.7**)

CURRICULUM ▶ Connection

Canary in a Coal Mine

Have you ever heard the expression "a canary in a coal mine"? It means someone or something that warns of danger. Digging coal in a deep underground mine can be a dangerous job. One risk to coal miners is a poisonous gas, carbon monoxide. You cannot see it, and you cannot smell it. Today, miners carry electronic detectors that warn them of carbon monoxide. How did miners check for toxic gas before the detectors existed?

After a fire or explosion, mine rescuers carried a small caged bird, a canary. Because canaries are more sensitive to carbon monoxide than people, the miner would watch the bird. If carbon monoxide was present, the bird would stop singing or start swaying on its perch. The miner knew that it was time to quickly return to the surface.

Infer Carbon from coal and oxygen from air combine to form carbon monoxide. What process produces the gas?

How do we find 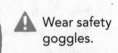 oil?

Engineers use echoes from underground to decide where to drill for oil. What methods can you use to find a balloon buried in sand?

Design and Build

☐ **1.** Bury the balloon that is filled with water in the sand in the box. Make sure that the sand is level and that you cannot see the balloon. Trade boxes with another group.

☐ **2.** Write a plan to use energy to find the water buried in sand. Have your teacher review your plan before you start. Record your observations.

Materials
- small balloon filled with water
- large plastic box with sand
- safety goggles

Suggested Materials
- wooden spoon
- wooden skewer

Observations

⚠ Wear safety goggles.

Engineering Practice

Engineers compare methods used by others.

Evaluate Your Design

3. Analyze What forms of energy did you use to search for the hidden balloon? Was your search successful?

_____

_____

4. Collaborate Compare your procedure with those of other groups. Which procedure was most successful in finding the water? Why do you think that is so?

_____

_____

_____

Lesson 2 Nonrenewable Energy Sources   217

Connecting Concepts ▸ Toolbox

Energy and Matter Energy and matter flow in and out of systems. In books or Internet articles, read about the connection between fossil fuels and environmental pollution. Share the information you find with classmates.

Fossil Fuels

Much of the energy that people use comes from fossil fuels. **Fossil fuels** are materials that formed as ancient plants and animals decayed underground. The three main fossil fuels are coal, petroleum, and natural gas. These fuels react with oxygen in the air during combustion, releasing heat and light. Fossil fuels are a nonrenewable source of energy. The supply is limited because it takes millions of years to change living materials into fossil fuels. Burning fossil fuels can have a harmful **outcome**, or result, on the enviroment. It can cause significant environmental problems, such as air pollution and acidic rivers and lakes.

Coal

Many millions of years ago, swamps covered large areas of Earth's surface. When the plants in these swamps died, they sank to the bottom. Layer after layer of dead plants built up over a very long time. These layers were covered by soil and rock. Chemical changes transformed the plant stems and leaves into a hard, black substance, called **coal**. The amount of coal that exists in the world today will last for more than a hundred years at current rates of production. But coal is not a renewable energy source. As it is used up, no more coal replaces it.

☑ **READING CHECK Use Text Features** Headings are the section labels in large type. What do the headings on this page tell you about the paragraphs that follow them?

_____

_____

The energy of fossil fuels originally comes from the sun. Your Quest is to run a motor using power from human motion. How does that energy also come from the sun?

_____

_____

_____

Petroleum

What do you buy at a gas station? Not a gas, but gasoline. The most important fuels for transportation in most of the world—gasoline and diesel—are made from petroleum. **Petroleum** is a liquid fossil fuel formed by the decay of ancient plants and animals. It is not found in as many places as coal. Saudi Arabia, Russia, and the United States produce the most petroleum. It is shipped to distant places using pipelines, trains, trucks, and large ships. Huge factories, called refineries, separate different parts of the petroleum. These are used as fuel and to make many different products that include plastics, textiles, fertilizers, and medicines.

Reflect These oil rigs drill and remove petroleum from beneath the ground. In your science notebook, write how this process might affect the environment.

Where do FOSSIL FUELS come from?

It takes a long time for plants and animals to change into fossil fuels. Much of the coal and petroleum that we use today began to form long ago.

COAL

When plants died and fell into the water, they decomposed and formed layers of peat.

After a very long time, heat from inside Earth and pressure from soil and rock changed the peat into coal.

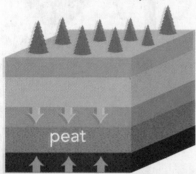

The whole change took more than 10 million years.

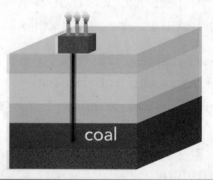

! **Predict** What do you think would happen if coal did not form?

_____

_____

PETROLEUM

When plants and animals died in the ocean, they fell to the bottom. Most of these organisms were single-celled plankton and algae.

Sediment covered them. Over a long time, these plants and animals decomposed and formed oil and natural gas.

Today, these materials fill small gaps and pores in rock deep below the surface.

! Infer Why do you think coal and petroleum are different?

_____

_____

_____

Natural Gas

Engineers often find another fossil fuel in or near petroleum. **Natural gas** is a fossil fuel that occurs in the gas state. Like petroleum, it formed by the decay of ancient plants and animals. In many places, natural gas flows through pipes to homes and businesses. In homes, it is used for heating, cooking, and water heating. Natural gas is also an important fuel for producing electricity. Some modern vehicles use natural gas as a fuel. Because it is a gas, natural gas is harder to store and transport than coal or petroleum. It is usually stored and shipped in containers at very high pressure. Many of these containers are spheres because a sphere is very strong.

Design It! An engineer is evaluating use of fossil fuels for a power plant. List some criteria and constraints that would affect use of a fossil fuel.

Nuclear Fuel

Beginning in the second half of the twentieth century, people used nuclear energy to produce electrical energy. Nuclear energy comes from changes inside particles of matter. The unstable elements that produce this energy in power plants are the **nuclear fuel**. Most nuclear power plants use the element **uranium**. Uranium is found in underground rocks. Miners dig up the rocks, and the uranium is collected from them. Uranium is a nonrenewable energy source because only a limited amount of it can be mined. Nuclear power plants work in a similar way as fossil fuel plants, but the fuel is not burned. Instead uranium atoms are split apart to produce heat energy. The heat energy makes steam that drives a turbine and generator.

......uBe a Scientist ....

Make It Turn

Hold a toy pinwheel outdoors on a day when a breeze is blowing. Observe what happens to the pinwheel. How could wind power be used as a source of energy?

✓ Lesson 2 Check

SC.4.P.10.2

1. **Assess** Explain how the remains of plants and animals become fossil fuels. Why are they considered nonrenewable resources?

_____

_____

_____

_____

2. **Identify** What are three ways that people use natural resources?

_____

How can you use a battery to produce Motion?

Engineers use criteria, or standards, to evaluate whether a solution works. How can you design a device that uses a battery to produce motion?

Materials
- battery in battery holder
- insulated copper wire
- switch
- electric motor
- safety goggles

Suggested Materials
- movable parts from construction sets

Design and Build

☐ **1.** Decide how you will build a device that uses a battery to produce motion. List the criteria.

_____

_____

_____

⚠ Wear safety goggles.

Engineering Practice

Engineers use their knowledge to design solutions to engineering problems.

☐ **2.** Make a diagram that shows how you will arrange the materials. Label the components. Show your diagram to your teacher before you begin.

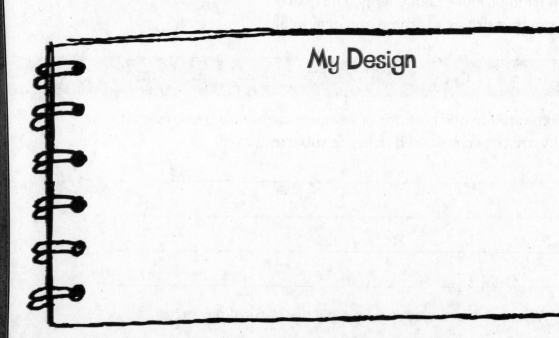

My Design

3. Build your device. If it does not work, revise your drawing and rebuild the device.

Evaluate Your Design

4. **Use Evidence** Does your solution meet the criteria that it makes the motor run? Provide evidence to support your answer.

_____

_____

_____

_____

5. **Hypothesize** How could you replace the battery with some type of mechanical energy to make the motor run?

_____

_____

_____

_____

Renewable Energy Sources

I can...

Distinguish between renewable and nonrenewable energy sources.
Give examples of renewable energy sources.

Literacy Skill
Use Text Features

Vocabulary
geothermal energy
hydropower

Academic Vocabulary
available

▶ **VIDEO**

Watch a video about geothermal energy.

SC.4.P.10.4 Describe how moving water and air are sources of energy and can be used to move things. (Also **SC.4.N.1.1, SC.4.N.2.1, SC.4.N.3.1**)

ENGINEERING ⟩ Connection

The most abundant source of energy on Earth is not actually on the planet. Every day, the sun provides 10,000 times more energy to Earth than people use. Because this energy is spread out across the planet, people have developed systems to concentrate and use it. The United States already has more than 1 million solar energy systems. As engineers improve solar energy devices, this number will increase.

Solar energy in a home is used in two common ways. In one method, sunlight directly heats the house or heats water for washing and laundry. The other method uses photovoltaic cells. These devices are often placed on the roof of a building. The cells use sunlight to produce electric current. The electricity from these cells can be used immediately or stored in a battery for later use. Solar energy can also be changed to electrical energy in large facilities that then deliver it to customers.

📓 **Write About It** Engineers are designing a solar energy system to meet all the energy needs of a home. In your science notebook, write what constraints they must consider.

How does a windmill capture wind energy?

Scientists and engineers have developed devices that change energy from one form to another. How can you design a way to capture energy from moving air?

Suggested Materials

- construction paper
- plastic drinking straws
- straight pins
- modeling clay
- stapler
- paper glue
- safety goggles

 Wear safety goggles.

Science Practice

Scientists make models to answer scientific questions.

Procedure

☐ 1. Plan a way to make a device that rotates when wind blows on it. Include a method to test the device. Show your plan to your teacher before you begin.

☐ 2. Observe how wind direction affects the way that your device moves. Record your observations.

☐ 3. Based on your observations, make improvements to your device. Test it again. Record your observations.

Analyze and Interpret Data

4. **Infer** Use what you observed about your model and what you know about generators to describe how a windmill might produce electrical energy.

_____

_____

_____

_____

_____

_____

_____

Observations

Visual Literacy Connection

Is renewable energy all around?

Renewable energy sources contribute more to our total power needs every year. They do not run out as we use them. Some energy can be used directly. Other forms of renewable energy are changed to electrical energy or chemical fuels before we use them.

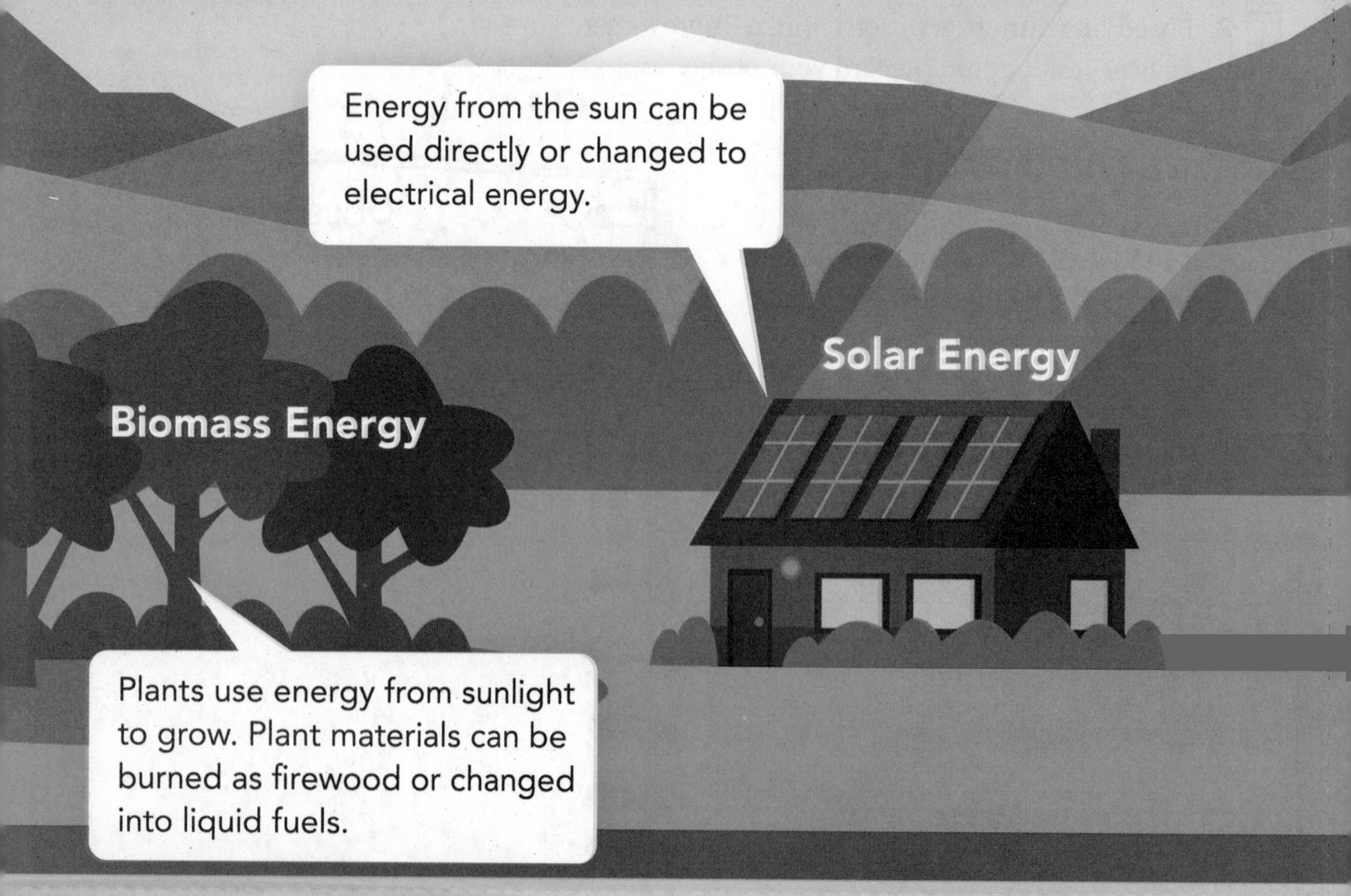

Energy from the sun can be used directly or changed to electrical energy.
Solar Energy
Biomass Energy
Plants use energy from sunlight to grow. Plant materials can be burned as firewood or changed into liquid fuels.

! **Describe** Circle the renewable energy sources you would use to provide electricity to your school.

As the sun heats the atmosphere, air moves around. Wind turbines change that motion to electrical energy.

Solar energy causes water to evaporate. After water condenses and falls as rain or snow, the energy of flowing rivers can be used to generate electrical energy.

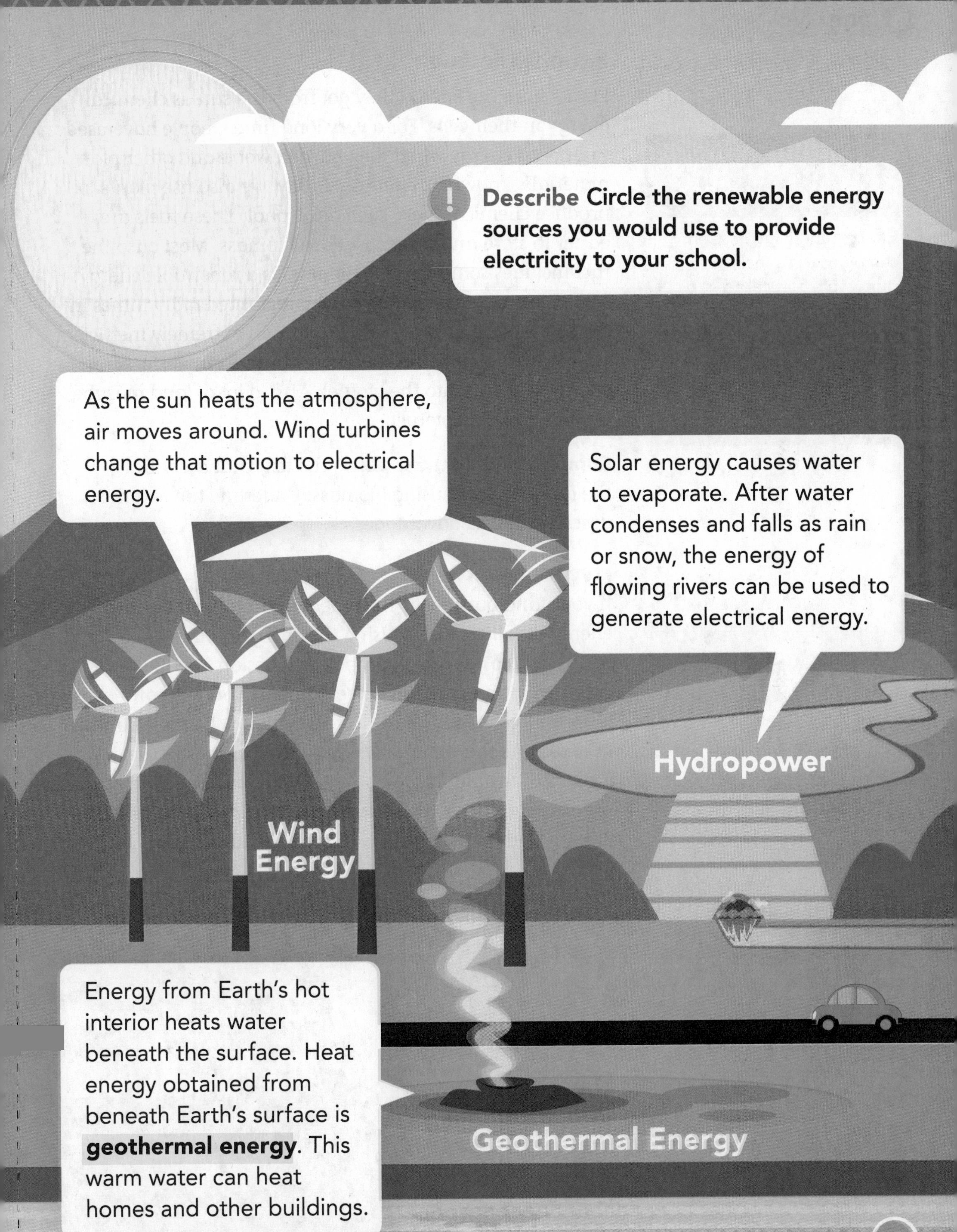

Hydropower

Wind Energy

Energy from Earth's hot interior heats water beneath the surface. Heat energy obtained from beneath Earth's surface is **geothermal energy**. This warm water can heat homes and other buildings.

Geothermal Energy

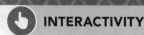
INTERACTIVITY

Do an activity about natural resources.

Connecting Concepts ► Toolbox

Energy and Matter Corn can be used to make a renewable fuel called ethanol. Corn is also an important food in many diets. How does using corn for fuel affect the supply of corn for food?

Renewable Fuel

Plants store the energy they get from the sun as chemical energy in their cells. For a very long time, people have used the stored energy when they burned wood and other plant materials, known as biomass. Today, we also use plants to produce chemical fuels, such as alcohol. These fuels are easier to store and transport than biomass. Most gasoline fuel includes some alcohol. Biomass is a renewable energy source because new plants can be replanted many times in the same place. However, biomass is an extremely inefficient way to store energy. Much less than 1 percent of the sun's energy makes it into the biofuel. Also, a lot of land must be used to grow the biofuel.

Compare and Contrast Circle the text that describes the advantages of using biomass. Underline the text that describes the disadvantages.

Hydropower

If you stand outside during a heavy rainfall, you can feel the energy of falling water. Using the energy of moving water is called **hydropower**. Hydropower relies on flowing water to create motion, such as a wheel turning. Today, hydropower is an important source of electrical energy. Dams hold water in a lake. As the water flows through openings in the dam, it turns a turbine. The turning turbine causes a generator to produce electricity. The moving water of flowing rivers can also be the source of energy to turn the turbine.

Energy That Does Not Run Out

Biomass is a renewable energy source because we can grow more plants. However, some energy sources do not need to be replaced. They are produced continually by nature. Wind energy is completely renewable. As the atmosphere absorbs energy from the sun, temperature differences in the atmosphere cause wind to blow. While the wind may stop now and then, we can rely on it to start blowing again.

Solar energy is another source of energy that does not run out—at least for the next few billion years! As long as the sun shines, it will continue to provide energy to Earth. We use some solar energy directly to heat water or the air in a building. Solar energy can also be changed into electrical energy. Then energy can be transmitted to users far from the site of the energy cells. One limit of solar energy is that it is not available at night. When something is **available**, it is able to be had.

Describe How can air be used as an energy source?

_____

_____

_____

> ### uBe a Scientist
>
> **Balancing Act**
> On a sunny day, put two pieces of construction paper—one white and one black—side by side in the sun. Tape them in place if there is wind. After about an hour, place one hand on top of each piece of paper. What do you observe about the paper? Explain why this happens.

✓ Lesson 3 Check

 SC.4.P.10.4

1. **Use Reasoning** Kim holds a pinwheel in the air and says it can be used to model a source of energy. Identify the type of energy that Kim's pinwheel models. Explain how the energy source can be used.

_____

_____

_____

2. **Evaluate** Farmers can grow crops, such as corn, that can be turned into fuel for vehicles. Is fuel made from corn a renewable resource? Justify your response.

_____

_____

How can the sun make a motor work?

In the last Quest Check-In, you powered an electric motor with a battery. How can you make your electric motor run using a solar cell rather than a battery?

Materials
- small solar panel
- insulated copper wire
- switch
- electric motor

Suggested Materials
- desk lamp

Design and Build

☐ 1. Make a diagram that shows how you will arrange the materials to use a solar cell to run the motor. Label the components. Show your diagram to your teacher before you continue.

Engineering Practice

Engineers design solutions to a problem.

☐ 2. Build your device. If it does not work, revise your drawing and rebuild the device.

Evaluate Your Solution

3. **Evaluate** How well does the solar device work compared to the battery device? Explain how you compared them.

_____

_____

_____

One important math tool is a bar graph. A bar graph can show how something changes over time. When two things are related, a double bar graph can show how one factor changes the other. A double bar graph compares two sets of data.

The blue bars in the graph show the amount of electrical energy produced from hydropower every five years between 1995 and 2015. The green bars show the amount of electrical energy produced from other renewable sources over the same time. Notice how the amount of electrical energy from hydropower changes. Then notice what happens to the amount of electrical energy from other renewable sources. The data on the double bar graph shows the connection between the electrical energy produced by hydropower and the electrical energy produced by other renewable sources.

Draw Conclusions What does the double bar graph show about the connection between hydroelectricity and other renewable energy sources?

_____

_____

_____

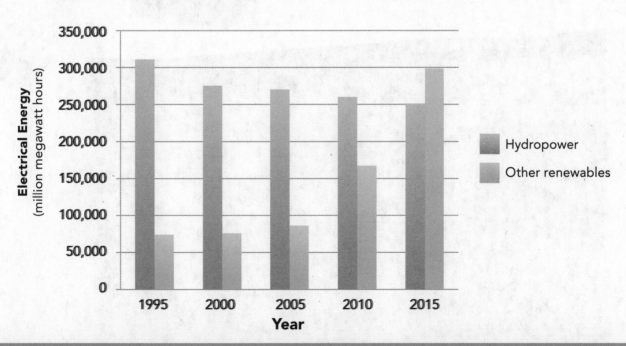

Hydropower and other renewable electricity generation (1995–2015)

VIDEO

Go online to see how plastics are recycled.

Hold *That* **Phone**

The earliest mobile phones were very large. People sometimes called them "bricks" because of their shape and size. Their mass was more than a kilogram! Think about how different that is from today's smart phone. Technology allows modern phones to be much smaller and use energy more efficiently.

Engineers consider many different criteria when they design a new phone. Some people want a very small phone that fits in a pocket. Other people want a phone with a large screen that can run a lot of apps. Each phone design has some features that users want, but it may not meet the needs of other users. How would you design a phone that meets your preferences?

Engineers do not change everything in a phone at one time. When they redesign a phone that is already used, first they evaluate that phone. Then they decide how to make it better.

Improve It

Suppose that you work for a company that makes cell phones. Your job is to redesign the current phone so that it has the features people want. The first step is to decide what would make the phone better.

- [ ] Think about the phones that you and your friends use. What feature would you change to make the phone better?

- [ ] Brainstorm ways you could redesign a smart phone to add the new feature.

- [ ] Draw your new phone.

Environmental Impacts of Using Energy

I can...

Describe how the use of different natural energy resources affects the local and global environments. Evaluate how technology can improve the environmental effects of using a given energy resource.

Literacy Skill
Use Text Features

Vocabulary
emission
pollutant
scrubber
greenhouse gas

Academic Vocabulary
impact

SC.4.P.10.1 Observe and describe some basic forms of energy, including light, heat, sound, electrical, and the energy of motion. (Also **SC.4.N.1.1, SC.4.N.3.1**)

STEM › Connection

As you pass a modern power plant, you are likely to see tall towers, such as those shown in the photograph. They appear to release smoke, but they are not smokestacks. What you see coming from the towers is water vapor. As the vapor cools in the air above the towers, it forms small droplets. You are actually looking at a cloud in the sky above the tower!

Power plants make a lot of steam to run turbines. The steam condenses to make hot water. In the past, the hot water often was dumped into a river or lake. In towers like these, some of the hot water evaporates from the water surface to form water vapor. Since it takes energy to make water vapor, the remaining water becomes cooler. When it has cooled enough, the water is recycled to make new steam.

Analyze What would be some effects on the environment of dumping hot water from a power plant into a river? Do you think this practice should be allowed?

_____

_____

_____

uInvestigate Lab

Why is **oil** cleanup so hard?

When crude oil spills on a beach, scientists develop ways to clean up the oil. Why is it hard to separate crude oil from sand?

Procedure

☐ 1. Drop a spoonful of oil into a bowl of sand and mix it.

☐ 2. Make a plan to separate the oil from the sand. Show your plan to your teacher before you begin. Record your observations.

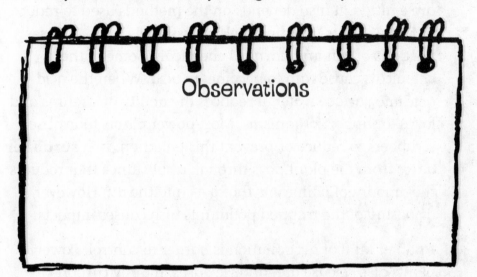

Observations

☐ 3. Think of other methods that you could use to separate the oil from the sand. Try one of those methods. Record your observations.

Analyze and Interpret Data

4. **Analyze** Why was the oil hard to separate from the sand?

_____

_____

5. **Use a Model** What did your model show you about pollution on a beach?

_____

_____

Materials
• model oil
• sand
• bowl
• safety goggles
• plastic gloves
• spoons

Suggested Materials
• paper towels
• sieve

⚠ Wear safety goggles and gloves.

⚠ Do not taste lab materials.

Science Practice

Scientists use models to help understand phenomena.

Have an adult help you look up the amount of carbon dioxide, or CO_2, in the atmosphere for the past 10 years. Make a graph with the data you collect. What patterns do you see in the data?

Impact of Energy Production

The human use of energy has **impacts**, or effects, on the environment. These impacts occur when humans change the land to build a structure or to remove a resource. They can also occur during energy production. **Emissions** are the release of substances into the environment. Some emissions can have a harmful impact on the environment. For example, releasing a **pollutant**, or harmful substance, during energy production can poison land, water, and air.

The impact that a power plant has on the environment depends on how the power is generated and what pollutants are emitted. It also depends on the methods used to reduce harmful effects. Burning fuel in fossil-fuel plants releases particles of ash and harmful chemicals. Some of these chemicals cause rain to become an acid. When the acid gets into surface water, it reduces the ability of streams and lakes to support organisms. Most power plants today use scrubbers to reduce or prevent this pollution. In a **scrubber**, gases from the plant pass through a substance that reduces the amount of pollutants that gets into the air. However, disposing of the trapped pollutants also causes impacts.

Another kind of air pollution is harder to control. Power plants also release greenhouse gases, mainly carbon dioxide. A **greenhouse gas** is a pollutant that increases the atmosphere's ability to hold heat. Because carbon dioxide is always produced by combustion, fossil-fuel power plants are a major source of this impact.

READING CHECK Use Text Features Choose one of the vocabulary words on the page. How does it relate to the title of this section?

_____

_____

_____

_____

Impacts of Nuclear Power

Nuclear power plants do not produce air pollutants, but they produce solid waste that remains dangerous for thousands to millions of years. Nuclear power plants also produce large amounts of hot water.

Analyze How could the release of very hot water affect the environment and its living things?

_____

_____

Science Practice ▸ Toolbox

Obtaining and Evaluating Information What are some sources of information on environmental impacts of using energy? Which source is more reliable, a government website or an oil company website? Why?

Impact of Obtaining Fuel

Some fuels that power plants use must be mined. This process can change the land surface. Often forests and fields are removed to get to the fuel beneath them. Coal mines can leave large areas completely changed. Some mined materials dissolve in water when they are uncovered. They can wash away and pollute streams and rivers.

Drilling is also used to get fuels. Drillers must make roads and cut down forest areas to make a place for the drilling equipment. Some drilling methods use toxic materials to force the oil and gas to the surface. These materials can spill and pollute the land and water around the drilling site.

Cause and Effect Underline two harmful effects of obtaining fuel.

Quest Connection

Why does an energy source that does not use fuel have a smaller environmental impact?

_____

_____

How can the use of energy damage Ecosystems?

Energy use can affect ecosystems in many ways. Some types of impact on the environment due to energy use are listed below.

! Draw a line from each description to a place that illustrates the impact.

surface mine

Disturbing land can pollute streams and rivers.

Roads can break up habitat areas.

Mining can cause a loss of habitat for plants and animals.

Fossil fuel combustion can pollute the atmosphere.

coal power plant

hydropower dam

Building dams can damage stream habitats.

Impact of Transporting Fuels

Large pipes carry natural gas and crude oil to where the fuels are used. The largest pipes are over one meter in diameter. They carry fuel distances of thousands of kilometers. Sometimes, a pipeline starts to leak. If the leak is not noticed quickly, a lot of fuel can spill. Oil spills are very hard to clean up. Crude oil is very sticky. It covers anything it touches. Natural gas leaks add a lot of greenhouse gases to the atmosphere.

Another risk of transporting oil comes from shipping it across the ocean. Huge ships carry giant containers of crude oil from one continent to another. If a ship collides with something, a massive amount of oil can spill. The oil floats on the water, and currents can spread it over a large area.

Apply What is one harmful effect that the oil spill shown in the photo could cause?

_____

_____

✓ Lesson 4 Check

1. **Critique** A classmate tells you that power plants do not affect the environment. Are they correct? Justify your response.

_____

_____

_____

_____

2. **Analyze** How do scrubbers help to reduce pollution?

_____

_____

_____

Impact Inspections

You found a source of energy other than a battery for the motor. Now consider the environmental impact of that device.

1. Does using solar energy to run a motor have any negative impacts on the environment? Explain.

_____

_____

_____

_____

2. Contrast the environmental impact of the solar energy with that of a battery and the mechanical energy produced by a human.

_____

_____

_____

_____

3. What is a disadvantage of using human power compared to using a battery or solar energy?

_____

_____

_____

_____

👆 **INTERACTIVITY**

Evaluate your design to support your Quest Findings.

STEM Power from the People

How can a device convert energy from one form to another?

Test Your Solution

You have learned how electrical energy can make a motor run. Design a device that uses human energy to provide power to an electric motor. Show your design to your teacher before you build the device.

Discuss how you can develop a test that compares different solutions to the problem. What criteria would you use to determine which device works best? On the card, write the steps of a test that can compare devices.

Redesign and Retest

Think of a change that you can make to your device that might make it work better. How will you know whether the new design is an improvement?

_____

_____

Make the change to your design. Retest the device. Did your change improve the device? Explain your answer.

_____

_____

Test Steps
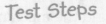
_____

_____

_____

_____

_____

Electrical Engineer

Electrical engineers work with electronics, electromagnetism, or electricity. They design, test, and produce electrical equipment that can range from small devices to large, impressive systems.

Electrical engineering is a relatively new addition to the engineering field. It has opened a whole new range of careers for engineers. An electrical engineer can work in developing solutions for problems dealing with aerospace, power generation, and automotive industries. For example, power generation engineering has become more important as interest in renewable energy has increased. Engineers who work in power engineering create more efficient ways of conducting electricity across equipment that generates energy from renewable resources.

Write About It

Electrical engineers develop solutions to big problems. What are some problems in the world today that an electrical engineer might be able to solve? How could he or she do it?

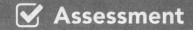
Read each question and choose or write the best answer.

1. **Use Diagrams** This diagram shows a turbine and generator used in a hydropower plant.

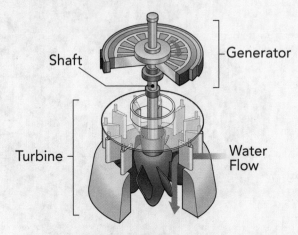

Shaft
Generator
Turbine
Water Flow

What is the function of the turbine in the power plant?

A. It pushes water through the dam.

B. It causes the generator to move.

C. It produces electricity that flows into power lines.

D. It heats the water to produce steam that turns the generator.

2. **Identify** Which is a renewable energy source?

A. biomass

B. coal

C. petroleum

D. uranium

3. **Critique** An article states, "The energy for some fuels used in combustion comes from the sun." How could the sentence be changed to make it more accurate?

A. Change *some* to *all*, because all fuels originally came from plants which used sunlight as an energy source.

B. Change *some* to *all*, because all fuels originally came from plants which used sunlight as an energy source or from animals that ate plants.

C. Keep the sentence as is, as some combustion is formed from the use of nonrenewable resources.

D. Keep the sentence as is, as some combustion is formed using wind or water power.

4. **Construct** Explain a similarity and a difference between how coal and petroleum form. Construct a supported argument to explain how these energy resources affect the environment.

_____

_____

_____

_____

_____

_____

_____

_____

5. Interpret Graphs The graph shows the types of energy used in a recent year.

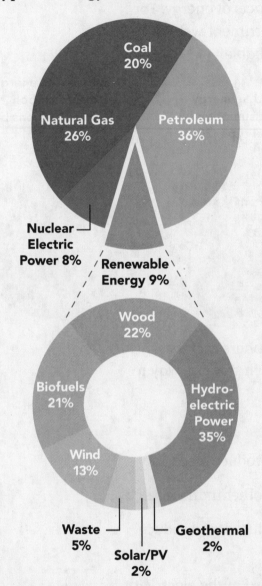

Coal 20%

Natural Gas 26%

Petroleum 36%

Nuclear Electric Power 8%

Renewable Energy 9%

Wood 22%

Biofuels 21%

Hydro-electric Power 35%

Wind 13%

Waste 5%

Solar/PV 2%

Geothermal 2%

What was the largest renewable energy source during that year?

A. hydro-electric power

B. natural gas

C. petroleum

D. wind

6. Use Reasoning A letter to a newspaper is written. It explains why building a nuclear power plant to produce electricity is a better option than building a coal power plant. Identify at least one fact that can be used to support this opinion. Provide one fact to support an opinion that opposes the use of nuclear power plants.

_____

_____

_____

_____

_____

The Essential Question

How do we convert energy to meet our needs?

Show What You Learned

Many energy sources are converted to usable electrical energy. What are some reasons that people use electrical energy instead of using other sources directly?

_____

_____

_____

_____

_____

_____

Read the scenario and answer questions 1–2.

Manny wrote a report about the environmental impacts of energy. For his report, Manny found these graphs on a U.S. government website. His teacher said that information from that website is reliable.

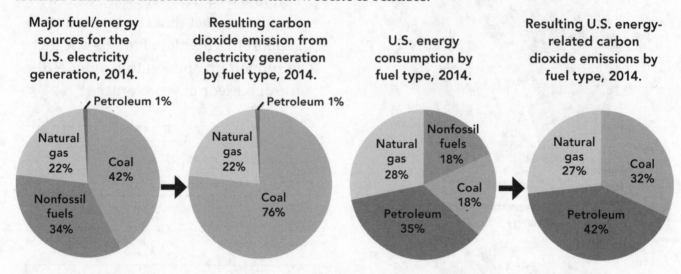

Major fuel/energy sources for the U.S. electricity generation, 2014.

Resulting carbon dioxide emission from electricity generation by fuel type, 2014.

U.S. energy consumption by fuel type, 2014.

Resulting U.S. energy-related carbon dioxide emissions by fuel type, 2014.

1 As the amount of greenhouse gases in the atmosphere increases, the atmosphere's ability to hold heat increases. What is one way to prevent higher average global temperatures?

Ⓐ use more petroleum to produce electricity

Ⓑ use more nonfossil fuel sources of energy to produce electricity

Ⓒ only use fossil fuels to produce energy in forms other than electricity

Ⓓ increase the amount of electricity that is produced and reduce other kinds of energy use

2 Nonfossil fuels are used to produce about one-third of the electricity used in the United States. In the graphs, analyze the data about carbon dioxide emissions. What could Manny conclude about the production of carbon dioxide by nonfossil fuels?

Ⓕ Nonfossil fuels do not produce carbon dioxide.

Ⓖ Nonfossil fuels produce less carbon dioxide than using coal.

Ⓗ Nonfossil fuels produce almost half of carbon dioxide emissions.

Ⓘ Nonfossil fuels produce more carbon dioxide than using petroleum.

Read the scenario and answer questions 3–5.

Scientists are hoping to expand the areas where renewable energy sources can be gathered. They are planning to use the two sites below for renewable energy farms.

③ Why is location 1 a good site for a wind turbine farm to be built?

Ⓐ because there are large cliffs

Ⓑ because there are mountains

Ⓒ because the ocean produces a lot of wind

Ⓓ because it does not rain often

④ Which type of renewable energy farm would best be built in location 2?

Ⓕ geothermal energy because the desert is very warm and the water beneath Earth's surface would be hotter there

Ⓖ hydropower because the Hoover Dam, a huge source of hydropower, is near a desert

Ⓗ solar power because this is a very sunny area free of many trees and homes

Ⓘ biomass energy because there is a lot of open area where trees can be planted to be used as fuel

⑤ Which is a benefit of renewable energy sources, such as wind turbines, being used to generate electricity?

Ⓐ Renewable energy sources are expensive.

Ⓑ There is no carbon dioxide emitted from using renewable energy sources.

Ⓒ There is no cost to build a wind turbine because wind is freely produced.

Ⓓ Renewable energy sources run out as we use them.

How can energy resource usage change?

Materials
- 200 tokens
- 6-sided number cube

In the uConnect game, you modeled how energy supplies were different when the sources were nonrenewable or renewable. In real world usage, conditions sometimes change. How can you modify the game to investigate how a change in condition affects the energy supply?

Science Practice

Scientists **construct explanations** for the observations and the results of investigations.

Procedure

☐ **1.** Review the uConnect game and your results. Choose one or more of these changes or make up a change of your own.

- Demand for energy increases, so users need more energy each year.
- New renewable technologies are invented, so more renewable energy is available.
- Improved technologies reduce the demand for energy by both users.
- The demand for energy changes from year to year.

   Circle which change or changes in energy supply or demand you will model.

☐ **2.** Design a solution to the new problem by writing a set of rules that show how energy is used in the model after the change.

_____

_____

_____

_____

☐ **3.** Explain how your rules model the change.

_____

_____

_____

4. Make a hypothesis about how the change will affect the results of energy supply and use in the game.

_____

_____

_____

_____

5. Play the game using your new rules. Use the table to record your data.

Analyze and Interpret Data

6. Use Evidence Did your evidence support your hypothesis? Explain.

_____

_____

_____

_____

7. Predict Will renewable energy sources always last longer than nonrenewable sources when you change the model? Explain.

Turn	Supplier A			Supplier B		
	Added	Used	Total	Added	Used	Total
0						
1						
2						
3						
4						
5						
6						
7						
8						

_____

_____

_____

_____

Plants and Animals

Lesson 1 Life Cycles of Florida Plants

Lesson 2 Life Cycles of Florida Animals

Lesson 3 Plant and Animal Characteristics

Lesson 4 Animal Behavior

SC.4.L.16.1 Identify processes of sexual reproduction in flowering plants, including pollination, fertilization (seed production), seed dispersal, and germination. **SC.4.L.16.2** Explain that although characteristics of plants and animals are inherited, some characteristics can be affected by the environment. **SC.4.L.16.3** Recognize that animal behaviors may be shaped by heredity and learning. **SC.4.L.16.4** Compare and contrast the major stages in the life cycles of Florida plants and animals, such as those that undergo incomplete and complete metamorphosis, and flowering and nonflowering seed-bearing plants. (Also **SC.4.N.1.4, SC.4.N.1.5, SC.4.N.1.6, SC.4.N.3.1, LAFS.4.RI.1.2,** and **MAFS.4.G.1.3**)

Go online to access
your digital course.

▶ VIDEO

📖 eTEXT

👆 INTERACTIVITY

🧪 VIRTUAL LAB

🎮 GAME

☑ ASSESSMENT

The Essential Question

How do living things grow and change?

Show What You Know

What structures do you think the honeybee and flower have that help them survive?

_____

_____

_____

STEM Design a Wetland Exhibit

How can you help others observe Florida plants and animals?

Hi, I'm Samuel Alcorta. Have you ever thought about how lucky you are to live in Florida? The state has so many different kinds of habitats with an amazing variety of plants and animals. Some of these plants and animals are very rare.

I work as a zoo engineer, and right now I'm working on a wetland exhibit. I need your help to design the exhibit. In this problem-based learning activity, you will design a wetland exhibit of your choice.

Follow the path to learn how you will complete the Quest. The Quest activities in each lesson will help you complete the Quest! Check off your progress on the path when you complete an activity with a QUEST CHECK ✓ OFF. Go online for more Quest activities.

Quest Check-In 1

Lesson 1

Learn about different kinds of plant life cycles to decide whether to include the white water lily in your exhibit.

SC.4.L.16.4 Compare and contrast the major stages in the life cycles of Florida plants and animals, such as those that undergo incomplete and complete metamorphosis, and flowering and nonflowering seed-bearing plants

Quest Check-In Lab 3

Lesson 3

Find out about how a flamingo responds to factors in its habitat. Decide how your exhibit could meet the needs of flamingos.

▶ VIDEO
Watch a video about a zoo engineer.

GIFT SHOP

Quest Check-In 4

Lesson 4

Consider the behavior of the rainbow snake as a factor in your decision whether to include this reptile in your wetlaInd exhibit.

Quest Check-In 2

Lesson 2

Use what you learn about the life cycle of an amphibian to decide whether to include a marbled salamander in your exhibit.

Quest Findings

You are ready to design your exhibit! Use the knowledge you have gained on your Quest to design a wetland habitat for zoo visitors to experience.

uConnect Lab

How far can a seed travel on its own?

HANDS-ON LAB

SC.4.L.16.1, SC.4.N.3.1

Scientists use models to study nature. How can you use a model to see which features help a seed travel farthest?

Procedure

☐ **1.** Which features help seeds travel the farthest distance in the wind?

_____

_____

☐ **2.** Design 2 seeds. Each should have different features. Draw your model seeds. Get your teacher's approval before you make your models.

☐ **3.** Test your models by placing them in the air blown by a fan. Drop each model from the same place and height. Measure and record how far each travels.

Analyze and Interpret Data

4. Compare Results Compare your results with those of other students. What features do the model seeds that traveled farthest share?

_____

_____

_____

_____

_____

_____

Materials

- scissors
- fan
- meterstick
- safety goggles

Suggested Materials

- paper clips
- feathers
- tape or glue
- paper

⚠ Be careful using scissors.

⚠ Wear safety goggles.

Science Practice

Scientists use models to investigate.

My Model Seeds

Main Idea and Details

The main idea is the big idea that the writer wants you to understand about a piece of text. Identifying the main idea helps readers recall the most important information in the text.

As you read, ask yourself these questions:

- What are some important facts or ideas in the text?
- What does the writer want me to understand by telling me these facts or ideas?

Read the text about the Citrus Wizard. Look for the main idea and details.

⚙ LAFS.4.RI.1.2

GAME

Practice what you learn with the Mini Games.

The Citrus Wizard

A farmworker helped Florida grow better citrus fruits. His name was Lue Gim Gong. Lue was born in China and came to the United States at the age of 12. During the 1894–95 winter, Florida had one of its worst freezes in history. Nearly all the fruit trees in the orange groves died. Lue experimented to make a new kind of orange tree. He watched bees to see how they carried pollen from one plant to another. In 1911, he grew a new orange that ripened in the early fall. When the oranges ripened, they could be harvested before the frost, and the citrus crop would not be ruined. The orange is still grown today and is the basis of Florida's modern citrus industry.

✓ **READING CHECK** **Main Idea and Details** Circle the main idea. Underline two supporting details.

Lesson 1

Life Cycles of Florida Plants

I can...

Identify different ways that flowering plants reproduce.
Compare and contrast the life cycles of Florida plants.

Literacy Skill
Main Idea and Details

Vocabulary
germinate
sepal
pistil
stamen
pollination
fertilization

Academic Vocabulary
disperse

▶ VIDEO

Watch a video about the life cycles of plants.

SC.4.L.16.1 Identify processes of sexual reproduction in flowering plants, including pollination, fertilization (seed production), seed dispersal, and germination. **SC.4.L.16.4** Compare and contrast the major stages in the life cycles of Florida plants and animals, such as those that undergo incomplete and complete metamorphosis, and flowering and nonflowering seed-bearing plants. (Also **SC.4.N.3.1, LAFS.4.RI.1.2**)

STEM ▶ Connection

When scientists find fossil plant pollen, how do you think they identify the kind of pollen trapped in the rock? Scientists study pollen from both living plants and fossils. Scientists use powerful microscopes and detective skills to study the pollen. They identify and count the different kinds of pollen in rocks of a particular time. They get clues to what the climate was like when the plants lived. They can also figure out what the land looked like. By studying the rock and pollen fossils, scientists can figure out what made up an entire ancient forest.

📖 **Write About It** Suppose you are a scientist that has just found a new fossil of plant pollen. What questions about the fossil would you investigate? How would you find the answers?

HANDS-ON LAB

SC.4.L.16.1, SC.4.N.3.1

How do insects help
plants reproduce?

Materials
- 2 magnets
- magnetic objects
- paper

When designing exhibits, zoo engineers often use models to help visitors understand how a natural system works. How can you model what happens when insects move pollen from one flower to another?

Science Practice

Scientists make and use models to understand processes in nature.

Procedure

☐ **1.** Make a plan to model what happens when insects move pollen from one flower to another flower. Tell what each material in your model represents and what processes will be modeled.

☐ **2.** Show your procedure to your teacher before you begin. Record your observations.

Observations

Analyze and Interpret Data

3. Analyze How does your model help you understand how insects move pollen?

_____

_____

Visual Literacy Connection

What are the life cycles of plants?

Compare the life cycles of these two Florida plants. Other than the way they make seeds, their life cycles are similar.

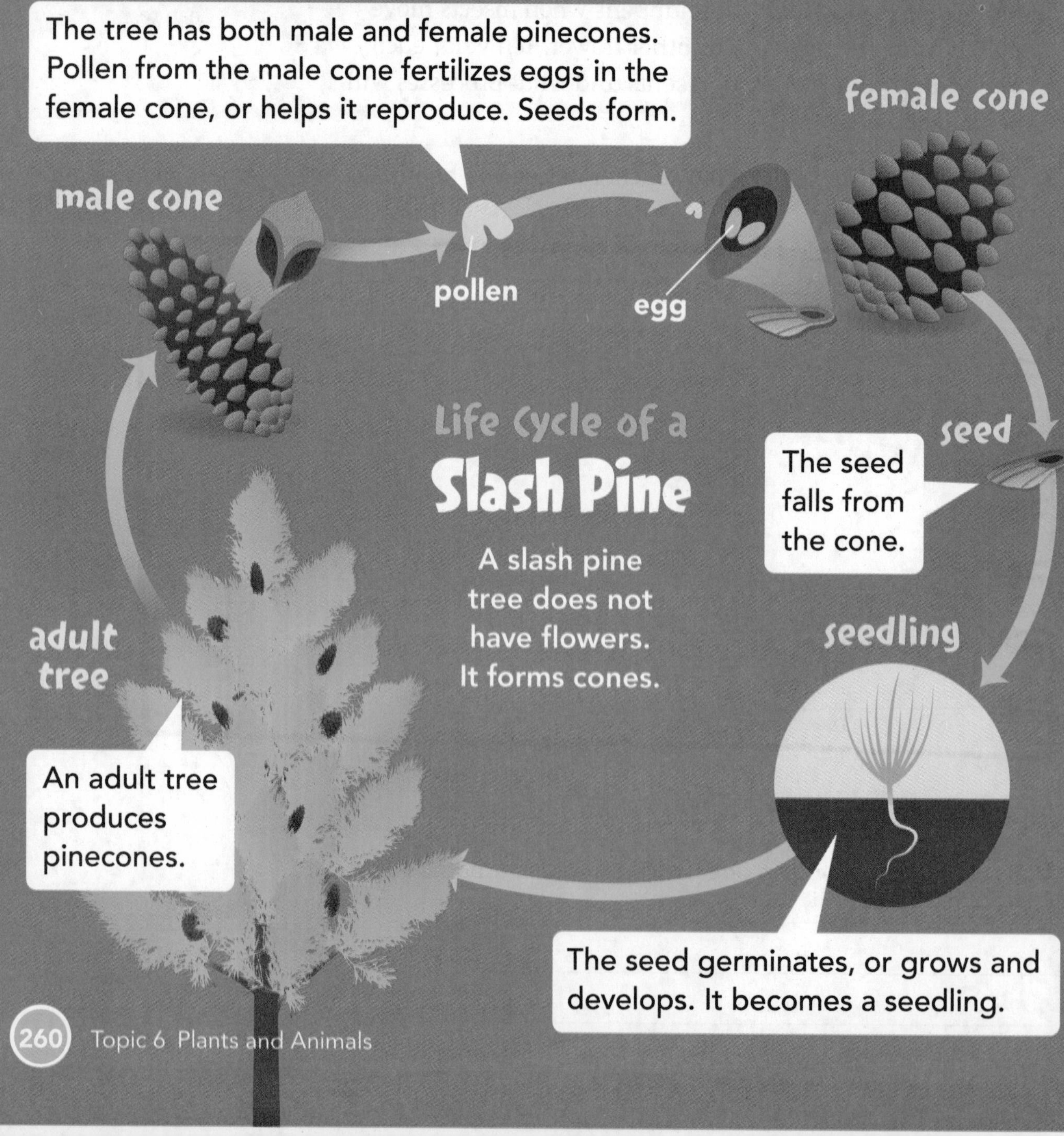

The tree has both male and female pinecones. Pollen from the male cone fertilizes eggs in the female cone, or helps it reproduce. Seeds form.
female cone
male cone
pollen
egg
Life Cycle of a
Slash Pine
A slash pine tree does not have flowers. It forms cones.
seed
The seed falls from the cone.
seedling
adult tree
An adult tree produces pinecones.
The seed germinates, or grows and develops. It becomes a seedling.

What similarities can you identify in the two different life cycles?

_____

_____

The orange fruit and its seeds fall to the ground.

A seed germinates and grows into a seedling.

seed

The young plant is called a seedling. Its leaves make food for the plant as it grows into an adult plant.

Life Cycle of a
Orange Tree

An orange tree is a flowering plant. The flowers produce seeds.

fruit

seedling

The tree gets larger and begins to grow flowers. Flowers are pollinated when pollen is transferred to the female part of the flower. Pollinated flowers produce seeds.

Fruit grows around the seed.

adult tree

Dissect a Flower

A good way to learn about flowers is to take one apart. Try this! Get a simple flower from a florist or garden. Carefully take apart the flower. Observe the parts with a hand lens. As you work, draw your flower and label its parts.

How Flowers Make Seeds

The life cycle of most flowering plants starts with a seed. The seed germinates, and a new plant grows from the seed. The plant continues to grow until the adult plant produces more seeds.

In flowering plants, the flowers are the plant parts that make seeds. The flowers of different kinds of plants have different sizes and shapes. Most flowers have four main parts.

A. The **sepals** are the green leaf-like parts that cover and protect the flower before it opens.

B. The color and smell of the petals help attract insects, birds, and other living things.

C. The **pistil** is the female part of the flower. A pistil extends into the flower. At its bottom is the ovary, where the egg cells are produced. Seeds will form there.

D. The **stamens** are the male part of the flower. Stamens surround the pistil and produce the pollen. These small grains contain the sperm cells. They join with the egg cells to make seeds.

Describe How do flowering plants reproduce?

_____

_____

_____

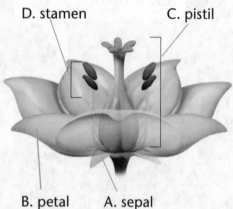

D. stamen   C. pistil

B. petal   A. sepal

Quest Connection

How can you represent the relationship between plants and their pollinators in your wetland exhibit?

_____

How Pollen Moves

In order for seeds to form, pollen must get from the stamen to a pistil. This movement of pollen from stamen to pistil is called **pollination**. Animals often play a part in pollination. Animals that transfer pollen are called pollinators. The bee in the photo is a pollinator. The bright colors of the flower attract the bee to it.

Many flowers make a sweet liquid called nectar. This provides a food source for bees, bats, butterflies, and birds. As the animal feeds, pollen from the stamens rubs onto its body. The pollen may then rub off onto the pistil of the same flower or onto another flower.

Wind and water can also transfer pollen from one flower to another. Wind pollination is common in trees and grasses. These plants do not have big flowers with colorful petals to attract animals.

Once a pollen grain lands on a pistil, a thin tube grows down through the pistil to the ovary. The pollen travels down the tube to the ovary. The sperm cell of the pollen combines with the egg cell in a process called **fertilization**.

Explain Draw a picture that shows what happens after a pollen grain lands on a pistil.

Literacy ▸ Toolbox

Main Idea and Details

The main idea is the big idea the writer is trying to tell. Underline the main idea in the paragraph about pollination.

LAFS.4.RI.1.2

Shell Design The seed in the photo is dispersed by water. How could you change the seed's design so that it is dispersed in a different way?

How Seeds Grow and Change

After fertilization, the flower changes. The petals and stamens dry up and fall off the flower. The fertilized egg in the ovary develops into a seed. The ovary grows into a fruit that covers and protects the seed. When the fruit is ripe, the seed is ready to change into a new plant.

Plants have different ways to **disperse**, or scatter, their seeds. Many seeds are built to spread with the wind. Other seeds, such as this coconut, can float in water. Some seeds, such as burrs, have tiny hooks that stick to an animal's fur. As the animal goes from one place to another, it disperses the seeds. Tasty fruits also help scatter seeds. When an animal picks or eats the fruit, it often scatters its seeds.

☑ Lesson 1 Check

SC.4.L.16.1, SC.4.L.16.4

1. Identify Patterns Draw and label a model of a flowering fruit tree, such as an apple tree. Include at least 4 stages in your diagram.

2. Critique You overhear someone say that bees are pests and only impact the environment in negative ways. Critique their statement.

_____

_____

_____

Life Cycle of a
White Water Lily

Florida has many kinds of plants growing in its wetlands. One of the most easily recognized plants is the white water lily. The white water lily is a flowering plant that grows in shallow freshwater. The plants have large, flat, rounded leaves that enable the flowers and leaves to float. The leaves can be 30 cm (about 12 in) wide. The lily's flowers can be 25 cm (about 10 in) wide. It has rootlike structures. These structures grow from seeds that have sunk to the bottom of the pond. Each spring, the plants grow up through the water from the rootlike structures.

Describe How would you include the white water lily in the design of your wetland exhibit? Underline two details that you will include in your design. Draw your design.

My Design

▶ VIDEO

Go online to learn about technology and pollination.

Here's the Buzz

Many farmers and orchard owners are facing a problem. They depend on honeybees to pollinate the flowers of their crops, but the number of honeybees is getting much smaller. As a result, flowers have fewer pollinators. Without pollinators, crops and orchards will not produce fruits and vegetables.

To help solve the problem, engineers have built a robotic bee that flies in groups to pollinate flowers. The robot is called RoboBee. How does RoboBee know where to go and what to do? Computer codes tell a robot what to do.

Design It

Help the bee transfer pollen from one flower to the other flower and then return to its hive. Develop a code to help bees pollinate flowers in a garden. You can use numbers or letters or add directional arrows to the code, if you choose.

☐ Use a coin to represent the bee. Place the coin on the bee at the entrance to the flower garden. The bee cannot fly through the black squares.

☐ Write your code symbols and your coded instructions in the boxes.

Your code symbols	
Move right one space.	Move down one space.
Move left one space.	Move up one space.
Your code							
1.	2.	3.	4.	5.	6.	7.	8.
9.	10.	11.	12.	13.	14.	15.	16.

☐ Exchange codes with another student. Have the partner try your code by moving the coin through the maze.

Life Cycles of Florida Animals

I can...
Compare and contrast the life cycles of Florida animals.

Literacy Skill
Main Idea and Details

Vocabulary
metamorphosis
larva
pupa
molt

Academic Vocabulary
transform

▶ **VIDEO**

Watch a video about the life cycles of Florida animals.

SC.4.L.16.4 Compare and contrast the major stages in the life cycles of Florida plants and animals, such as those that undergo incomplete and complete metamorphosis, and flowering and nonflowering seed-bearing plants. (Also SC.4.N.1.4)

ENGINEERING ▶ Connection

Have you seen a leatherback sea turtle on the beach? Leatherback sea turtles live in the ocean for most of the year. However, mother turtles must return to the beach to lay their eggs. A mother turtle digs a nest in the sand. Then she lays her eggs and returns to the ocean. After two months, the eggs begin to hatch. The hatchlings, or young turtles, crawl at night toward the ocean. The hatchlings look exactly like adult sea turtles, only smaller. They will be adults in about 12 to 15 years.

Young turtles have only a 25 percent chance that they will make it to the ocean. With the help of civil engineers, property owners in coastal areas of Florida are developing ways to help the leatherback sea turtles nest safely and survive the journey from nest to ocean.

📓 **Write About It** In your science notebook, explain why you think it is important to help protect sea turtles. How can civil engineers help reduce the human threats to sea turtle nesting grounds? What should they consider about how sea turtles nest when they plan coastal building projects?

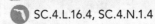

How does a sea turtle change in its *life cycle?*

Some scientists, called herpetologists, study the life cycles of reptiles and amphibians. How can you compare a leatherback sea turtle in different stages of its life cycle?

Science Practice

Scientists attempt reasonable answers to scientific questions.

Procedure

☐ 1. Observe the photos of the leatherback sea turtles in different stages of their life cycle. Choose one feature of the sea turtle to compare at each stage.

☐ 2. Record your observations about each life stage in the table.

Body feature being compared _____

Life stage	Observation
Egg	
Hatchling	
Young adult	
Adult	

Analyze and Interpret Data

3. Describe How does the sea turtle change during its life cycle?

_____

_____

Be a Scientist

Life Cycle Illustrator

Research the life cycle of an animal you have observed in your neighborhood. Draw the life cycle and label the life cycle stages in your drawings.

Life Cycle of a Reptile

Like plants, animals go through life cycles. Some animals change more during their lives than others. Mammal and reptile young look very much like their parents.

The American alligator is a large reptile. It has a life cycle similar to the life cycle of the sea turtle, but there are also differences.

1. The mother alligator builds a nest of plants and mud. She stays close to the nest.

2. The mother helps the babies hatch.

3. The hatchlings stay with their mother for about a year.

4. At the age of 11 or 12, the alligators are adults.

Question It!

Suppose you were studying the growth and development of reptiles. What are some questions you might ask about the hatchling stage of the reptiles?

_____

_____

_____

_____

Life Cycle of an Insect

Insects go through a **metamorphosis**, or a change in form, as they grow. The metamorphosis can be complete or incomplete. In complete metamorphosis, the insect goes through four different life stages: egg, larva, pupa, and adult. These stages are so different that you might not even recognize them as the same animal. In incomplete metamorphosis, the change is more gradual. Insects with incomplete metamorphosis go through three stages: egg, nymph, and adult.

In both kinds of metamorphosis, the insect **transforms**, or changes, from egg to adult. The word *incomplete* does not mean that the insect does not become an adult. It means that it does not change completely from one stage to the next. A chrysalis, or butterfly pupa, is very different from an adult butterfly. Its change is complete. A young grasshopper, however, looks like an adult grasshopper. It just needs bigger wings and some extra weight.

✓ READING CHECK **Main Idea and Details** Circle the number of different life stages in complete metamorphosis. Underline the number of different life stages in incomplete metamorphosis.

egg

larva

pupa

Quest Connection

How would you design your wetland habitat to support animals that go through metamorphosis? Record your ideas.

_____

_____

_____

_____

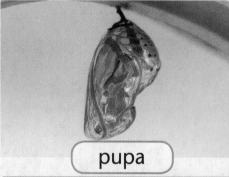

adult

What are **complete** and **incomplete** metamorphosis?

Insects change form as they grow. This change is called metamorphosis. It can be complete or incomplete. Follow the diagram to understand how the life cycles of two different insects are similar and different. Complete the drawing and summary.

1 egg

2 **larva,** or growth stage

3 **pupa,** or resting stage, where the body changes

4 adult

Complete metamorphosis

The young insect **looks very different** from the adult.

INTERACTIVITY

Complete an activity on the life cycles of Florida animals.

1 egg

2 nymph

Incomplete metamorphosis

The young insect **looks very similar** to the the adult, only smaller.

3 adult

! **Draw the missing nymph.**

As the nymph grows, it **molts**. This means that it sheds its outer layer.

! Summarize how the two forms of metamorphosis are similar and how they are different.

_____

_____

_____

Life Cycle of a Mammal

Like most mammals, Florida panthers give birth to live babies. Florida panthers are often born in late spring. At first, they cannot walk or open their eyes. Mammal babies drink milk from their mother. Within two months, their mother takes them with her when she hunts. The young cats remain with their mother until they can hunt and live on their own. When the panthers are between the ages of two and three, they may have kittens of their own. The panther life cycle begins again.

☑ **READING CHECK** **Main Idea and Details** What is one detail in this paragraph? How does it help you understand the main idea?

_____

_____

_____

_____

Connecting Concepts ▸ Toolbox

Patterns A pattern is the way something appears or happens over and over in the same order. Why is a life cycle a pattern?

☑ **Lesson 2 Check**   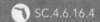 SC.4.6.16.4

1. Compare How are the life cycles of a sea turtle and a Florida panther different?

_____

_____

_____

2. Infer A bee goes through complete metamorphosis. A cockroach goes through incomplete metamorphosis. Differentiate between complete and incomplete metamorphosis.

_____

_____

Life Cycle of a Salamander

Marbled salamanders live in the wetlands of northern Florida. They dig burrows under rocks or logs near riverbanks. They are amphibians. Unlike most amphibians, marbled salamanders mate on land instead of water. A female salamander digs out a hiding place under a log, leaves, or a rock and lays her eggs. The eggs need water to hatch. So, the mother stays with the eggs in her nest until it rains. Once the nest fills with water, the hatchlings are on their own.

A hatchling salamander is called a larva. The larval salamander has feathery gills to breathe underwater. The larva grows quickly. Within a few weeks, its legs begin to grow, and its gills begin to disappear. It breathes air near the water's surface. After a few months, the young salamander leaves the water and enters the forest. The adult salamander can reproduce when it is between 17 and 26 months old. This starts the cycle all over again.

1. **Explain** Why is the marbled salamander a good animal to include in your wetland exhibit? Explain your reasoning.

_____

_____

_____

2. **Describe** How could you design an exhibit to include a salamander and a water lily?

_____

_____

_____

_____

Plant and Animal Characteristics

I can...

Explain that plant and animal characteristics are inherited but sometimes can be affected by the environment.

Literacy Skill
Main Idea and Details

Vocabulary

inherit
heredity
environment

Academic Vocabulary

characteristic

▶ **VIDEO**

Watch a video about plant and animal characteristics.

SC.4.L.16.2 Explain that although characteristics of plants and animals are inherited, some characteristics can be affected by the environment. (Also **SC.4.N.1.5, SC.4.N.3.1**)

LOCAL-TO-GLOBAL ▶ Connection

Did you know that oranges are unknown in the wild? The fruit that many of us enjoy as a breakfast drink is the result of producing plants from two other citrus fruits—a tangerine and a light-green grapefruit, called the pomelo. Both plants have been grown in Southeast Asia since ancient times.

Climate affects the features of citrus fruits. Color is one of those features. Ripe oranges grown in the tropics are not orange in color. They are bright green on the outside. The fruit's skin contains chlorophyll, the same chemical that gives green leaves their color. The orange color of the fruit's outer covering only shows when the chlorophyll disappears. Cool weather—about 13°C (55°F)—is needed for citrus fruits to change color while on the trees. The more the fruits are exposed to cooler weather, the faster their color changes. In tropical countries where temperatures are warm all year, oranges stay green or yellow.

Explain Why are oranges green when they are grown in tropical climates?

_____

_____

uInvestigate Lab

How can pollution affect an organism?

Climate is only one factor that affects living things. How can pollution affect living things?

Materials
- safety goggles
- water
- graduated cylinder
- plastic cups
- vinegar
- measuring spoon
- yeast
- clock
- sugar

Procedure

☐ **1.** Using all the materials, make a plan to investigate how pollution affects yeast. (A yeast is a single-celled organism that is related to mushrooms. Live yeast produce a gas, carbon dioxide, when they use sugar as food.)

☐ **2.** Show your plan to your teacher before you begin. Record your observations.

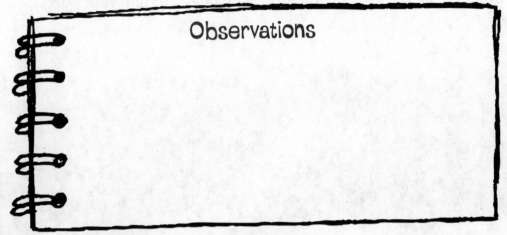

Observations

⚠ Wear safety goggles.

⚠ Do not taste any of the materials.

Science Practice

Scientists compare their results with those of others.

Analyze and Interpret Data

3. Compare and Contrast Compare your results with those of classmates. Explain any differences.

_____

_____

_____

_____

_____

Develop a Model The patterns on a giraffe help it blend in with its environment. How do you think that characteristic helps the giraffe survive? Design a model to test your hypothesis.

Animal Characteristics and Heredity

Giraffes have patterned skin. The patterned skin is a **characteristic**, or trait, of all giraffes. Young giraffes look like their parents because they inherit their characteristics. When a plant or animal **inherits** a characteristic, it gets the characteristic from its parents. Animals and plants will pass the characteristics that they inherit on to their own offspring. The passing of characteristics from parents to offspring is known as **heredity**. All plants and animals inherit characteristics from their parents.

You probably would not confuse a giraffe for any other animal. Different kinds of animals have their own sets of inherited characteristics. Their offspring will all have the same traits as their parents.

Reflect In your science notebook, write what characteristics you think you inherited from your parents.

Plant Characteristics and Heredity

Like animals, plants inherit their characteristics from parent plants.

Compare and Contrast Compare the two prickly pear cacti. What traits do they share? What traits are different?

_____

_____

_____

_____

_____

Plants that live in dry regions inherit structures to help them survive with very little water. The prickly pear cactus plant has paddle-shaped pads. These pads are actually stems that act as leaves. These stems are a good place for the plants to store water. The cacti also have a waxy coating to hold in moisture. Instead of leaves, they have spines. The spines help protect them from animals that might eat them. The prickly pear cactus has flowers that make seeds. Those seeds will make plants that have the same characteristics as the cacti you see.

☑ **READING CHECK** **Main Idea and Details** Circle the main idea about the prickly pear cactus. Underline two details that support the main idea.

WHAT ENVIRONMENTAL FACTORS affect animal characteristics?

Factors in the environment can affect animal characteristics. An **environment** is everything that surrounds a living thing.

TEMPERATURE

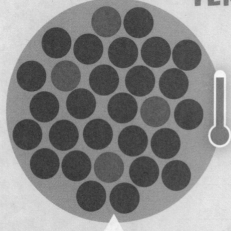

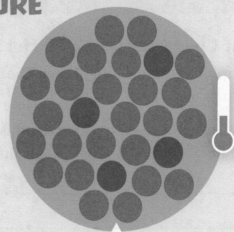

In a warm sea turtle nest, many more **female** sea turtles will develop (●).

In a cool nest, many more **male** sea turtles will develop (●).

CLIMATE

The Himalayan rabbit normally has dark hair only on parts of its body that are cool.

If the rabbit lives in a hot climate, it does not have any dark hair.

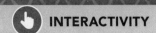

DIET

A flamingo's feathers are actually white.

The feathers turn pink when a flamingo eats shrimp and algae, which contain carotene.

POLLUTION

A certain chemical in water pollution can cause male fish to develop eggs in their bodies.

! **Describe an environmental factor that could affect you.**

_____

_____

Be a Scientist

Nature Notebook
Take a field trip in your neighborhood. Keep a nature notebook. Record evidence that you find of how the environment affects the plants and animals you observe.

Plants and Environmental Characteristics

It is easy to see how the environment affects the tree in the picture. Strong winds that blow in one direction have caused the tree to grow sideways. The effects of the enviroment are not always that obvious. The hydrangea flowers in the picture are the same kind of plant, but their color is different. The amount of acid in the soil where the plant grows determines whether the hydrangea flower will be pink or blue. The flowers of hydrangeas that grow in soil that is acidic will likely be blue. In soils that are not acidic, the flowers tend to be pink.

Draw Conclusions What factors other than wind might affect this tree? Label the factors on the photo.

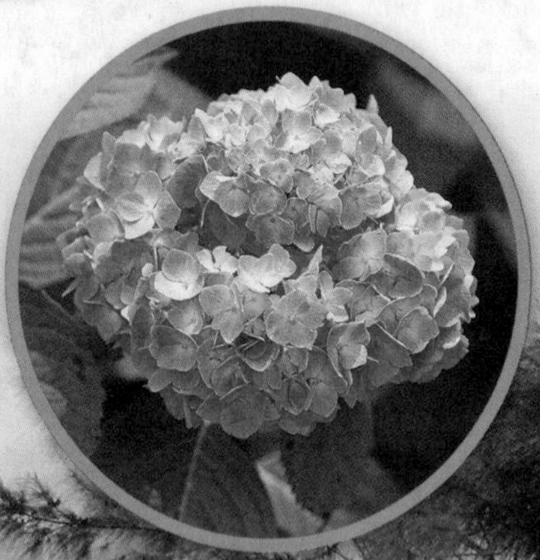

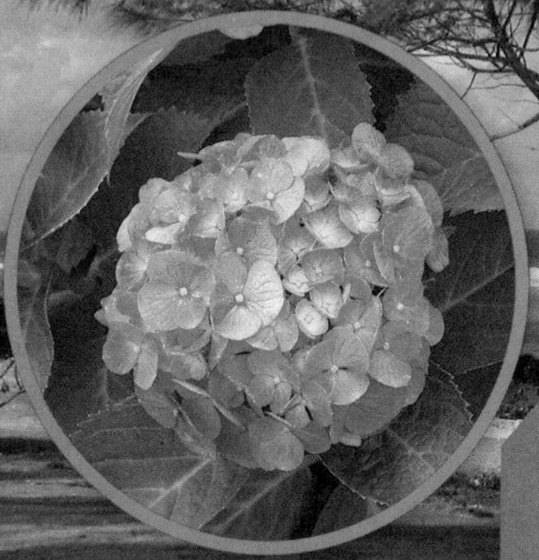

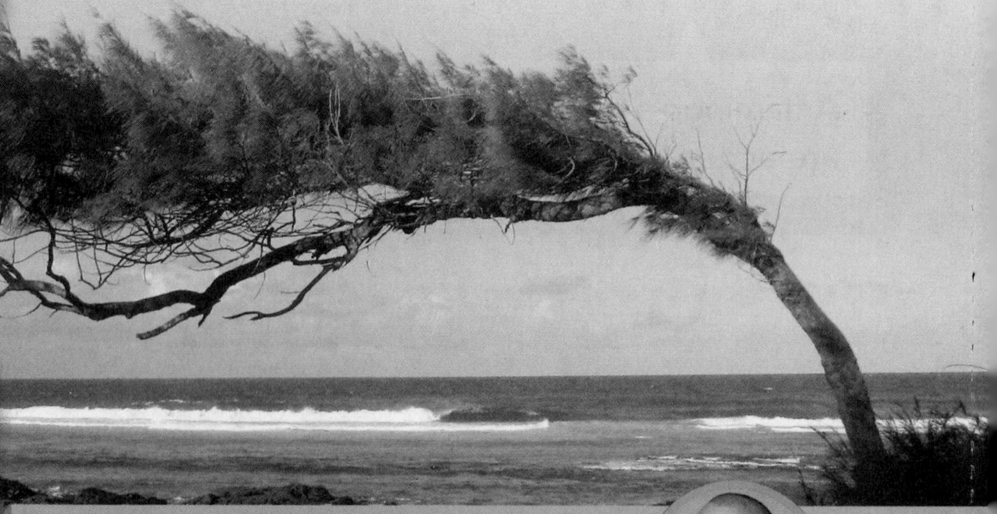

Quest Connection

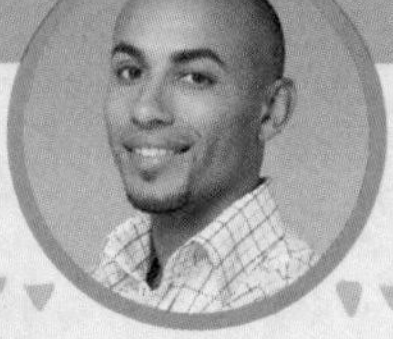

What kinds of environmental factors may affect plants in your exhibit?

____

____

____

____

Even though this potted plant grows indoors, it still has an environment. The shape of this bonsai tree does not result from heredity. A gardener closely controls the amount of soil and water the tree receives to keep it from growing too much. The small pan that it grows in also limits how much it can grow. The gardener also trims and uses wires to shape the tree. These characteristics of the tree are due to its environment.

✓ Lesson 3 Check

1. **Assess** One of your peers says that all cacti can grow in dry and wet environments. Critique their statement using evidence to support your ideas.

_____

_____

_____

2. **Organize Data** Choose one plant and one animal. Write their names in the first column of the chart. List an inherited trait of each in the second column. In the third column, tell how their environments affect each trait.

Living thing	Inherited trait	How the environment affects trait

Why do the colors of flamingos vary?

Environmental factors, such as the food birds eat, can cause changes to their bodies. How does a flamingo's food affect its color?

Materials
• Flamingo Colors sheets
• scissors
• colored pencils
• paper fastener
• paper

 Be careful handling scissors.

Procedure

☐ **1.** A flamingo's feather colors may appear to have more color when it eats a diet high in carotene, a protein found in its food.

Engineering Practice

Engineers **use models** to investigate the scientific world.

☐ **2.** Use the Flamingo Colors sheets, scissors, and paper fastener to make a cause and effect wheel that shows the relationship between food and feather color. Vary the color of the flamingos based on different diets ranging from no carotene to high levels of carotene.

☐ **3.** Write a question that you want to ask about how the environment affects another animal. How could you use a similar wheel to show the cause and effect relationship?

_____

_____

_____

☐ **4.** Build the wheel and write a series of questions that another group can answer using the wheel. Trade wheels with another group.

_____

_____

Analyze and Interpret Data

5. Analyze What information does your wheel show about flamingos?

_____

_____

6. How will this information be helpful in your wetland exhibit?

_____

_____

_____

7. Analyze Use the second wheel from a different group. What
environmental factor and effect does it show?

_____

_____

Animal Behavior

I can...

Explain how animal behaviors are shaped by heredity and learning.

Literacy Skill
Main Idea and Details

Vocabulary
instinct

Academic Vocabulary
distinguish

▶ **VIDEO**

Watch a video about songbird behavior.

SC.4.L.16.3 Recognize that animal behaviors may be shaped by heredity and learning. (Also **SC.4.N.1.6, MAFS.4.G.1.3**)

LOCAL-TO-GLOBAL ⟩ **Connection**

Each fall, monarch butterflies migrate south in great numbers from Canada and the eastern United States to Mexico. These insects migrate to an area where the temperature is warmer. Their winter home can be almost 5000 kilometers (3,000 miles) away. The monarchs spend the winter hibernating and then leave Mexico in the spring. They lay eggs on milkweed plants as they travel north.

Scientists think that Florida's monarch butterflies stay in the state year-round, unlike monarch butterflies in colder areas.

Infer Why do you think the monarchs in Florida stay year-round?

_____

_____

Do mealworms prefer damp or dry places?

The monarch butterflies migrate to environments that best meet their needs. What environmental conditions do mealworms prefer?

Materials
- 10 mealworms
- plastic gloves
- paper towels
- plastic spoons
- water
- tray

Procedure

☐ **1.** Observe the mealworms. Write a hypothesis about whether mealworms prefer a damp place or a dry place.

_____

_____

_____

☐ **2.** Plan an investigation to test your hypothesis. Have your teacher approve your plan before you begin.

☐ **3.** Record your observations. Be sure to distinguish observations from ideas and inferences about the observations.

 Be careful handling animals.

 Wear plastic gloves.

⚠ Wash your hands.

Science Practice

Scientists make inferences from observations.

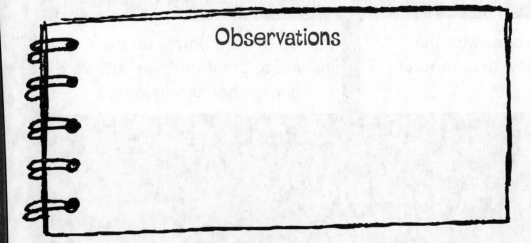

Observations

Analyze and Interpret Data

4. Infer From what you observed, can you infer why mealworms behave this way? Explain.

_____

_____

WHAT ARE SOME animal instincts?

An **instinct** is a behavior that an animal inherits from its parents. Animals are born with instincts to do certain behaviors that help them survive.

Protection

Ducklings are born with the instinct to follow their mother to stay safe.

Porcupines are born with the instinct to point their quills toward an enemy when threatened.

Food and Shelter

Spiders are born with the instinct to weave webs. They use their webs to trap insects and lay their eggs.

Migration

Antelope are born with the instinct to migrate. Herds of antelope migrate long distances in search of food.

Hibernation

Some squirrels are born with the instinct to hibernate. When outside temperatures are cold, squirrels remain inactive to conserve energy.

! **Draw an animal you know.**

Write about one of its instincts.

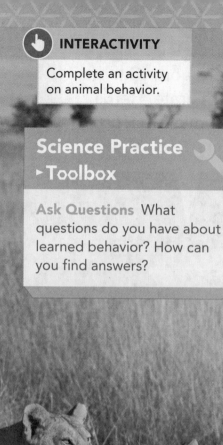

INTERACTIVITY

Complete an activity on animal behavior.

Science Practice
► Toolbox

Ask Questions What questions do you have about learned behavior? How can you find answers?

Learned Behavior

Many animals learn to get food by watching their parents. Lion cubs learn to hunt by watching older lions. A pride, or group of lions, often hunts together. Zebras are common prey for lions. A herd of zebras keeps safe from attack by staying together. When a zebra is separated from the herd, the lions will chase it toward a group of lions that is hiding. The lions will then pounce on their prey. A lion cub learns to pounce on its prey by pouncing on its mother's twitching tail.

Scientists found that when monkeys learn new things, they teach other monkeys what they have learned. In one investigation, scientists dropped sweet potatoes near a group of monkeys. The potatoes landed in sand. The monkeys liked the potatoes, but they did not like the sand that stuck to the potatoes. One of the younger monkeys found that she could wash the sand off in a nearby stream. She taught her mother how to wash off the sand too.

📖 **Reflect** In your science notebook, write about a behavior that you have learned.

Quest Connection

What kinds of learned behaviors may an animal learn in the wild? What kinds of behaviors may an animal learn in a zoo?

_____

_____

_____

Learning and Instinct Combined

Some behaviors are partly instinctive and partly learned. Birds build nests as a result of instinct, but they get better with practice. Their choices of materials to use may change over time as they watch their parents or other birds.

Bird song is another behavior that can be both instinctive and learned. This young white-crowned sparrow inherits the ability to **distinguish**, or tell the difference between, a white-crowned sparrow's song and the songs of other kinds of birds. But learning the song is not inherited. Young sparrows that are separated from their parents never learn to sing the complete song.

Infer Why is it important for the white-crowned sparrow to sing the same song that is sung by other birds of the same kind?

_____

_____

_____

✓ Lesson 4 Check

SC.4.L.16.3

1. **Separate** Ella gets a new puppy. The puppy has some behaviors that are instinctual and some that are learned. What is an example of each type of behavior the puppy might show?

   _____

   _____

2. **Explain Phenomena in Terms of Concepts** Can the behavior of an animal be shaped by both learning and heredity? Provide an example to support your argument.

   _____

   _____

   _____

Rainbow Snake Behavior

The common rainbow snake is a large reptile that lives in wetlands or slow-moving streams. In Florida, the rainbow snake is found in the panhandle and in the northern part of the state.

Rainbow snakes are not seen often. They spend much of their life hiding under floating water plants and logs. They also burrow within the banks at the water's edge. These snakes rarely bask in sunlight out of the water. They are active at night. They are excellent swimmers, but they usually hunt along the bottom of a body of water. The adult rainbow snake eats mainly eels and salamanders. The snakes eat their prey alive, swallowing them head first. However, they rarely bite humans if they are captured.

Think about the behavior of a rainbow snake. How does its behavior affect your decision to include it in the wetland exhibit?

_____

_____

_____

_____

_____

_____

_____

_____

_____

_____

MAFS.4.G.1.3

Lines of Symmetry

Something has symmetry if one side matches the other side when you draw a line to divide it in half. Almost all animal bodies show some form of symmetry.

Identify Simple shapes, such as the circle, rectangle, and triangle, have symmetry. Draw lines of symmetry on the three shapes.

  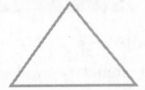

Identify It is easier to find out whether something in a picture is symmetrical by drawing a line. Draw a line through the center of each animal to show its symmetry.

INTERACTIVITY

Organize data to support your Quest Findings.

STEM Design a Wetland Exhibit

How can you help others observe Florida's plants and animals?

Identify Exhibit Parts

List the plants and animals you will include in your wetlands exhibit design.

_____

_____

What concepts or interactions will your exhibit explain to visitors?

_____

_____

Communicate Your Design

Complete the design for your wetland exhibit. Then present your plan by using a design model of your choice.

My Design

Zoo Engineer

Zoo engineers are responsible for designing new zoo habitats that meet the needs of the animals that live there. They try to meet the animals' needs while providing an educational experience for the visitors. They oversee all aspects of the exhibit design process. They draw up the plans and supervise the building process. They work for zoos, animal parks, museums, aquariums, and other cultural institutions.

Zoo engineers must have experience with building construction, budgeting, and managing projects. It helps to have a background in zoology and wildlife biology. Some zoo engineers are self-employed, while others work for companies that employ a team of experts. Still others work directly for museums, aquariums, and zoos. Ideally, a zoo engineer has a love of nature, a passion for artistry, and a desire to help animals.

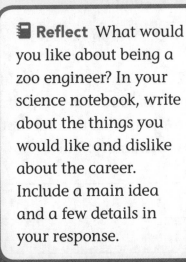

Reflect What would you like about being a zoo engineer? In your science notebook, write about the things you would like and dislike about the career. Include a main idea and a few details in your response.

☑ Assessment

Read each question and chose or write the best answer.

1. Recognize A grasshopper goes through different stages during its life cycle.

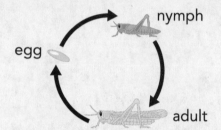

Which stage in the grasshopper's life cycle is found only in animals that undergo incomplete metamorphosis?

   A. egg

   B. larva

   C. adult

   D. nymph

2. Compare How is the life cycle of a mammal different from the life cycle of an animal that undergoes metamorphosis?

_____

_____

_____

_____

_____

_____

_____

_____

3. Formulate Sujin wants to model the life cycle of a mammal. Which choice describes how she should build the model?

   A. construct a time line starting at birth and ending at death

   B. construct a pyramid showing what the mammal eats throughout its life

   C. construct a circular diagram showing only growth and death

   D. construct a Venn diagram showing how a mammal's life is similar to another organism's life

4. Identify Which of the following describes pollination?

   A. movement of pollen from a stamen to a pistil

   B. movement of pollen from a sepal to a pistil

   C. movement of pollen from a pistil to a stamen

   D. movement of pollen from a stamen to an ovary

5. Predict The picture shows three different kinds of seeds.

Dandelion   Maple   Pine

How are these seeds most likely spread?

A. by wind

B. by water

C. by animals

D. none of the above

6. Develop a Logical Argument Many people grow plants in pots in their homes. How are the characteristics of a potted plant shaped by the plant's environment and by heredity?

_____

_____

_____

_____

_____

_____

7. Investigate Animals inherit certain behaviors from their parents. They also learn certain behaviors. Which behavior results from both instinct and learning?

A. A cat shakes water from its fur.

B. A baby kangaroo climbs into it mother's pouch as soon as it is born.

C. A dog sits in front of its owner when a treat is offered.

D. A cat pounces on a mouse.

The Essential Question *How do living things grow and change?*

Show What You Learned

Choose one plant and one animal. Describe the stages in the life cycle of the plant and animal of your choice.

_____

_____

_____

_____

_____

_____

_____

_____

_____

Look at the picture and answer questions 1–2.

The picture shows a family of crows.

1 Which statement supports the claim that an inherited trait in crows is black feathers?

  Ⓐ The parents and young in the picture all have black feathers.

  Ⓑ The young are smaller than the parents.

  Ⓒ Black feathers help keep the crows cool in warm weather.

  Ⓓ The young crows have the same parents.

2 These crows are likely to join other crows to form flocks. Which is **not** an advantage of joining a large flock of other crows?

  Ⓕ Individuals in a flock are less likely to eaten by predators.

  Ⓖ Individuals in a flock can keep each other warm during cold weather.

  Ⓗ Individuals in a flock can inherit new traits from each other.

  Ⓘ Individuals in a flock can learn from each other.

3 Diet is one of many factors that affect animal characteristics. How does diet affect the characteristics of birds such as flamingos?

  Ⓐ It affects the kind of nests they build.

  Ⓑ It affects the kind of songs their species sings.

  Ⓒ It affects the color of their feathers.

  Ⓓ It affects the length of their migration routes.

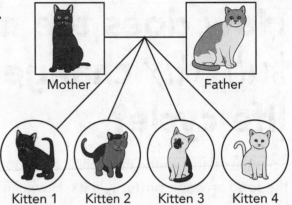
Mother   Father

Kitten 1   Kitten 2   Kitten 3   Kitten 4

Read the scenario and answer questions 4–6.

Angelina's family had two cats that had four kittens. The parent cats and their offspring are shown in the pictures.

4 All of the kittens, except Kitten 2, grew to be about the same size as the parents. Which plan would be best for Angelina to investigate why Kitten 2 is smaller?

(F) Observe and record the sounds each kitten makes.

(G) Observe and record how much food each kitten eats.

(H) Observe and record which kitten's fur changed the most.

(I) Observe and record how much each kitten sleeps for a month.

5 Angelina observed that all the kittens ran toward her whenever they heard the sound of the can opener. She used the can opener to open cat food cans. Which description best explains this behavior?

(A) The kittens were born with instincts to react to certain sounds similar to the can opener sound.

(B) The kittens learned that the sound of the can opener was often related to getting food.

(C) The kittens smelled the cat food as the can was being opened.

(D) The kittens learned from their mother how to get food.

6 The kittens may have young of their own when they become adults. Which statement is **not** true of the life cycles of the kittens and Angelina's pet lizard?

(F) Both lizards and kittens stay with their mother for a while after they are born.

(G) Kittens inherit traits from their parents, but lizards do not.

(H) Both lizards and kittens become adults at some time in their life cycles.

(I) Both lizards and kittens look like their parents when they are born.

uDemonstrate Lab

How does the mouth of a *butterfly* change during its life cycle?

Suggested Materials
- modeling clay
- pipe cleaners
- pinch clip
- scissors
- paper square
- cup of water
- straw

Scientists know that a caterpillar eats food that is different from the food an adult butterfly eats. How can you model the way the caterpillar and the butterfly eat?

⚠ Do not taste anything in the lab.

Procedure

☐ **1.** Look at the photos of the caterpillar eating a leaf and the butterfly sucking nectar. Write how the mouthparts of the caterpillar and the butterfly might be different.

Science Practice

Scientists use models to investigate.

_____

_____

_____

_____

☐ **2.** What materials could you use to model how the caterpillar eats and how the butterfly eats? How can you test your models to see whether they work? Write a plan. Show your plan to your teacher before you begin.

_____

_____

_____

_____

_____

_____

_____

☐ **3.** Test your models. Record your observations.

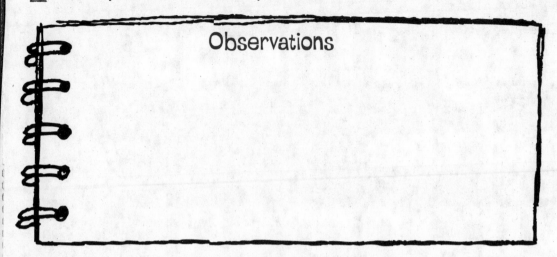

Observations

Analyze and Interpret Data

4. Compare and Contrast Compare your models with the models of other students. Which models worked best?

_____

_____

_____

_____

_____

5. Compare and Contrast Explain how the mouthparts of the caterpillar and the butterfly help each get the food they need.

_____

_____

_____

_____

_____

Living Things and the Environment

 SC.4.L.17.1 Compare the seasonal changes in Florida plants and animals to those in other regions of the country. **SC.4.L.17.2** Explain that animals, including humans, cannot make their own food and that when animals eat plants or other animals, the energy stored in the food source is passed to them. **SC.4.L.17.3** Trace the flow of energy from the Sun as it is transferred along the food chain through the producers to the consumers. **SC.4.L.17.4** Recognize ways plants and animals, including humans, can impact the environment. (Also **SC.4.N.1.3, SC.4.N.1.4, SC.4.N.1.5, SC.4.N.3.1,** and **LAFS.4.RI.3.7**)

Go online to access
your digital course.

▶ VIDEO

📖 eTEXT

👆 INTERACTIVITY

🎮 GAME

☑ ASSESSMENT

The Essential Question

How do living things interact with their environment?

Show What You Know

Animals often interact with each other to satisfy their basic needs. What do you think are some of the basic needs of the animals in the picture?

_____

_____

_____

Find a Home for Zoo Animals

Should animals be kept in a zoo?

Hi, my name is Sam Branton, and I am an ecologist who works at the local zoo. I have been asked to provide the zoo with an evaluation about whether living in a zoo is helpful or harmful for an animal. I am hoping that you can help me with this important task.

In this problem-based learning activity, you will evaluate different aspects of animals' lives in a zoo and compare them with animals living in their natural habitats. This is a hard decision, so get ready to debate the issue!

Follow the path to learn how you will complete the Quest. The Quest activities in the lessons will help you complete the Quest! Check off your progress on the path when you complete an activity with a

QUEST CHECK ✓ OFF . Go online for more Quest activities.

Quest Check-In Lab 1

Lesson 1

Determine whether zoo animals can survive in a different climate than that found in their natural habitats.

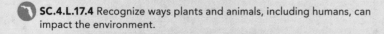

SC.4.L.17.4 Recognize ways plants and animals, including humans, can impact the environment.

Quest Check-In 3

Lesson 3

Use what you learn about how energy flows through ecosystems in natural habitats to decide where zoo animals belong in food chains.

Quest Check-In 4

Lesson 4

Apply what you learn about how organisms, including humans, change natural habitats to explore the good and bad of having animals in zoos.

Quest Check-In 2

Lesson 2

Learn about what animals eat in their natural habitats and whether that food is available in a zoo.

Quest Findings

Complete the Quest! Use what you have learned to decide whether animals should be kept in zoos. Propose solutions to improve the lives of zoo animals.

HANDS-ON LAB

SC.4.L.17.4, SC.4.N.3.1

What happens to animals when plant life decreases?

Materials
- green paper squares
- brown paper squares

Ecologists investigate how changes in one part of an ecosystem affect other parts of the ecosystem. How can you use a model to help explain what happens in an ecosystem if the number of plants decreases?

Science Practice

Scientists use models to help explain the world around them.

Procedure

☐ **1.** Predict what will happen to plant eaters if the number of plants in an ecosystem decreases.

_____

_____

☐ **2.** The green squares represent plants, and brown squares represent animals. Write a plan to test your prediction. Show your plan to your teacher before you begin. Record your observations.

Analyze and Interpret Data

3. **Use Evidence** What happens to plant-eating animals if plant life decreases in an area? Use evidence from the lab to support your answer.

_____

_____

_____

_____

Observations

Use Evidence from Text

LAFS.4.RI.3.7

GAME Practice what you learn with the Mini Games.

When you read carefully, you look for evidence. Use these strategies to find evidence.

- Read the text. Then reread it more carefully.
- Underline important facts.

Read the text to learn about annual and perennial plants.

Annuals and Perennials

Some plants go through a complete life cycle within a single year. Their roots, stems, and leaves die as cold weather appears. These plants are called annuals. In one year, an annual plant will sprout from a seed, grow, flower, reproduce, and die.

Other plants can live for many growing seasons. These plants are called perennials. They do not die when winter arrives. The parts of the plant aboveground die each year. However, the roots do not die. In spring, the plant grows new stems and leaves.

perennial flower

✓ **READING CHECK** **Use Evidence from Text** Suppose you live in a place with cold winters and you have perennial plants in your garden. What will happen to the plants during the winter months? Underline the important facts from the text that support your claim with evidence.

_____

_____

_____

_____

annual flower

Seasons Affect Plants and Animals

I can...

Explain how seasons affect plants and animals.
List examples of ecosystems.

Literacy Skill
Use Evidence from Text

Vocabulary
climate
ecosystem
dormant
hibernate
migrate

Academic Vocabulary
respond

SC.4.L.17.1 Compare the seasonal changes in Florida plants and animals to those in other regions of the country. (Also **SC.4.N.3.1, LAFS.4.RI.3.7**)

CURRICULUM Connection

Many birds fly south during the winter months. Many humans also move from the northern areas of the United States to the southern areas of the United States, such as Florida. Unlike the movement of other animals, this form of human movement is not necessary for survival. Reasons for this human movement might include vacation, work, or simply to escape the changing seasons. Humans who participate in this migration are often referred to as "snowbirds."

Compare and Contrast How do the reasons why humans and birds move south during the winter differ?

_____

_____

_____

_____

_____

uInvestigate Lab

How can you see 👁 👁 seasonal patterns in birds?

Ecologists use evidence to understand how animal behavior changes with the seasons. How can you use evidence to understand patterns of bird migration?

Materials
- Map of the United States
- colored circle stickers
- colored markers

Migratory Florida Birds			
Species	Arrive in Florida	Depart from Florida	Migrates to
American redstart	September	June	all states north of Florida and east of the Missouri River
Painted bunting	September	April	Texas, Louisiana, Arkansas, Oklahoma
Gray Catbird	September	April	Most states east of the Rocky Mountains

Science Practice

Scientists use evidence to answer questions and explain observations.

Procedure

☐ **1.** Read the information in the table about some Florida birds that migrate.

☐ **2.** Decide how you will represent this information on the map to show bird migration. Mark the map.

Analyze and Interpret Data

3. Identify Patterns Describe the patterns in bird migration that you see. What evidence supports your answer?

_____

_____

_____

4. Compare Compare the patterns you identified with the patterns of other students. Explain any differences.

_____

_____

Changing Seasons and Climate

Is it warm and wet where you live? Do you notice a pattern of weather that repeats year after year? Different places in the United States have different seasons and climates. **Climate** is the average weather conditions in one place over a long time. Climate does not change as much as weather. Weather is all the conditions in one place at one time.

Apply Concepts Mark the statement about weather with a *W*. Mark the statement about climate with a *C*.

_____ Summers are hot and humid along the Gulf Coast.

_____ Tomorrow will be partly cloudy with a high of 21°C (70°F).

Florida's seasons are generally warm compared to the seasons in the northern regions in the United States. Seasons in Florida vary by the amount of precipitation. Most of the state receives at least 122 centimeters of rain yearly.

Use Graphs Circle the month when the average rainfall in Florida is greatest.

Average Monthly Rainfall in Tallahassee, Florida

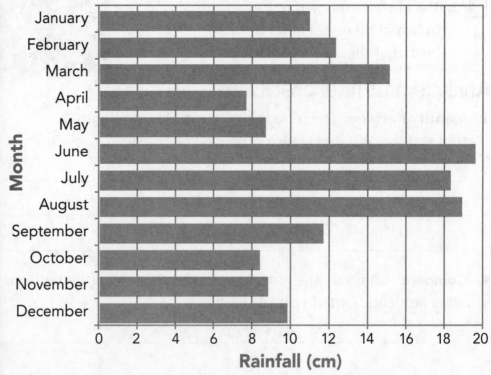

Seasonal Changes in Florida Plants and Animals

An **ecosystem** is all the living and nonliving things that interact in an area. Many ecosystems change with the seasons. Living things **respond**, or react, to the change. The same changes happen each year.

Think about changes in plants and animals in a Florida ecosystem. Since Florida's winters are not as cold as in most regions in the United States, plants have longer growing seasons. The bougainvillea and many other Florida plants do not have long **dormant**, or inactive, periods.

Some animals in northern Florida, such as this Florida box turtle, **hibernate**, or become less active, during the winter. Other animals, such as the white pelican, **migrate**, or move, in large groups to the warm south in fall. Then they migrate to the north in spring.

Literacy ▸ Toolbox

Use Evidence from Text
Facts from a text support a main idea. Find and underline evidence that supports that some animals live in different places in different seasons.

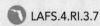 LAFS.4.RI.3.7

How do organisms change with seasons?

Many plants and animals change with seasons.

loss of leaves

Bald cypress trees have needle-like leaves that they lose when the season changes to winter.

color change

INTERACTIVITY

Do an activity about seasons and living things.

The Florida maple is bright green and lush during summer.

The leaves change colors from green to red, orange, and sometimes yellow during fall.

In the winter, most of the leaves fall from the branches.

Use the caption to help you draw a Florida maple in winter.

Everglades National Park

hibernation

In the summer, the American bullfrog can be found in the grasses of coastal dunes.

In the winter, the bullfrog digs a hole in the mud and hibernates underwater.

Seasonal Changes in Plants and Animals in Different Regions

Plants and animals live all over the United States in different regions with different seasons. Some southwestern states, such as Arizona and New Mexico, have mostly desert ecosystems. The seasons there are usually warm and dry throughout the year. Summers are very hot, and winters have little rainfall. Plant seeds usually grow in spring when water is more plentiful. In spring, the desert bighorn sheep at Joshua Tree National Park in California get water from the grasses and plants they eat. At other times, the sheep must travel to narrow canyons to find water.

✔ **READING CHECK Use Evidence from Text** Circle a fact from the text that explains how seasonal changes in spring help desert bighorn sheep survive.

In deciduous forests, precipitation can fall all year. Winters are long and cold, and water is often frozen. Trees store energy in spring and summer. In winter, many trees remain dormant. Animals, like moose, eat a variety of food in different seasons. A moose might eat leafy plants in summer and woody twigs and bark in winter.

Quest Connection

What would a moose from a deciduous forest need in order to survive in a zoo in Florida?

_____

_____

_____

The Midwest has prairie ecosystems. The prairie is a grassland ecosystem with hot summers and cold winters. It has many summer grasses and nonflowering plants. Few plants grow in winter. Animals may migrate, hibernate, or stay to gather food. The brown and white coat of the weasel changes to a white coat in winter. The white coat is camouflage that hides the weasel from both predators and prey in snow.

📔 **Reflect** Identify an example of a plant or animal in your state that responds to a seasonal change. How does the response help the plant or animal survive?

........ᴜ**Be a Scientist** ....

Nature Hike
Go on a nature hike. Draw a table with two columns. Label the columns "Plant Features" and "Animal Features." Observe different plants and animals. Draw each kind you see in the correct table column. Circle the parts that show characteristics that might help organisms live in your area in a particular season.

☑ **Lesson 1 Check**   🕐 SC.4.L.17.1

1. **Recall** How does the changing coat of a weasel help it survive?

_____

_____

_____

2. **Differentiate** Compare how flowering plants in Florida may be different from flowering plants in a northern state during the winter months.

_____

_____

_____

Lesson 1 Seasons Affect Plants and Animals   (315)

How can polar bears survive in Florida?

Zoo keepers make sure that a zoo habitat has conditions similar to the climate where an animal lives in nature. How can you model a habitat for a polar bear?

Materials
- ice cubes
- small container
- thermometer

Suggested Materials
- aluminum foil
- wool fabric
- cotton balls
- waxed paper
- masking tape
- newspaper

Design a Solution

☐ **1.** The table shows the temperature range where polar bears live in the Arctic. Research the average temperature range where you live. Fill in the table with your data.

Engineering Practice

Engineers use models to solve problems.

Temperature Range	
Where polar bears live	**Where I live**
–30°C to –10°C	

☐ **2.** What criteria would your local zoo need to meet when building a habitat for a polar bear?

_____

_____

_____

_____

☐ **3.** Make a plan to see how long you can keep the container at the right temperature for a polar bear. Choose your materials.

☐ **4.** Show your plan to your teacher before you begin. Test it and record your observations.

Observations

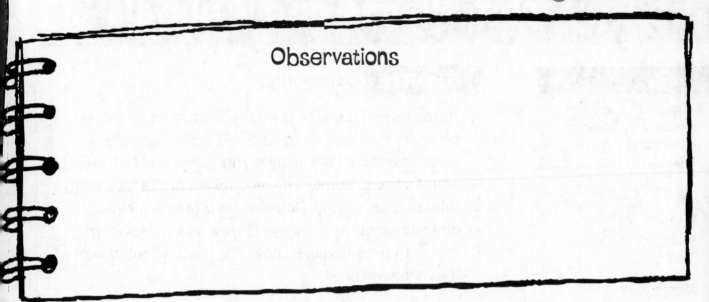

Evaluate Your Design

5. **Compare** Compare your results with other groups. Which model habitats stayed within the temperature range for a polar bear for the longest time?

_____

_____

6. **Evaluate** How could you improve your design to keep the model at the right temperature for a longer time?

_____

_____

7. **Use Evidence** How could you advise a local zoo to prepare a habitat with the right temperature for your zoo animal? Why is this important?

_____

_____

_____

_____

Energy from Plants and Animals

I can...

Explain that animals get energy from the plants and animals they eat.

Literacy Skill
Use Evidence from Text

Vocabulary
producer
consumer
herbivore
carnivore
omnivore

Academic Vocabulary
source

SC.4.L.17.2 Explain that animals, including humans, cannot make their own food and that when animals eat plants or other animals, the energy stored in the food source is passed to them. (Also **SC.4.N.1.3**)

SPORTS ▸ Connection

Humans need a source of energy to carry on all the processes that keep them alive. For example, soccer players need a lot of energy to run, jump, and kick the ball. Anything humans do requires energy. In fact, even thinking uses energy. Different kinds of activities require different amounts of energy. Playing soccer uses more energy than resting in a chair. The foods we eat provide the energy we need.

Humans are not the only animals that need a source of energy. All animals must eat food to stay alive.

Identify What activities do you do that require a lot of energy? Where do you get your energy to carry out these activities?

_____

_____

Where do animals get their energy?

Ecologists are interested in finding out how living things get energy. What are some energy sources of different animals?

Materials
• index cards
• paper
• yarn
• tape
• scissors

Procedure

☐ **1.** Think of at least one plant and four animals that live in the same ecosystem. Draw each on a separate index card.

☐ **2.** Think about what each animal eats. Record the information in the table.

⚠ Be careful when using scissors.

Science Practice

Scientists use models to answer questions about the natural world.

Animal	What the animal eats

☐ **3.** Make a plan to use the animal pictures, the paper, and the yarn to model how animals get food.

Analyze and Interpret Data

4. Explain What does your model show about how animals get energy?

_____

_____

_____

_____

Conduct Investigations In science, when you investigate to answer a question, you gather information by researching or testing. How could you investigate what a plant needs, other than sunlight, to survive?

Producers Make Food

All living things need water, nutrients, and space to grow and reproduce. They also need a source of energy. A **source** is a starting place. The source of all energy in an ecosystem begins with sunlight. The sun's energy enters the ecosystem and flows through all living things in the ecosystem. It changes form as it moves throughout the ecosystem.

The sun's energy enters an ecosystem through plants. During a process called photosynthesis, plants use energy from sunlight to change carbon dioxide and water into food and oxygen. Plants store the energy from the food they make until the energy is needed for processes in the plant. Plants are called **producers** because they produce, or make, their own food. In almost all land ecosystems, green plants are the main producers.

Describe How do plants use energy from the sun?

_____

_____

_____

_____

_____

Consumers Eat Food

You may have seen a bird eating a worm or an armadillo eating a plant.

INTERACTIVITY

Do an activity about producers and consumers.

These and all other animals get energy by consuming, or eating, plants or other animals. Living things that eat other living things are called **consumers**. When an animal eats a plant or another animal, the energy stored in this food flows to the animal that eats it.

Reflect As a human, you are a consumer. How do you rely on producers and other consumers?

u Be a Scientist

Build a Bird Feeder
Work with an adult. Hollow out half of an orange. Make 3 small, equally spaced holes 1 cm from the edge. Put a different string through each hole, and tie the string to make a loop. Hang the 3 loops on a branch. Fill the orange with birdseed. Observe for several days. Record the number and types of birds you see.

Quest Connection

What are two ways that a zoo could provide food to an animal that eats plants?

_____

_____

_____

_____

_____

It eats WHAT?

Suppose you have discovered a fossil skull of a dinosaur. You know an animal's teeth give clues about what the animal eats.

! **What do you think the dinosaur ate when it was alive? Support your answer with evidence.**

_____

_____

_____

_____

_____

_____

Herbivores are consumers that eat plants. Herbivores that eat leaves have broad, flat teeth with rough surfaces in the backs of their mouths. The teeth help grind up tough plants.

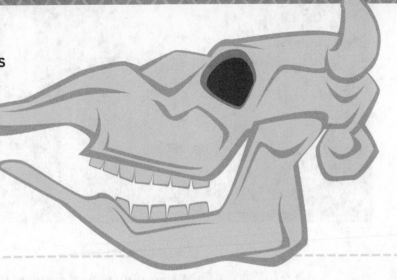

! Circle the teeth that support the herbivore classification.

Carnivores are consumers that eat other animals. They usually have long, sharp front teeth. These teeth help to catch prey. They also help to tear apart the animal's food.

! Circle the teeth that support the carnivore classification.

Omnivores are consumers that eat both plants and animals. Their back teeth are flat for grinding a variety of food. The front teeth are wide and shaped like chisels. This helps the animal bite off chunks of meat or plants.

! Circle the teeth that support the omnivore classification.

Decomposers

When plants and animals die or leave wastes, what happens to the unused energy in these materials? Bacteria and other organisms, such as this mushroom and this earthworm, break down the dead materials or the wastes. Organisms that break down plant and animal remains and wastes are called decomposers. They get energy that is stored in the dead plants and animals and wastes.

Identify Describe the flow of energy from the sun to the decomposer.

_____

_____

☑ Lesson 2 Check

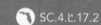

SC.4.L.17.2

1. **☑ READING CHECK Use Evidence from Text** Can a producer survive without a consumer? Cite evidence from the text and use your background knowledge to explain your answer.

_____

_____

_____

2. **Identify** What is the source of all energy in an ecosystem?

_____

_____

_____

Feeding Zoo Animals

Choose a zoo animal. Research what the animal eats in
its natural habitat. Then find out whether that food is
available in Florida. Record what you find.

Kind of animal_____	
What does it eat?	**Does it live in Florida?**

Use the information you found to describe what a zoo might have to do if
it wants to keep the animal you researched.

_____

_____

_____

_____

Food Chains and Food Webs

I can...

Describe how energy flows in food chains and food webs.

Literacy Skill
Use Evidence from Text

Vocabulary
food chain
food web

▶ **VIDEO**

Watch a video about food chains.

SC.4.L.17.3 Trace the flow of energy from the Sun as it is transferred along the food chain through the producers to the consumers (Also SC.4.N.3.1)

LOCAL-TO-GLOBAL ⟩ **Connection**

Humans are consumers, but we can consume plants, animals, or both. Some people choose to not eat animals. Those individuals are called vegetarians. Throughout the world, the number of vegetarians varies greatly. In India, about 30 percent of the population follows a vegetarian diet. In the United States, about 2 percent of the population follows a vegetarian diet.

Compare Explain why you think the percentage of vegetarians in the United States is lower than the percentage of vegetarians in India.

_____

_____

_____

_____

uInvestigate Lab

How does energy flow from organism to organism?

Materials
• 5 index cards
• large sheet of paper
• glue
• yarn
• markers
• scissors

Ecologists use models to find out how living organisms in an ecosystem are connected. How can you use a model to explain how organisms are connected?

⚠ Be careful when using scissors.

Procedure

☐ 1. Think of an insect that eats plants. Draw the insect on an index card. Label the card with the name of the insect.

☐ 2. Draw and label a plant the insect eats on a separate card.

☐ 3. Draw and label an animal that eats your insect.

☐ 4. Draw and label an animal that eats your animal.

☐ 5. Using the cards and other materials, make a model to show how the plant, insect, and the other two animals are connected.

☐ 6. What important factor is missing from your model? Make an index card for this factor, and add it to your model.

Science Practice

Scientists use models to explain the world around them.

Analyze and Interpret Data

7. **Analyze** Suppose you removed an organism from your model. How would that affect your model?

_____

_____

_____

_____

Visual Literacy Connection

How does energy flow through food chains?

A **food chain** is a model that shows the transfer of energy from one organism to another. Food chains begin with energy from the sun. Arrows between organisms show the flow of energy. Arrows point from the "eaten" to the "eater."

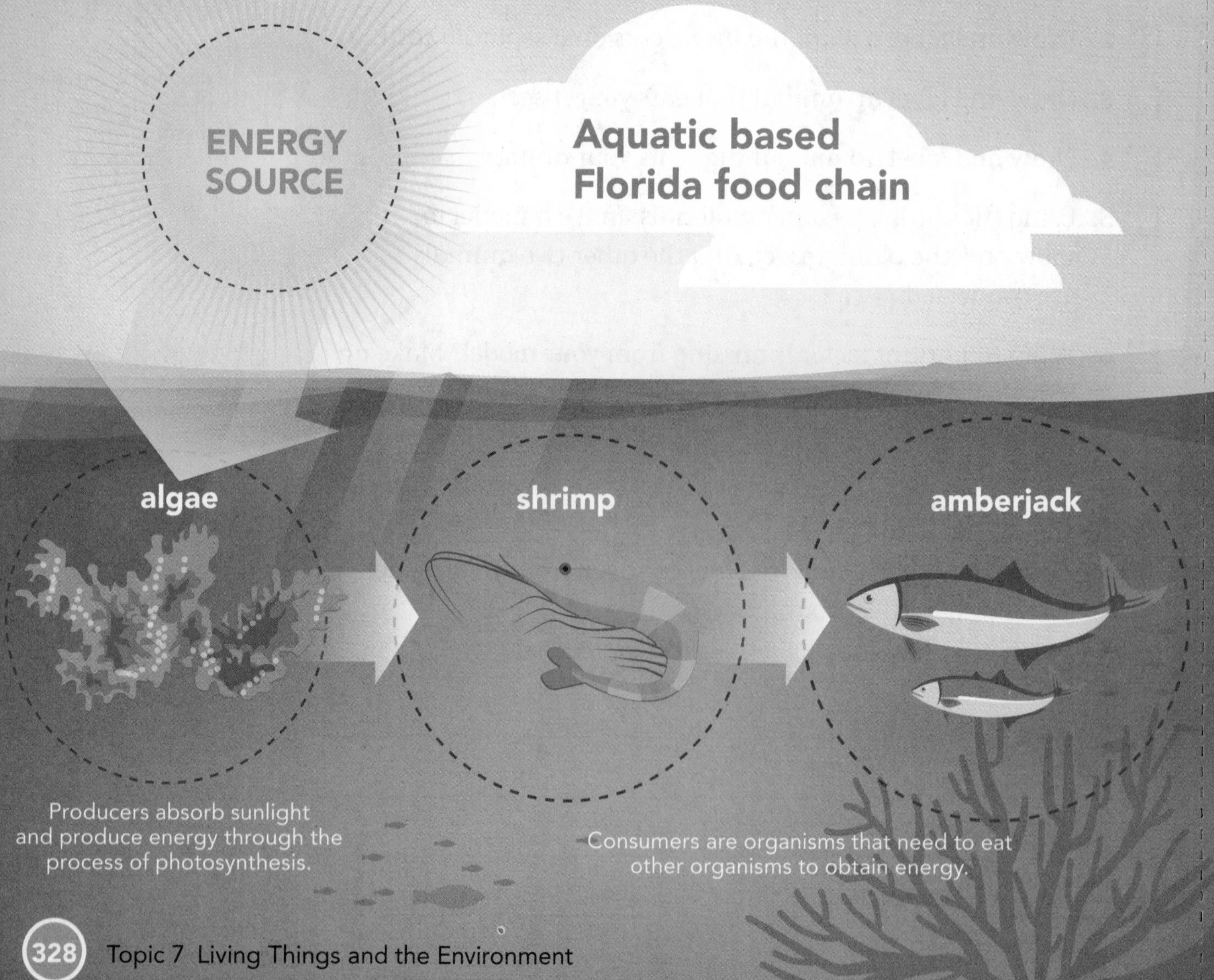

ENERGY SOURCE
Aquatic based Florida food chain
algae
shrimp
amberjack
Producers absorb sunlight and produce energy through the process of photosynthesis.
Consumers are organisms that need to eat other organisms to obtain energy.

ENERGY SOURCE

Land based Florida food chain

Complete this food chain.
Write a label for each organism.

red fox

_____ → _____ →

Connecting Concepts ▸ Toolbox

System Models Models
can help you represent and
understand ideas. For example,
the arrows in a food chain or
food web show the flow of
energy. The arrows represent
the flow of energy *from* the
organism that is the food *to*
the organism eating this food.
How can you use the arrows in a
food web to better understand
an ecosystem?

Energy Flow Through a Food Web

The same food source in an ecosystem can be part
of more than one food chain. As a result, one food
chain often overlaps with other food chains to form a
food web. A **food web** is a model of overlapping food
chains in which the flow of energy branches out in
many directions. In the food web shown, some of the
producers and consumers are eaten by more than one
kind of organism.

A change in one part of a food web can affect some or
all parts of the web. For example, too few or too many
of a type of organism can cause an imbalance in the
ecosystem. A healthy ecosystem has many different
organisms that can meet the needs of its consumers.

📖 **Reflect** How do you fit into a food web? In your science
notebook, describe a food web that includes you.

Quest Connection

How do feeding patterns in the zoo differ from a typical
food web in the wild?

_____

_____

_____

Model It! Food webs are models. Draw a model of a food web using five organisms of your choosing.

☑ Lesson 3 Check

 SC.4.L.17.3

1. **Explain** Draw a food chain with a producer and two consumers. Label the diagram with arrows and words to describe how energy is transferred throughout the food chain.

2. **Formulate** Suppose that an ecosystem experiences a decline in a major species of consumer. How might the ecosystem's food web be affected?

_____

_____

Zoo Food Chains

Even animals in a zoo are part of a food chain. Make a food chain for a zoo animal.

Choose your favorite zoo animal.

_____

Answer the following questions to determine your zoo animal's place in a food chain.

1. What does your zoo animal eat in its natural habitat?

_____

_____

2. Does your zoo animal get eaten by other animals? If so, which ones?

_____

_____

The diagram shows an incomplete food chain. Draw and label your animal in the correct circle. Draw and label anything that eats or is eaten by your animal in the other two circles.

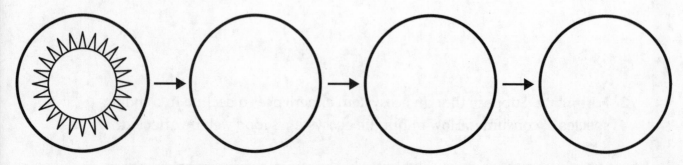

What if all animals became vegetarians?

Moose, zebras, and rabbits are all herbivores. What do you think would happen if lions, sharks, spiders, and all other carnivores became herbivores too?

The best way to answer this question is to consider evidence and then use your reasoning skills. Complete the table to organize your evidence. If you are not sure what one animal eats, use reliable online or printed sources to find the answer.

Carnivore	What it eats	What the prey eats
lion	Lions eat zebras and impalas	Zebras eat grasses and shrubs.

Now, use the evidence in your table to complete the following **science-based claim**: If all animals became herbivores, then carnivores would stop eating prey animals. Over time, the numbers of the prey animals would likely

_____.

The carnivores would begin to eat plants to get their energy. Therefore, the total number of animals eating plants would _____.

After several years, it is likely that _____

_____

_____

Plants, Animals, and Humans Affect the Environment

I can...

Explain how plants, animals, and humans can affect the environment.

Literacy Skill
Use Evidence from Text

Vocabulary
environment
competition
overpopulation

Academic Vocabulary
interact
benefits

SC.4.L.17.4 Recognize ways plants and animals, including humans, can impact the environment. (Also **SC.4.N.1.5, SC.4.N.3.1, SC.4.N.1.5**)

ENGINEERING ⟩ Connection

Animals in the wild often must compete for space with other animals, including humans. When people build roads or make other changes, their actions can divide habitats. Animals with large habitats, such as deer, are especially harmed when habitats are divided. The deer must cross roads, which can be dangerous. Other animals may not be able to travel from one part of the habitat to another. This happens when human actions have blocked any ways that the animals might move from one habitat to another.

Some people have built bridges, called wildlife crossings, to help solve the problem. The bridges might cross over roads, human-made bodies of water, or other barriers. The wildlife crossings allow animals to safely cross over the obstacles.

Propose What is another way that people could help animals cross roads safely?

_____

_____

uInvestigate Lab

How do **wolves** and **deer** affect each other?

Scientists must understand how carnivores and herbivores interact. How can you model the relationship between deer and wolves?

Materials
• pennies
• nickels
• graph paper

Procedure

Science Practice

Scientists use models to investigate scientific questions.

☐ **1.** Predict how more wolves will affect the number of deer in a habitat.

_____

_____

☐ **2.** Develop a model using the materials to show how deer and wolves interact. Start with 3 deer for every wolf. You cannot have more deer and wolves than can fit in the habitat. Deer and wolves can be added if the habitat still has space. Record your results in the table.

Ecosystem Model Results		
	Number of deer remaining	**Number of wolves remaining**
Round 1 – add/subtract _____ deer		
Round 2 – add/subtract _____ deer		
Round 3 – add/subtract _____ deer		
Round 4 – add/subtract _____ deer		

Analyze and Interpret Data

3. Predict If all of the wolves were removed permanently, what would happen to the deer population?

_____

_____

Competition in Environments

Living things, including humans, **interact** with, or depend on, one another and their environment. The **environment** is the living and nonliving surroundings in which an organism lives. The environment provides resources to satisfy the needs of organisms.

When resources are not plentiful, living things may have to compete for them. **Competition** occurs when two or more living things need the same limited resources to survive. For example, two tree seeds might sprout on a log in the forest. The young trees are in competition with each other and the other trees to meet their needs. Some trees get enough light and other resources. As their branches grow, they shade nearby plants. The environment changes for nearby plants that now may not get enough light to survive.

Quest Connection

How might animals in a zoo compete? How could the problem be solved?

_____

_____

_____

_____

Animals Impact the Environment

Some animals change the environment to meet their needs. A beaver, for example, needs deep water. If the stream where it lives is too shallow, the beaver cuts down trees with its teeth. It uses the wood to build a dam across the stream. The blocked water forms a pond behind the dam.

A beaver that changes its environment **benefits**, or helps, plants and animals that need to live in water. However, beaver dams can harm some plants and animals when their homes are flooded.

The table shows some other ways animals can be helpful and harmful to the environment.

How animals are helpful	How animals are harmful
Predator-prey balance	Destruction
Predator animals like the brown pelican help keep the number of prey animals in check.	Termites damage homes as they eat the sugars in the wood.
Food source	Poisonous/dangerous
Animals, such as cows, provide food for humans.	Some animals, such as this brown recluse spider, may bite humans when threatened or disturbed.

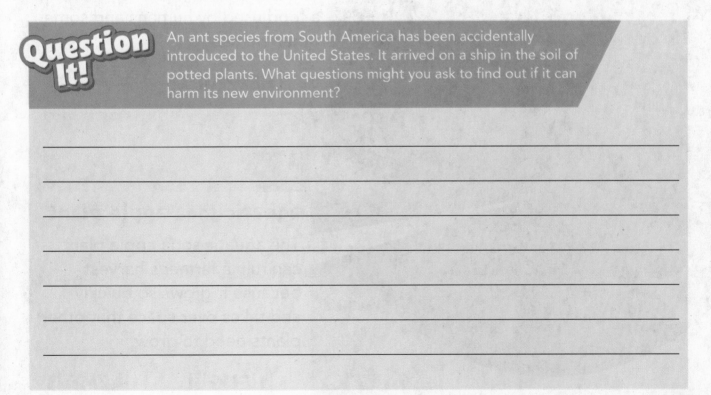

Question It! An ant species from South America has been accidentally introduced to the United States. It arrived on a ship in the soil of potted plants. What questions might you ask to find out if it can harm its new environment?

_____

_____

_____

_____

_____

_____

_____

Visual Literacy Connection

How can plants impact the environment?

Plants can impact the environment in positive and negative ways.

! Check HELPFUL or HARMFUL for each plant, using the description as a guide.

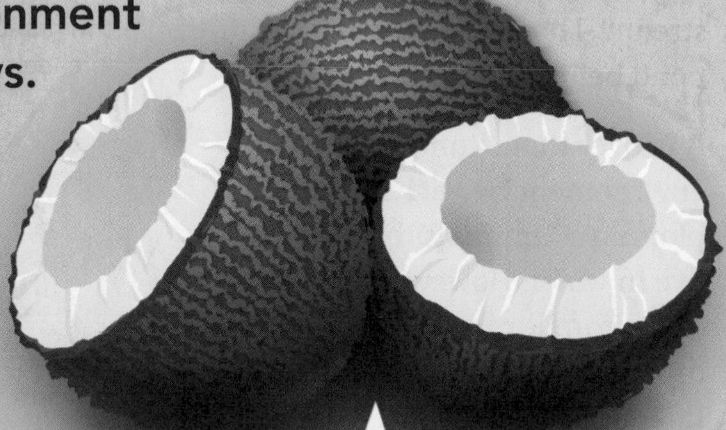

coconut palms

Coconut palms produce coconuts, a food used by humans and some other animals.

☐ HELPFUL ☐ HARMFUL

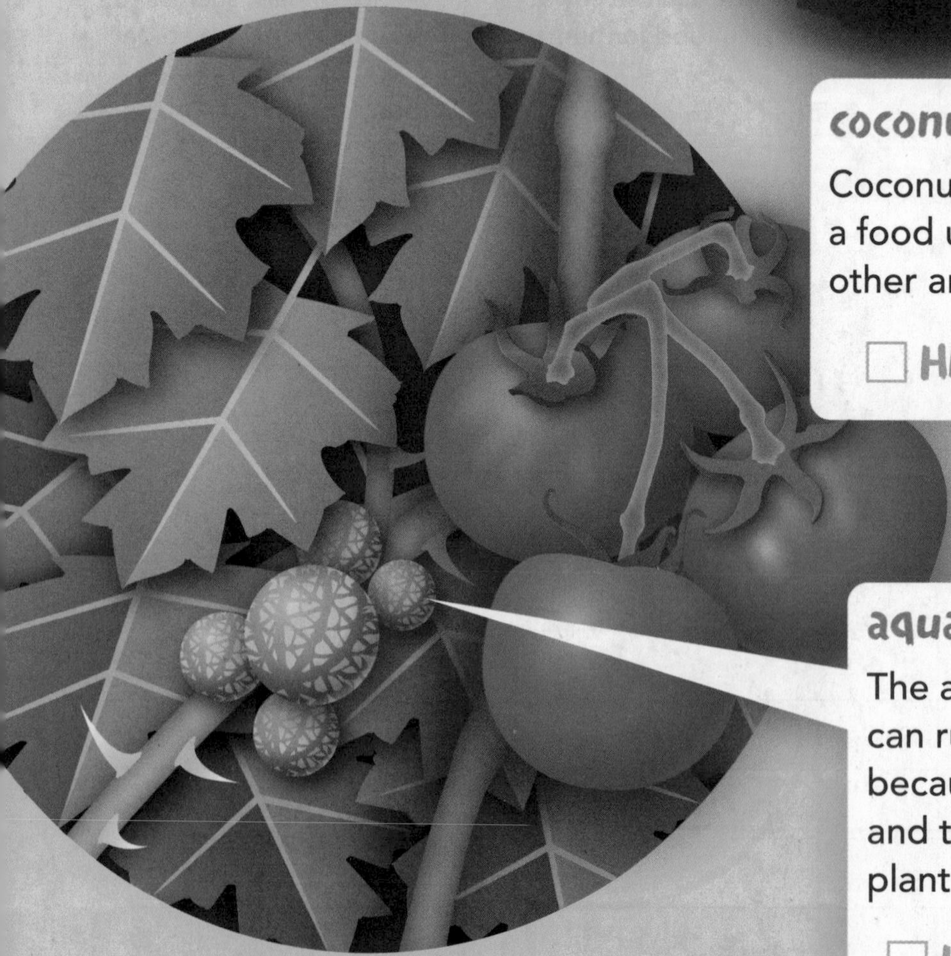

aquatic soda apple plant

The aquatic soda apple plant can ruin a farmer's harvest because it grows so quickly and takes over space that other plants need to grow.

☐ HELPFUL ☐ HARMFUL

red mangroves

Red mangroves provide habitats to many coastal animals: white egret (bird) and French grunt (fish).

☐ HELPFUL ☐ HARMFUL

poison ivy

Poison ivy is a poisonous plant. Touching it can cause an allergic reaction.

☐ HELPFUL ☐ HARMFUL

⚠ CAUTION

POISON IVY

netted chain ferns

People plant netted chain ferns to help keep soil from washing away when it rains.

☐ HELPFUL ☐ HARMFUL

INTERACTIVITY

Do an activity about the effects of humans on the environment.

Humans Impact the Environment

People need resources just as other living things do. When people build homes, they change the environment. They may cut down forests and plow up grasslands to make room for houses. Each of these changes affects the environment. Sometimes animals and humans compete for space because people move to places where animals live. This explains why people might find coyotes in their backyards or a deer walking alongside a busy road.

Human **overpopulation** is a condition where the number of people in the population is greater than the number of people that Earth can provide for without harming the environment. Overpopulation contributes to many of the current environmental problems, such as climate change, pollution, habitat loss, and depletion of Earth's resources.

Explain How might humans impact the habitat of animals?

_____

_____

_____

☑ Lesson 4 Check

SC.4.L.17.4

1. **✓ READING CHECK Use Evidence from Text** Whitney says that humans only affect the environment in negative ways. Is she correct? Use your experiences as evidence to support your answer.

_____

_____

_____

_____

2. **Describe** What are two ways that plants help the environment?

_____

_____

Zoos Can Help Animals

Zoos provide an important way that people can help wildlife. Zoos employ many scientists, such as ecologists, who study the animals that live there. Sometimes, scientists working in the field rescue animals that may be injured or orphaned. For these animals, zoos are a lifeline.

Zoos also provide a substitute for an animal's natural habitat. Many kinds of animals are threatened or endangered because of habitat destruction and disease. For animals such as these, zoos might help save them from extinction.

Evaluate Think about your favorite zoo animal. How might your animal benefit from living in a zoo? How might living in a zoo be harmful for your animal?

_____

_____

_____

_____

_____

_____

QUEST CHECK ✓ OFF 341

µEngineer It! · Define · STEM

INTERACTIVITY

Go online to learn about habitat restoration.

Living Things to the Rescue!

Around the world, coastal environments have been badly damaged. Two major problems facing coastal areas are habitat loss and pollution. Scientists and engineers work together to solve problems facing ecosystems. Sometimes, they use living things to help solve problems. One such solution is the Fantasy Island Oyster Habitat Restoration Project. Oysters are great for ocean environments. As they grow and reproduce, they can build islands. They also filter water as they collect food. In this project, oysters are being used to build a habitat along the shoreline of an island in Florida. The oysters will help to stabilize the shoreline, which has been eroding for many years. This project will also improve the quality of water for the Tampa Bay ecosystem. Scientists hope the project will revitalize the fish and wildlife habitats along the shore.

Define It

You are an environmental engineer who has been hired by a city. Near the city is a large hill. It used to have a forest growing on it, but the trees were all cut down for lumber. Recently, residents have been complaining about rocks falling down the hill. Dirt and mud also have been building up on the road below the hill. Some people are worried the problem may get worse soon.

☐ Summarize the problem the city faces.

_____

_____

_____

☐ Make a list of criteria that you will have to meet to solve the problem.

_____

_____

_____

☐ What are some materials you could use to help solve the problem? Explain why you think the materials you choose would be good to use.

_____

_____

_____

_____

_____

_____

Find a Home for Zoo Animals

Should animals be kept in a zoo?

INTERACTIVITY

Organize data to support your Quest Findings.

Organize Information

Review the information you have gathered in this Quest to decide whether animals should be kept in zoos. How do zoos provide an advantage for animals? How can living in a zoo be a disadvantage for animals? Organize the information in the table.

Advantages	Disadvantages

Make an Argument

Now it is your turn to decide what you think is best for the animals. Present your findings in a format such as a written report, a digital presentation, or a public message. If you think that animals should be kept in zoos, propose two things that must be done in a zoo to care for the animals. If you do not believe that animals should be kept in zoos, propose two solutions other than zoos to help animals in the way that zoos do.

QUEST CHECK ✓ OFF

Ecologist

An ecologist studies the relationship between organisms and their environments. Ecologists conduct research on plants and animals in forests, deserts, swamps, and other environments. They work hard to protect ecosystems around the world. Some ecologists choose to work in zoos, while others choose to work in the wild. Some ecologists do both. Animals and plants are the main focus of ecologists, but they also research the impact that humans have on the planet.

Ecologists love nature. They also love working outdoors. Ecologists do research in difficult working environments. Their research can help other people make decisions about how to treat the environment. The world needs ecologists because they help us understand the natural world.

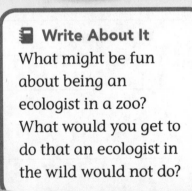

📔 Write About It
What might be fun about being an ecologist in a zoo? What would you get to do that an ecologist in the wild would not do?

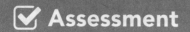

Read each question and choose or write the best answer.

1. Draw Conclusions The pictures show the same place in two different years: 2000 and 2015.

What has happened over time to cause the changes in this landscape?

_____

_____

_____

_____

_____

_____

_____

2. Vocabulary Which kind of living thing can make its own food?

A. carnivore

B. producer

C. consumer

D. omnivore

3. Cause and Effect A certain kind of plant is found throughout much of the United States, including Florida. In most states, the plant does not grow for part of the year. In Florida, the plant grows throughout the year. Which statement explains this difference?

A. The lengths of Florida's seasons are different from the lengths in the rest of the country.

B. Florida's winters are not as cold as those of most regions in the United States.

C. Florida has a longer coastline than the coastlines of most other states.

D. Florida's soil is drier than soil in most other states.

4. Summarize Florida has different climates in different parts of the state. Which of the following describes the climate of an area?

A. South Florida has a rainy season from May through October.

B. The high temperature in Miami tomorrow will be between 90°F and 95°F.

C. High tides and hurricane winds and rain caused flooding on Florida's east coast.

D. The central parts of Florida are having a severe drought.

5. Hypothesize Two food chains from the same grassland are shown.

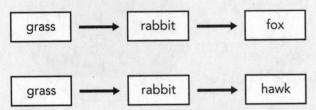

Suppose in one year the grassland has many more hawks than in previous years. How will this **most likely** affect the number of foxes? Why?

_____

_____

_____

_____

6. Infer How do animals get the energy they need to survive? Explain your answer.

_____

_____

_____

7. Analyze How do plants impact the environment in helpful and harmful ways?

_____

_____

_____

_____

The Essential Question

How do living things interact with their environment?

Show What You Learned

Based on the evidence you studied, how do plants and animals interact with and impact their environment all year-round? Give examples.

_____

_____

_____

_____

_____

_____

_____

_____

_____

_____

_____

_____

_____

_____

_____

_____

_____

_____

Read the scenario and answer questions 1–3.

Emma is developing a model of a forest ecosystem. The diagram shows her planned model.

1 Emma plans to include stones and dirt in her ecosystem model. Which of the choices **best** explains why she should or should not include rocks and dirt?

Ⓐ She should not include them because they are not living things.

Ⓑ She should include them because living things interact with them.

Ⓒ She should not include them because they are not in a food web.

Ⓓ She should include them because a forest would look wrong without them.

2 As plants in Emma's ecosystem die, she plans to remove the plant remains. How might this affect the ecosystem over time?

Ⓕ Less energy will be available in the ecosystem.

Ⓖ The air will be cleaner.

Ⓗ The plants will need less water.

Ⓘ More water will be available to plants.

3 Emma wants to investigate the effect of light on the forest ecosystem. She will cover all the sides and the top of the terrarium with black paper. Is this a good setup to test this variable? Why?

Ⓐ Yes, because then no sunlight can get into the terrarium.

Ⓑ Yes, because the temperature in the terrarium will remain constant.

Ⓒ No, because she will have to remove the paper to make observations.

Ⓓ No, because she does not have an ecosystem with light to compare her results.

Read the scenario and answer questions 4–6.

A group of bird watchers recorded how many birds of certain kinds they saw throughout the year. Then they organized their data into a table. They included the average temperature for the periods they recorded in the table.

Type of Bird	Number of Birds at Feeder			
	Jan–Mar 17°C	Apr–Jun 25°C	Jul–Sep 28°C	Oct–Dec 20°C
blackbird	8	22	30	15
crow	5	16	25	9
limpkin	9	28	36	23
sandpiper	11	27	33	22
woodpecker	4	19	24	13

4 What conclusion can the bird watchers make from the data?

   Ⓕ Birds migrate in cold weather.

   Ⓖ Birds hibernate in cold weather.

   Ⓗ Some birds prefer cold weather.

   Ⓘ Fewer birds are in the area in cold weather.

5 One bird watcher, Gavin, said that matter from trees can be found inside the body of the hawks they observe. Which statement best explains why Gavin is or is not correct?

   Ⓐ Gavin is not correct because hawks are predators that do not eat trees.

   Ⓑ Gavin is not correct because matter does not move between organisms.

   Ⓒ Gavin is correct because hawks eat animals that feed on products of trees.

   Ⓓ Gavin is correct because hawks build their nests in trees.

6 A plant loses its leaves in the fall and the plant stores food for winter. What is the **best** conclusion you can make?

   Ⓕ The plant will reproduce in winter.

   Ⓖ The plant will begin to hibernate.

   Ⓗ The plant is in a region with a cold winter.

   Ⓘ The plant is from a place with a warm climate.

How can you model human impact on the environment?

Materials
- sheet of paper
- sticky notes

Science Practice

Scientists use models to help explain the world around them.

Ecologists use what they know about human impacts on the environment to plan ways to prevent negative effects. How can you use a model to explain how cutting down forest trees affects an ecosystem?

Procedure

☐ 1. Place sticky notes on the sheet of paper so that they form 4 rows and 5 columns. The sticky notes represent trees in a forest.

☐ 2. Write a number on each sticky note. That number represents the number of animals that the tree supports.

☐ 3. Record the total number of animals that all the trees in the forest support.

☐ 4. Remove 3 to 5 trees. Record the number of animals that the remaining trees can support.

☐ 5. Repeat step 4, but remove more trees from the forest. The repeat step 4 again, but remove a lot more trees.

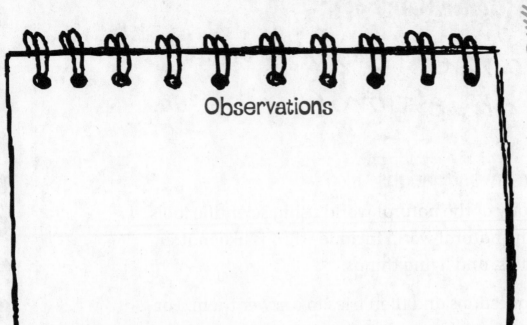

Observations

Analyze and Interpret Data

6. **Cause and Effect** How did the differences in the number of trees that were cut affect the impacts?

_____

_____

7. **Cause and Effect** How does cutting trees affect the flow of energy from the sun to other organisms in the ecosystem?

_____

_____

_____

_____

8. Do you think that the forest would recover more quickly when only a few trees are cut or when many trees are cut? Explain your answer.

_____

_____

_____

_____

SC.4.L.17.2, SC.4.N.3.1

HANDS-ON LAB

How do scientists ask and answer questions?

Questions and Investigations

Science is the study of the natural world using scientific tools and methods. The natural world includes things like matter, energy, the planets, and living things.

A scientist asks questions and then tries to answer them. For example, a scientist might wonder what causes ocean waves to move. The scientist could first study what others have already learned. Then the scientist could investigate, or look carefully at, questions that have not been answered.

Scientists look for answers by doing experiments and making observations. They keep records to share what they learn. They use their results to form explanations. A scientific explanation is an answer based on evidence. Evidence is what scientists gather from experiments and observations. For example, a scientist studying waves in the ocean might measure wind speed and wave sizes in an area. The data the scientist collects is evidence.

Ask Questions What questions would you ask about waves?

SC.4.N.1.1 Raise questions about the natural world, use appropriate reference materials that support understanding to obtain information (identifying the source), conduct both individual and team investigations through free exploration and systematic investigations, and generate appropriate explanations based on those explorations. **SC.4.N.1.8** Recognize that science involves creativity in designing experiments. **SC.4.N.2.1** Explain that science focuses solely on the natural world.

Reference Materials

Scientists use reference materials to learn more about their subjects. Reference materials include encyclopedias, books, journals, and certain websites on the Internet.

Scientists write articles in scientific journals to share what they learned. Other scientists read the articles to learn what others have already discovered.

Creativity

Science is focused on answering new questions. That often means that scientists must come up with new ways to answer questions. Designing a good experiment requires them to think of new ways to solve problems. They need to think about what could go wrong and how to fix it. For example, a scientist who studies tiny organisms in the ocean could use a machine that was first used in hospitals to count blood cells.

Plan Investigations Think about measuring the temperature of ocean water at different depths. How would you do it quickly and safely?

_____

_____

_____

These researchers are investigating nature to answer their questions.

How do scientists work together?

Comparing Results

When a scientific investigation is repeated in exactly the same way, the results should be the same. Scientists compare their results. For example, a scientist may observe that the water pressure in the ocean increases as the water gets deeper. If someone else measures the water pressure at the same locations, the results should be similar.

After an investigation is done, other scientists repeat the investigation. They use the same tools and the same conditions. Then they compare their results with the results of the first investigation. Usually the results are the same. If the results are different, it is important to find out why. Sometimes, a very small change in conditions can cause a big change in the results. Sometimes, more than one tool can be used in an investigation. The results should be the same. If not, the scientists will compare results and try to find the reason for the difference.

Ask Questions You and a classmate get different results in an investigation. What question should you ask to find out why?

_____

_____

SC.4.N.1.2 Compare the observations made by different groups using multiple tools and seek reasons to explain the differences across groups. **SC.4.N.1.5** Compare the methods and results of investigations done by other classmates. **SC.4.N.1.6** Keep records that describe observations made, carefully distinguishing actual observations from ideas and inferences about the observations.

Keeping Records

During an investigation, scientists keep records of what they observe. Records can be written notes, drawings, charts, or graphs. Sometimes, scientists write their records in a notebook. Other records are on a computer. These records show exactly what was done in the investigation.

Scientists record their observations.

Records should be accurate. If records are complete and accurate, someone else can use them to do the investigation in the same way. Good records can help find what was different if two investigations give different results.

Communication

Scientists communicate with other scientists to share what they learned. The words that scientists use sometimes have different meanings than the same words in everyday communication. *Current, heat,* and *record* are examples of words that have a specific meaning in science. In science, for example, heat refers to the flow of thermal energy. In everyday use, heat may refer to the temperature on a warm day.

Communicate Scientists communicate in different ways. How could a scientist use a computer to communicate with another scientist?

_____

_____

_____

How do scientists use evidence?

Empirical Evidence

Scientists use empirical evidence when they study nature. Empirical evidence is information that can be verified or disproven. It includes measurements and observations. Scientific conclusions are always based on evidence that can be tested.

For example, sea water tastes salty everywhere. Measurements and observations have shown that it contains different amounts of salt at different locations. It is usually less salty where rivers flow into the ocean.

These measurements can help answer questions about how water from a river mixes with water in the sea.

Measure Your friend thinks it is a hot day, but you think it is not hot. How could you get empirical evidence about the temperature of the air? Why is this empirical evidence?

_____

_____

_____

Opinion

Scientific observations are different from opinions. An opinion is a personal belief and is not always based on facts. An example of an opinion is that tuna tastes better than salmon. There are no facts to support the opinion. An example of a fact is that salmon lay their eggs in fresh water. This statement can be supported by observation.

Which fish tastes better? That is a matter of opinion.

Support Claims with Evidence

Scientists use evidence to support their conclusions. For example, the conclusion that whales migrate is based on evidence. Whales can be seen in some areas but not in others, depending on the season. Scientists can also track individual whales to see where they go.

Evaluate You read in an advertisement that sandy beaches are more beautiful than rocky cliffs. Can you prove whether that claim is true? Why or why not?

_____

_____

Scientists can recognize an individual humpback whale by the unique marks on its tail.

What are scientific models?

Models

Scientists often use models to help them understand something. You may be familiar with models like toy boats. A toy boat looks like a real boat, only smaller. It does not work like a real boat though. Models are objects or ideas that represent other things. A model shows only part of the object or system that it represents.

Models can help scientists understand things that are too big or too small to observe. A map of the ocean floor is a model that shows how underwater mountains and plains are arranged. We cannot see these features from the surface.

Scientists can learn about how things work using models.

Models can be two-dimensional or three-dimensional. A map of the ocean floor is a two-dimensional model. It shows some things about the ocean floor, but it cannot show the exact shape of the ocean's features. A toy boat is a three-dimensional model of a full-sized boat.

Scientists also use computers to make models. For example, a computer model can show how fast the water in an ocean current is moving and which way it flows.

SC.4.N.3.1 Explain that models can be three dimensional, two dimensional, an explanation in your mind, or a computer model.

Investigations and Experiments

Scientists observe the natural world to learn about how it works. There are different ways to learn about nature. One way to learn is through observation. When scientists make observations, they do not change anything. For example, scientists who want to learn about changes in climate can observe the ice near the North Pole. The scientists do not change anything about the ice. Instead, they look at how the ice changes over time and draw conclusions based on evidence from their observations.

Scientists also investigate the world using experiments. In an experiment, scientists make a change to the thing they are observing. Scientists who want to find out how quickly salt dissolves in water at different temperatures might do an experiment. They might put identical amounts of salt and water in several containers. One container is left at room temperature and stirred to dissolve the salt; this is the control. To do the experiment, the scientists will need to change something. The thing that they change is called the variable. In this case, the variable is temperature. The scientists change the temperature of other containers to see if this makes the salt dissolve more easily.

Plan Investigations You want to learn how far the water is moving in an ocean current. Would you do an experiment or make an observation? Why?

_____

_____

_____

_____

How do scientists investigate?

Scientific Investigations

Scientists use scientific methods as they work in the many different fields of science. Scientific methods are an organized way to answer questions and solve problems. They are also a way of discovering cause and effect. Scientific methods often include some or all of the steps on the card.

These steps enable scientists to perform investigations, but not every investigation follows all of these steps. All scientific investigations include collecting data. Scientific conclusions are always based on evidence.

- Ask a question and form a hypothesis.
- Use reference materials.
- Plan and carry out investigations.
- Collect and organize data in charts, tables, and graphics.
- Analyze and interpret data.
- Draw conclusions based on evidence.
- Report results.

Plan an Investigation A scientist is investigating life cycles of lobsters. What are some things the scientist should observe?

_____

_____

_____

SC.4.N.1.3 Explain that science does not always follow a rigidly defined method ("the scientific method") but that science does involve the use of observations and empirical evidence.

Evaluate Investigations

Scientists do not perform a single observation or experiment and then come to a conclusion. The results of a scientific investigation must be repeatable. Scientists perform investigations many times and compare the results before they draw a conclusion. If the results cannot be repeated, then some of the observations may include an error.

Scientists use observations to make their conclusions.

It is also important that scientific observations can be repeated by other researchers. Sometimes, other researchers cannot get the same result. Then the scientists compare their methods to find out what is different. It is possible that there is an error in one of the methods.

Being able to repeat results makes the conclusion more reliable, so communication among scientists is important. Scientists communicate their methods and results so other scientists can repeat and then compare them.

Evaluate A scientist repeats an experiment and gets a different result. What should the scientist do next?

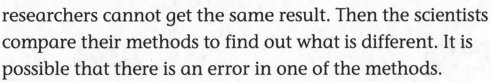

_____

_____

Glossary

The glossary uses letters and signs to show how words are pronounced. The mark " is placed after a syllable with a primary or heavy accent. The mark ' is placed after a syllable with a secondary or lighter accent.

Pronunciation Key

a	in hat, cap	k	in kind, seek	th	in thin, both
ā	in age, face	l	in land, coal	TH	in then, smooth
â	in care, fair	m	in me, am	u	in cup, butter
ä	in father, far	n	in no, in	u̇	in full, put
b	in bad, rob	ng	in long, bring	ü	in rule, move
ch	in child, much	o	in hot, rock	v	in very, save
d	in did, red	ō	in open, go	w	in will, woman
e	in let, best	ȯ	all, caught	y	in young, yet
ē	in equal, be	ô	in order	z	in zero, breeze
ėr	in term, learn	oi	in oil, voice	zh	in measure,
f	in fat, if	ou	in house, out		seizure
g	in go, bag	p	in paper, cup	ə a	in about,
h	in he, how	r	in run, try	e	in taken,
i	in it, pin	s	in say, yes	i	in pencil,
ī	in ice, five	sh	in she, rush	o	in lemon,
j	in jam, enjoy	t	in tell, it	u	in circus

appear (ə pir") the way objects seem based on how they look

available (ə vā" lə bəl) can be used

axis (ak" sis) an imaginary line that an object spins around

battery (bat" ər ē) an object that stores chemical energy that will change into electrical energy

benefit (ben" ə fit) an object or action that is helpful

butte (byüt) a steep hill with a small, flat top

canyon (kan" yən) a deep, narrow landform, usually found by mountains

carnivore (kär" nə vôr) an animal that eats only other animals for energy

characteristic (kâr' ik tə ris" tik) a trait that can help identify something

chemical change (kem" ə kəl chānj) the process where one or more kinds of matter changes into one or more different kinds of matter

climate (klī" mit) the average weather patterns of a place found by studying years of weather

coal (kōl) a solid fossil fuel that is burned to transfer energy

collision (kə lizh" ən) the action of one object bumping into another

compass-rose (kum" pəs rōz) a four pointed symbol that shows which directions are North, East, South, and West on a map

competition (kəm pə' tish" ən) when two or more organisms need to use the same limited resource to survive

compute (kəm pyüt") to find or calculate

conductor (kən duk" tər) a material that energy can easily flow through

constellation (kon' stə lā" shən) imaginary pictures formed by stars that are used to help identify stars

consumer (kən sü" mər) an organism that needs to eat another to survive, such as herbivores, carnivores, and omnivores

decay (di kā") a chemical change in dead organisms over time

device (di vis") objects made for a specific purpose

differentiate (dif' ə ren" shē āt) to identify the differences between two or more objects

disperse (dis pėrs") to spread out many objects, such as seeds

distinguish (dis ting" gwish) to recognize the differences between two objects

dormant (dôr" mənt) a state where a living thing slows its natural activity to survive winter

eclipse (i klips") the shadow cast by an object, such as the moon, when it moves between the Earth and the sun

ecosystem (ē" kō sis' təm or ek" ō sis' təm) the way living things and nonliving things interact

electric charge (i lek" trik chärj) a force caused by the movement of negative and positive particles

electric current (i lek" trik kėr" ənt) the flow of energy caused by the movement of negative and positive particles

ellipse (i lips") an oval shape that is used to describe the rotation of objects in space

emission (i mish" ən) something that is let out

energy (en" ər jē) the transferable ability to do work or cause change

environment (en vi" rən mət) the living and non-living things surrounding an organism

erosion (i rō" zhən) the slow process where particles are removed from solids by wind or water

evidence (ev" ə dəns) something easily observed that can be used to confirm or deny an idea

Glossary

fault (fȯlt) cracks in the Earth's crust that can cause earthquakes and volcano eruptions

features (fē" chər) a structure or form that is easy to recognize

fertilization (fėr' tl ə zā" shen) in plants, when an egg cell and a pollen cell combine and make a seed

food chain (füd chān) a model of the transfer of energy in some organisms in an ecosystem that is displayed as a straight line showing what consumes what

food web (füd web) a model of the transfer of energy that shows how all of the organisms in an ecosystem interact that looks like overlapping food chains

fossil fuel (fos" əl fyü" əl) a group of substances that are produced by pressure and decaying organisms that are used for energy

fuel (fyü" əl) a substance that could be used to make energy

gas (gas) matter with no definite mass or volume that is made of fast moving particles

generate (jen" ə rāt') to make something

generator (jen" ə rā' tər) an object designed to make something or change energy

geothermal energy (jē ō thėr" məl en" ər jē) energy created by pressure and heat underneath the earth's crust

germinate (jūr"mə nāt) to grow from a seed into a plant

greenhouse gas (grēn" hous') one of the gases that makes the atmosphere able to hold more heat, such as carbon dioxide and water vapor

hardness (härd" nis) the firmness of a solid

herbivore (ėr" bə vôr or hėr" bə vor) animals that eat only plants to get energy

heredity (hə red" ə tē) a characteristic that can be passed from parent to offspring

hibernate (hī" bər nāt) to go into a deep sleep during the winter months

hydropower (hī" drō pou" ər) energy from the movement of water

igneous (ig" nē əs) a group of rocks made from the products of a volcano eruption, such as magma

impact (im" pakt) to directly affect something

inherit (in her" it) to receive a trait from a parent

interact (in tər akt") to act or react to another organism

instinct (in" stingkt) a behavior that an animal knows as soon as it is born or hatched

kinetic energy (ki net" ik en" ər jē) the energy of motion

larva (lär" və) a recently hatched insect that eats to build up energy for the next stage of metamorphosis

legend (lej" ənd) an area on a map that explains the meaning of the symbols on the map

light (līt) energy that allows organisms to see

liquid (lik" wid) matter with a definite mass but no definite volume where particles easily slide around each other

magnet (mag" nit) a material that attracts metal because of an electric charge

mass (mas) the amount of matter an object has

metamorphic (met′ ə môr" fik) a group of rocks formed when particles of other rocks are combined by pressure

metamorphosis (met′ e môr" fə sis) the growth of an insect from egg to adulthood that has either three or four distinct stages

migrate (mī" grāt) to move from one place to another because the seasons changed

molt (mölt) to take off an outer layer, such as an exoskeleton or extra fur grown for winter

natural gas (nach" ər əl gas) a gas that is burned for energy

nonrenewable resource (non′ ri nü" ə bəl ri sôr" s or non′ ri nü" ə bəl rē" sôrs) a substance that there is a limited amount of or is used up faster than it is made

nuclear fuel (nü" klē ər fyü" əl) an energy source made from unstable elements, such as Uranium

omnivore (om" nə vôr′) animals that eat both plants and animals for energy

orbit (ôr" bit) the circular movement of an object, such as a planet or moon, around an object that can hold it in place with gravity (such as a sun or large planet)

organize (ôr" gə niz′) to sort organisms into groups to make them easier to compare

outcome (out" kum') the result of an event

overpopulation (ō' vər pop' yə lā" shən) the point where all of the members of a single species need more resources than what is there

pattern (pat" ərn) an observable event that happens in the same way again and again

perspective (pər spek" tiv) the view of an object from a different angle

petroleum (ō' vər pop" yə lā shən) a liquid that can be burned to transfer energy

phase (fāz) any of the shapes that the moon seems to be in as it moves around the Earth

physical change (fiz" ə kəl chānj) a change in traits—such as color, size, and shape—that does not change what a substance is made of

pistil (pis" tl) the part of a flower that receives pollen and makes the seed

pollination (pol' ə nāt" shən) the process where pollen is moved to different plant parts to produce a seed

pollutant (pə lüt" nt) substances made by human activity that have a bad effect

potential energy (pə ten" shəl en" ər jē) stored energy

primary (pri" mer' ē) the first or most important part

producer (prə dü" sər) an organism that can make its own nutrients, usually with energy from the sun

property (prop" ər tē) an observable trait of matter

pupa (pyü" pə) the third stage of an insect's life, where it rests so energy can be used to change to the final stage

radiation (ra' dē ā" shən) the outward spread of energy in all directions

renewable resource (ri nü" ə bəl ri sôr" s or ri nü" ə bəl rē" sôrs) a substance that cannot be used up

resistance (ri zis" təns) a trait of a material that makes electricity unable to flow through the material, such as rubber and wood

respond (ri spond") to react to a change or action

revolution (rev' ə lü" shən) the movement of one object around another

rotation (rō tā" shən) the spinning of an object when it moves

rust (rust) a brown-colored material that is made when oxygen and iron combine

scrubber (skrub" ər) a substance in a power plant that reduces the amount of harmful gases sent into the air

sedimentary (sed′ ə men" tər ē) a group of rocks formed when particles--such as dirt, sand, and fossils--settle into layers

sepal (sē" pəl) green, leaf-like part of a plant that protects a flower until it is ready to bloom

solid (sol" id) matter with a definite shape and volume that is made of vibrating particles

sound (sound) energy that can be heard

source (sôrs) the point that something comes from

speed (spēd) how fast something moves

stamen (stā" mən) the part of the flower that creates pollen

simulate (sim" yə lāt) to demonstrate or copy something to make it easier to understand

symbol (sim" bəl) pictures, colors, and lines that have a meaning

texture (teks" chər) how an object feels when it is touched, such as soft, rough, or smooth

thermal energy (thėr" mal en" ər jē) a form of energy that comes from rubbing objects together and produces heat

transfer (tran sfėr" or tran" sfėr) to change or move from one object to another

transform (tran sfôrm") the change of an organism into another organism with different properties

trench (trench) a landform in the ocean that is made when a long, narrow area of the ocean floor sinks deeper into the earth

turbine (tėr" bən or tėr" bin) an object that converts energy for human use with circular motion

uranium (yu̇ rā" nē əm) an unstable element used by humans as an energy source

volume (vol" yəm) the amount of space an object takes up

wave (wāv) a transfer of energy

weathering (weTH" ər ing) the process where particles are slowly moved off of a solid

Index

*Page numbers for charts, graphs, maps, and
pictures are printed in *italics*.

Illustrations

Aaron Ashley Illustration; Peter Bull Art Studio; Sara Lynn Cramb/
Astound US; Dan Crisp/The Bright Agency; Patrick Gnan/
IllustrationOnline.com; Stuart Holmes/Illustration Inc.; Mapping
Specialists, Ltd.; Bojan Orešković; Pronk Media Inc.; Rob Schuster;
Geoffrey P. Smith; Jim Steck/Steck Figures; Symmetry Creative
Productions; Sam Valentino/Bumblecat Design & Illustration, LLC;
Ralph Voltz/IllustrationOnline.com

Photographs

Photo locators denoted as follows: Top (T), Center (C), Bottom (B),
Left (L), Right (R), Background (Bkgd)

Front Cover: Klein & Hubert/Nature Picture Library;
Back Cover: Marinello/DigitalVision Vectors/Getty Images;

FM

iv: Tanarch/Shutterstock; vi: Kurhan/Fotolia; vii: Isuaneye/Fotolia;
viii: Ajr_images/Fotolia; ix: Hongqi Zhang Alamy Stock Photo;
x: Michaeljung/Fotolia; xi: BillionPhotos.com/Fotolia; xii: Felix
Mizioznikov/Fotolia; xiv Bkgrd: Iakov Kalinin/Fotolia; xiv TR:
Barry Tuck/Shutterstock

T01

000: One-image Photography/Alamy Stock Photo; 002: Kurhan/
Fotolia; 004: Elina Li/Shutterstock; 005: ESOlex/Shutterstock;
006: Mikelaptev/Fotolia; 008 T: Pekka Parviainen/Science
Source; 008 BL: xtock/Shutterstock; 009 Kurhan/Fotolia; 012
Bkgrd: RGB Ventures/SuperStock/Alamy Stock Photo; 012
BR: Peter Ptschelinzew/Alamy Stock Photo; 014: Kurhan/
Fotolia; 015: 3dsculptor/Fotolia; 016: LeeLook/Fotolia; 017:
MisterElements/Shutterstock; 018 BL: Pluto/Alamy Stock Photo;
018 T: Ad-hominem/Fotolia; 019: Kurhan/Fotolia; 022: Kurhan/
Fotolia; 023: Stuart O'Sullivan/Getty Images; 024: Ewoud/Fotolia;
025: makeitdouble/Shutterstock; 026 BR: Kurhan/Fotolia; 026 L:
natursports/123RF; 027: David Carillet/123RF; 028: Brian Kushner/
Alamy Stock Photo; 030: oorka/Shutterstock; 031: Kurhan/
Fotolia; 032 BL: Mclek/Shutterstock; 032 TR: ImageBroker/Alamy
Stock Photo; 034 Bkgrd: IMPhoto/Shutterstock; 034 CR: Kurhan/
Fotolia; 035 BR: Johnny Stockshooter/Alamy Stock Photo; 035 TR:
Stolk/iStock/Getty Images; 036: xtock/Shutterstock; 037: David
Carillet/123RF; 041 BL: MisterElements/Shutterstock; 041 BR:
Ad-hominem/Fotolia

T02

042: Michael Dorrington/Shutterstock; 044: Isuaneye/Fotolia;
047 Bkgrd: Bruce Roberts/Science Source; 047 CR: Bruce
Roberts/Science Source; 048: Dudarev Mikhail/Shutterstock;
049: Hchjjl/Shutterstock; 050: Isuaneye/Fotolia; 052: Iryna
Bezianova/Shutterstock; 055: Isuaneye/Fotolia; 056: Bjul/
Shutterstock; 057 CR: Padma Sanjaya/Shutterstock; 057 TR:
Jon Manjeot/Shutterstock; 058: Brisbane/Shutterstock; 060:
123rf.com; 065: stocker1970/Shutterstock; 066: Poravute
Siriphiroon/123RF; 067: LHF Graphics/Shutterstock; 068 BC:
Sonsam/Shutterstock; 068 BL: Vvoe/Shutterstock; 068 BR: Vvoe/
Fotolia; 068 CL: Sumikophoto/Shutterstock; 068 TCL: Siim Sepp/
Shutterstock; 068 TL: George Burba/123RF; 069 BC: Isuaneye/
Fotolia; 069 Bkgrd: Niti_Photo/Shutterstock; 069 CR: Sakdinon
kadchiangsaen/123RF; 072 BR: Albert Russ/Shutterstock;
072 BL: Mark A. Schneider/Science Source; 072 CL: Stefan
Malloch/Shutterstock; 074 CL: Nikolay Se/Shutterstock; 074 C:
PurpleImages/Getty Images; 074 CR: stocker1970/Shutterstock;
074 TC: Isuaneye/Fotolia; 076: Sherry V Smith/Shutterstock;
078: Photo Passion/Fotolia; 079 B: NNerto/Fotolia; 080: Paul
Hennessy/Alamy Stock Photo; 081: blickwinkel/Alamy Stock
Photo; 084: Atm2003/Shutterstock; 085: Isuaneye/Fotolia; 086:
IrinaK/Shutterstock; 087: Igor Malovic/Shutterstock; 088 BL:
Smileus/Shutterstock; 088 CL: Colin Stitt/Shutterstock; 088 R:
Jesus Keller/Shutterstock; 089: Sergiy Serdyuk/Fotolia; 090 TL:
Sde201982/Fotolia; 090 TR: Michal Durinik/Shutterstock; 091 TL:
Swapan Photography/Shutterstock; 091 TR: Mikesmithdesign/
Fotolia; 092 TR: ZUMA Press Inc/Alamy Stock Photo; 093 CR:
Aleksej Orel/123RF; 093 TR: Gorov/Fotolia; 094 Bkgrd: Alexander
Demyanenko/Fotolia; 094 CR: Isuaneye/Fotolia; 095 Bkgrd:
Jeremy Bishop/Science Source; 095 TR: William J. Wysession/
Courtesy of Michael Wysession; 097: Bildagentur Zoonar GmbH/
Shutterstock; 101: Doodleboards/Shutterstock

T03

102: JG Photography/Alamy Stock Photo; 104: Ajr_images/Fotolia;
107 CR: Akimov Igor/Shutterstock; 107 R: DuxX/Shutterstock; 108:
Bracas/Fotolia; 109: Elina Li/Shutterstock; 110 BR: Ajr_images/
Fotolia; 110 L: Valentina_G/Shutterstock; 111 B: Amanda Plank/
Fotolia; 111 BL: LuckyPhoto/Fotolia; 111 R: Fourmay/Fotolia; 114
C: Andre Bonn/Shutterstock; 114 TL: Cultura RM/Alamy Stock
Photo; 115: Ajr_images/Fotolia; 116 BL: Katsumi KASAHARA/
Getty Images; 116 TR: AFP/Stringer/Getty Images; 117: mhatzapa/
Shutterstock; 118: Anyaivanova/Getty Images; 119 BR: Anastacia
azzzya/Shutterstock; 119 CR: Dailin/Shutterstock; 120: Yazovskikh
Olga/Shutterstock; 121 B: Radoslaw Lecyk/Shutterstock; 121
BC: Ajr_images/Fotolia; 121 TR: Ase/Shutterstock; 124 L: Holly
Kuchera/Shutterstock; 124 R: Hemis/Alamy Stock Photo; 125 TL:
Ajr_images/Fotolia; 125 BR: redstallion/Getty Images; 126: Africa
Studio/Shutterstock; 127: Undrey/Shutterstock; 133: Ajr_images/
Fotolia; 134: Ajr_images/Fotolia; 135: Redfox331/Fotolia; 136
BL: Santi Rodríguez/Fotolia; 136 BR: Southtownboy/Fotolia; 137:
Elina Li/Shutterstock; 138: Catalin Petolea/Shutterstock; 139 BC:
Ajr_images/Fotolia; 139 CR: Valerii Zan/Fotolia; 139 TR: Grigoriy
K/Shutterstock; 142: Ajr_images/Fotolia; 143: Srki66/Fotolia; 144
Bkgrd: Tab62/Fotolia; 144 TR: Ajr_images/Fotolia; 145 Bkgrd:
BlackMac/Fotolia; 145 TR: HadelProductions/Getty Images 151:
Elina Li/Shutterstock

T04

152: ImageBROKER/Alamy Stock Photo; 154: Hongqi Zhang
Alamy Stock Photo; 157 C: Adil Yusifov/Fotolia; 157 R: Adil Yusifov/
Fotolia; 158: dpa picture alliance/Alamy Stock Photo; 160 BR:
Hongqi Zhang Alamy Stock Photo; 160 T: Ryhor Bruyeu/Alamy
Stock Photo; 161: Africa Studio/Fotolia; 164: Sergey Nivens/Alamy
Stock Photo; 165 BL: Matúš Lošonský/Alamy Stock Photo; 165 BR:
irishphoto.com/Alamy Stock Photo; 165 CR: iStockphoto_RAW/
Getty Images; 165 TL: Hongqi Zhang/Alamy Stock Photo; 166
BL: Andrew Twort/Alamy Stock Photo; 166 CL: krasyuk/Fotolia;
166 CR: photolife2016/Fotolia; 168 BL: JulieRob/Getty Images;

168 BR: Margoe Edwards/Shutterstock; 172 BR: Hongqi Zhang/ Alamy Stock Photo; 172 TL: Andresr/Shutterstock; 173: ErickN/ Shutterstock; 174: Honggi Zhang/Alamy Stock Photo; 176: Joseph Giacomin/Science Source; 181: Zastolskiy Victor/Shutterstock; 182 T: Janecat/Shutterstock; 182 CL: JGade/Shutterstock; 182 BR: Hongqi Zhang/Alamy Stock Photo; 184: Honggi Zhang/ Alamy Stock Photo; 185: Blend Images/Alamy Stock Photo; 186: 3drenderings/Shutterstock; 187: hchjjl/Shutterstock; 188 C: 5/ Shutterstock; 188 CL: Einar Muoni/Shutterstock; 189 BC: Honggi Zhang/Alamy Stock Photo; 189 R: maksimka37/Fotolia; 191: Marius Graf/Alamy Stock Photo; 192: Honggi Zhang/Alamy Stock Photo; 193: Robert Crum/Shutterstock; 194 Bkgrd: JTB MEDIA CREATION, Inc./Alamy Stock Photo; 194 TR: Honggi Zhang/Alamy Stock Photo; 195 B: Mark Scheuern/Alamy Stock Photo; 195 TR: Monty Rakusen/Getty Images

T05

202: Cultura Creative (RF)/Alamy Stock Photo; 204: Michaeljung/ Fotolia; 206: hchjjl/Shutterstock; 207: David Brimm/Shutterstock; 208: Idealink Photography/Alamy Stock Photo; 209: lineartestpilot/ Shutterstock; 210: Shutterlk/Shutterstock; 211: Africa Studio/ Fotolia; 214 CL: Scanrail/Fotolia; 214 CR: Michaeljung/Fotolia; 215: Michaeljung/Fotolia; 216 BL: Eric Isselee/Shutterstock; 216 BR: TomasSereda/Getty Images; 217: DesignPie.cc/Shutterstock; 218: Kustov/Shutterstock; 219 Bkgrd: huyangshu/Shutterstock; 219 TC: Michaeljung/Fotolia; 222: Unlisted Images, Inc./Alamy Stock Photo; 223: blickwinkel/Alamy Stock Photo; 224: Michaeljung/Fotolia; 225 BL: msk.nina/Fotolia; 225 BR: Alexander Potapov/Fotolia; 226: Nd700/Fotolia; 227: 1973kla/Shutterstock; 230: Elbud/Shutterstock; 232: Michaeljung/Fotolia; 234 B: Maicasaa/Fotolia; 234 C: Scyther5/ Shutterstock; 234 CR: Elbud/Shutterstock; 235: Tidarat Tiemjai/ Shutterstock; 236: Vaclav Volrab/Shutterstock; 238: Martin33/ Shutterstock; 239 BC: Michaeljung/Fotolia; 239 CR: Gudellaphoto/ Fotolia; 242: Tigergallery/Shutterstock; 243 TL: Michaeljung/ Fotolia; 243 B: buranasak wongsiriphakdee/Shutterstock; 244 Bkgrd: Chukov/Shutterstock; 244 CR: Michaeljung/Fotolia; 245 B: Jens Brüggemann/123RF; 245 TR: Kadmy/Fotolia

T06

252: Profimedia.CZ a.s./Alamy Stock Photo; 254: BillionPhotos. com/Fotolia; 256: Sergii Telesh/Alamy Stock Photo; 257 CR: Sherry Yates Young/Shutterstock; 257 R: alberto maisto/Alamy Stock Photo; 258: Keith Douglas/Alamy Stock Photo; 262: BillionPhotos. com/Fotolia; 263: Jacky Parker Photography/Getty Images; 264: Ethan Daniels/Alamy Stock Photo; 265 CR: imageBROKER/ Alamy Stock Photo; 265 TL: BillionPhotos.com/Fotolia; 265 TR: Artur Synenko/Fotolia; 266 B: Thierry Falise/LightRocket via Getty Image; 266 CL: Matgo/Shutterstock; 266 CR: Igor Podgorny/ Shutterstock; 266 TR: OntheCoastPhotography/Shutterstock; 268 B: Ellen McKnight/Alamy Stock Photo; 268 BL: Brian J. Skerry/ Getty Images; 269 BCR: makieni/Shutterstock; 269 BR: Françoise EMILY/Alamy Stock Photo; 269 TCR: Xavier Hoenner Photography/ Getty Images; 269 TR: Matt Jeppson/Shutterstock; 270 BC: All Canada Photos/Alamy Stock Photos; 270 CL: weerayut/Fotolia; 270 CR: Aggie 11/Shutterstock; 270 TC: Nature and Science/ Alamy Stock Photo; 271 BR: Nancy Bauer/Shutterstock; 271 C: BillionPhotos.com/Fotolia; 271 CR: tcareob72/Shutterstock; 271 TCR: Ron Rowan Photography/Shutterstock; 271 TR: Mau Horng/

Shutterstock; 274: Top-Pics TBK/Alamy Stock Photo; 275 BR: Jay Ondreicka/Shutterstock; 275 CR: Maslov Dmitry/123RF; 275 TL: BillionPhotos.com/Fotolia; 276: Nino Pavisic/Fotolia; 278: Alta Oosthuizen/Fotolia; 279 TC: Romasph/123RF; 279 CR: Elaine Giadone/123RF; 282 BCL: 123RF; 282 Bkgrd: Federica Grassi/ Flickr RF/Getty Images; 282 BR: BillionPhotos.com/Fotolia; 282 CL: Torsakarin/123RF; 283: Leeyiutung/Fotolia; 284: BillionPhotos. com/Fotolia; 285 B: Nikontiger/iStockphoto/Getty Images; 285 CR: Olgysha/Shutterstock; 286: Melinda Fawver/Fotolia; 290 L: Infocusphotos/Alamy Stock Photo; 290 BR: BillionPhotos.com/ Fotolia; 291: Blickwinkel/Alamy Stock Photo; 292 TL: BillionPhotos. com/Fotolia; 292 BR: Matthijs Kuijpers/Alamy Stock Photo; 293 BL: Abi Warner /123RF; 293 BR: Mitrarudra/Fotolia; 293 CL: Elizaveta Galitckaia/Shutterstock; 294 Bkgrd: Volgariver/Fotolia; 294 TR: BillionPhotos.com/Fotolia; 295 B: Ger Bosma/Alamy Stock Photo; 295 TR: Olesia Bilkei/Fotolia; 300 BR: Jessica Kuras/Shutterstock; 300 CR: Snvv/Shutterstock

T07

302: Adam Suto/Alamy Stock Photo; 304: Felix Mizioznikov/ Fotolia; 307 CR: Irisphoto1/Fotolia; 307 R: Surasaki/Shutterstock; 308 Bkgrd: Ruth P. Peterkin/Fotolia; 308 BL: Chiyacat/123RF; 309: Zizar2002/Fotolia; 310 L: Greg Dale/Getty Images; 311 B: Arinahabich/Fotolia; 311 CR: HHelene/Shutterstock; 311 TCR: Matt Jeppson/Shutterstock; 314 BL: Natureguy/Fotolia; 314 BR: Felix Mizioznikov/Fotolia; 314 TL: Neil Lockhart/Alamy Stock Photo; 315 TL: Victor Tyakht/Shutterstock; 315 TR: Stephan Morris/Fotolia; 316: Felix Mizioznikov/Fotolia; 318: Peter Mautsch/Hemera/Getty Images; 320: Vovan/Fotolia; 321 BC: Felix Mizioznikov/Fotolia; 321 TC: Arco Images GmbH/Alamy Stock Photo; 321 TL: Brian Pollard/Alamy Stock Photo; 324 TL: Rudy Umans/Shutterstock; 324 TR: Schankz/Shutterstock; 325 TL: Felix Mizioznikov/Fotolia; 325 TR: JoshSilverlock/iStockphoto/Getty Images; 326: Bonchan/ Shutterstock; 330 BR: Felix Mizioznikov/Fotolia; 330 TC: Gus Grosch/Getty Images; 330 TCL: Siriwut Theeratawatkul/123RF; 330 TL: Charles Brutlag/Shutterstock; 330 TR: Shackleford-Photography/Shutterstock; 331 TC: Critterbiz/Shutterstock; 331 TL: Charles Brutlag/Shutterstock; 331 TR: Earl Robbins/Fotolia; 332: Felix Mizioznikov/Fotolia; 333 BR: Alexey/Fotolia; 333 TR: Richardseeley/Fotolia; 334: Anita Tseng/EyeEm/Getty Images; 336 CR: Felix Mizioznikov/Fotolia; 336 Bkgrd: 886945/Shutterstock; 337 C: 123RF; 337 CR: Steve Collender/Shutterstock; 337 TC: Brian Lasenby/Fotolia; 337 TR: 7th Son Studio/Shutterstock; 340: pngstudio/Fotolia; 341 TL: Felix Mizioznikov/Fotolia; 341 B: Andamanec/Fotolia; 344 Bkgrd: Dennis MacDonald/age fotostock/Alamy Stock Photo; 344 TR: Felix Mizioznikov/Fotolia; 345 B: Yakoniva/Alamy Stock Photo; 345 TR: goodluz/123RF; 351: spetenfia/123RF; 352: AlinaMD/Shutterstock

EM

EM1: Goodluz/Shutterstock; EM3: Alexis Rosenfeld/Science Source; EM4: ImageBROKER/Alamy Stock Photo; EM5: Elvira Sa/ Shutterstock; EM6: Axel Heimken/AP Photo; EM8: DmitriMaruta/ iStock/Getty Images Plus/Getty Images; EM9: Monty Rakusen/ Cultura/Getty Images

My Notes and Designs

Draw, Write, Create

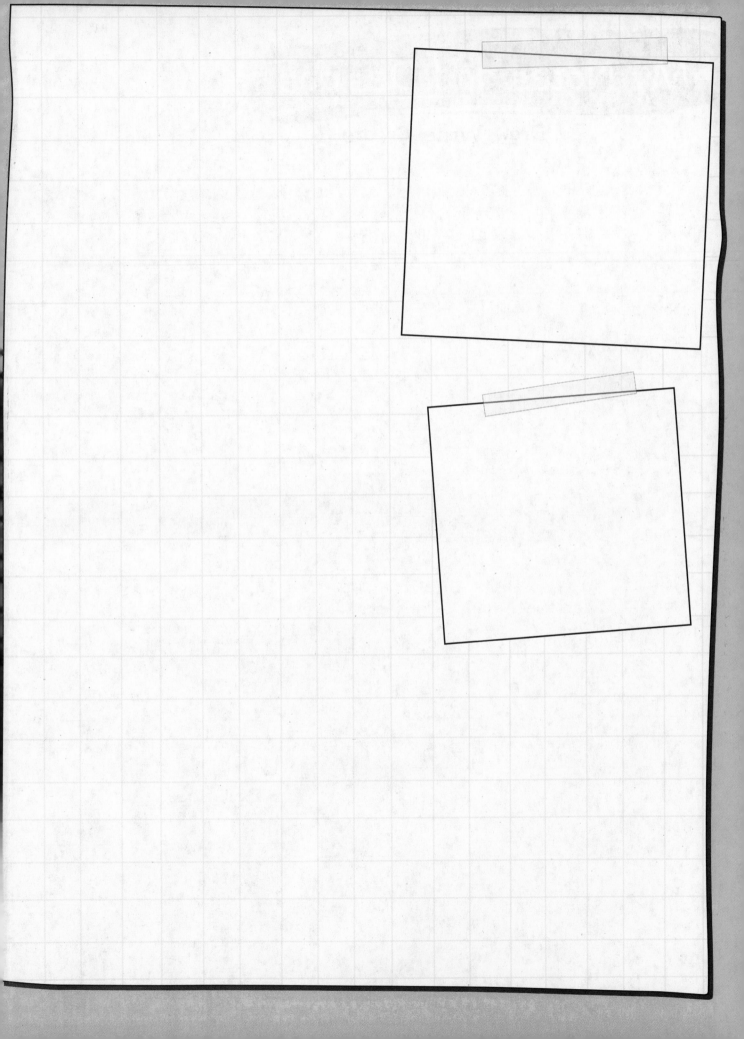

My Notes and Designs

Draw, Write, Create

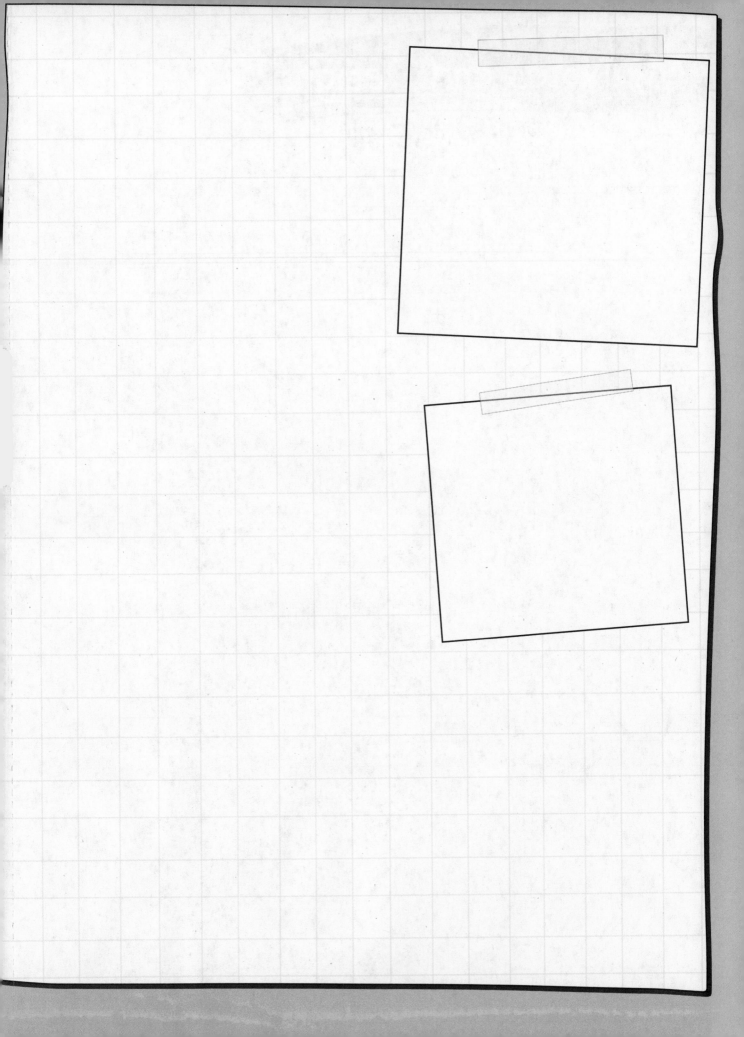

My Notes and Designs

Draw, Write, Create

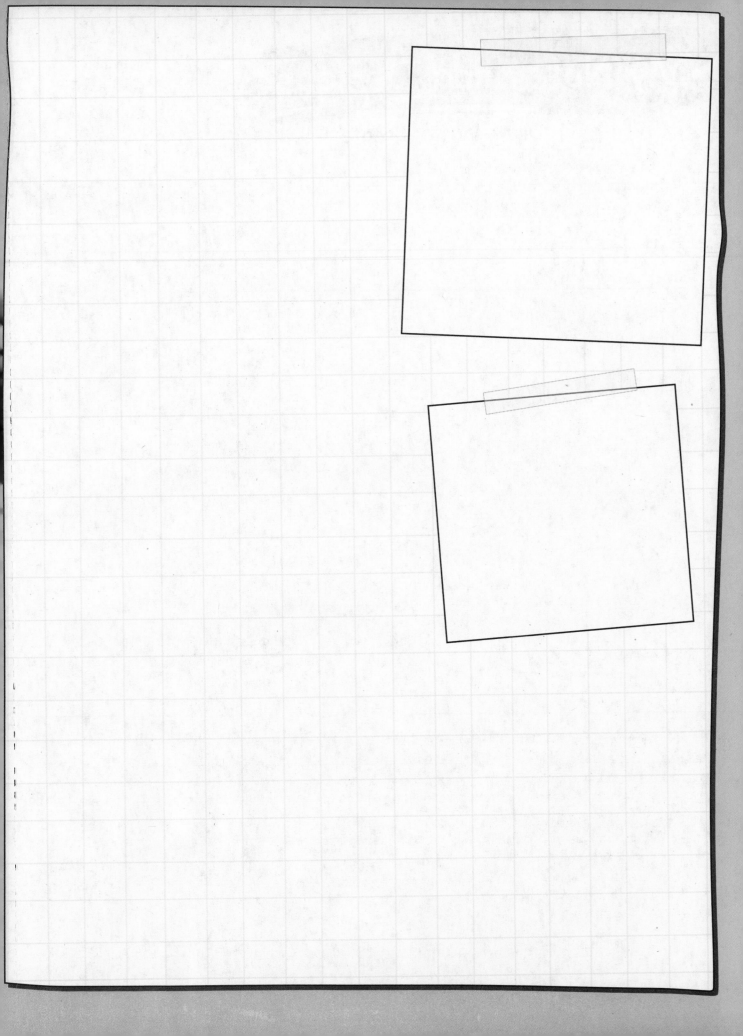

My Notes and Designs

Draw, Write, Create

My Notes and Designs

Draw, Write, Create

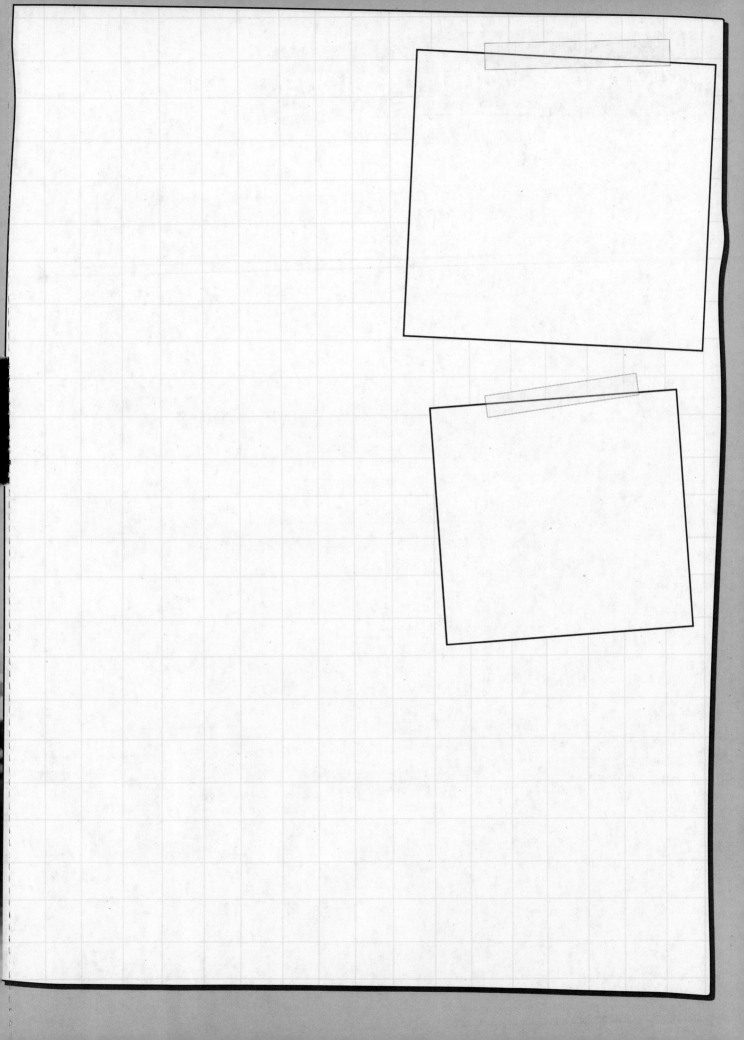

My Notes and Designs

Draw, Write, Create

My Notes and Designs

Draw, Write, Create

My Notes and Designs

Draw, Write, Create

My Notes and Designs

Draw, Write, Create

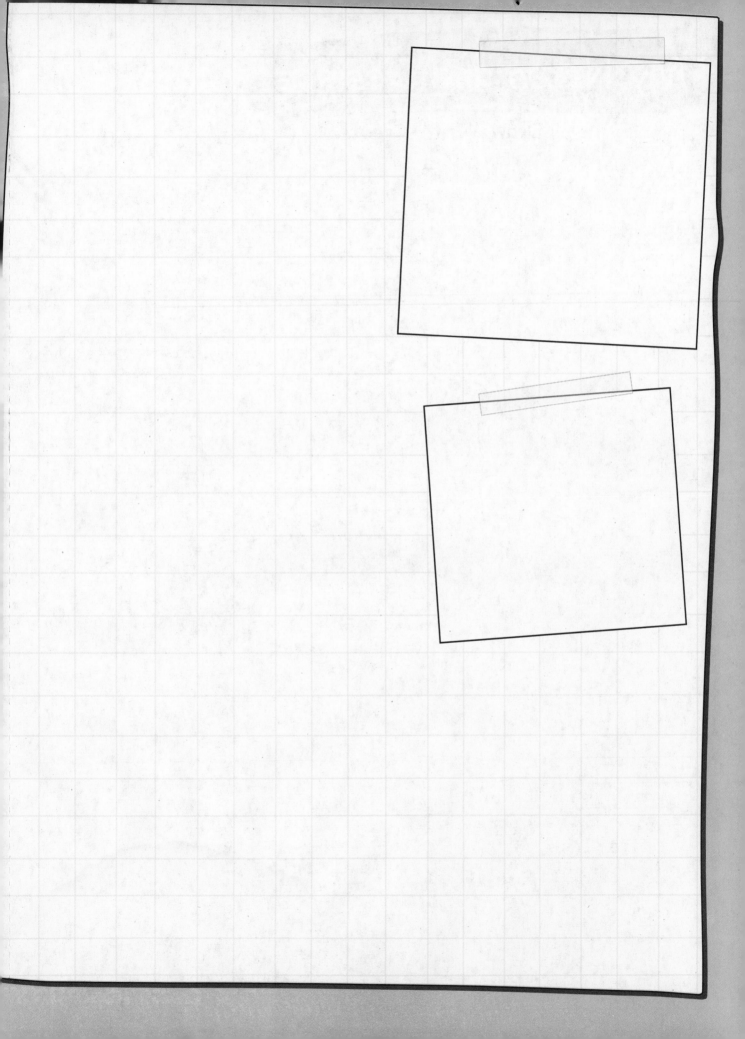

My Notes and Designs

Draw, Write, Create